Judy Moeller

P9-BYQ-300

HOW 4

A Handbook for Office Workers

Fourth Edition

James L. Clark
Chairman, Business Department
Pasadena City College

Lyn R. Clark
Professor, Office Administration Department
Los Angeles Pierce College

Kent Publishing Company
A Division of Wadsworth, Inc.
Boston, Massachusetts

Executive Editor: Richard C. Crews
Production Editor: Eve B. Mendelsohn
Interior Designer: Glenna Collett
Cover Designer: Nancy Lindgren
Production Coordinator: Linda Siegrist

Kent Publishing Company
A Division of Wadsworth, Inc.

© 1985, 1982, 1979, 1975 by Wadsworth, Inc., Belmont, California 94002. All rights reserved. No part of this book may be reproduced, stored in a retrieval system, or transcribed, in any form or by any means, electronic, mechanical, photocopying, recording, or otherwise, without the prior written permission of the publisher, Kent Publishing Company, 20 Park Plaza, Boston, Massachusetts, 02116.

Printed in the United States of America

4 5 6 7 8 9—93 92 91 90 89 88 87

Library of Congress Cataloging in Publication Data

Clark, James Leland, 1929–
    HOW 4: a handbook for office workers.

    Rev. ed. of: HOW 3. 3rd ed. 1982.
    Includes index.
    1. Commercial correspondence—Handbooks, manuals, etc. I. Clark, Lyn. II. Title. III. Title: H.O.W. 4.
HF5726.C55 1984   651.7′402   84-23366
ISBN 0-534-04542-1

Preface

How 4: A Handbook for Office Workers, Fourth Edition, is designed to assist students, office personnel, and business writers in preparing written business communications. Specific information for writing, typing or transcribing, and transmitting business documents may be found in this manual. The primary function of HOW 4 is to act as a reference book—to answer specific questions regarding punctuation, grammar, capitalization, number usage, word usage, forms of address, abbreviations, format, and document transmission as they relate to the preparation of business letters, memorandums, and reports.

HOW 4 may be used also as a supplementary classroom learning activity for potential secretaries, word processors, typists, and business writers. By using the *Workbook for HOW 4,* the instructor may teach and reinforce the major principles contained in the reference manual. Exercises are coordinated specifically with sections in HOW 4 and are designed to provide students with realistic learning materials, not just isolated sentence exercises. In addition, the *Instructor's Manual and Key* contains over 120 transparency masters that correspond directly with the principles in HOW 4 and the exercise materials in the workbook. Other teaching materials in the instructor's manual include a Familiarization Exercise, a complete set of dictation-transcription materials, and a series of business letter and memorandum problems.

Special Features

To increase the functional use of HOW 4 as a reference handbook, several special features, in addition to the table of contents and the index, are included:

1. *Chapter indexers*—edge-of-page printed tabulators so that major sections may be located quickly
2. *Solution Finders*—comprehensive topic indexes at the beginning of each chapter so that solutions to problems may be found easily
3. *Example headings*—italic headings that differentiate aspects of each rule so that specific applications can be isolated
4. *Two-color format*—rules are printed in red and examples are printed in black for ease in location, reading, and understanding
5. *Spiral binding*—a lie-flat feature so that office personnel may readily compare their problems with the examples

Finding Solutions to Problems

Information you need may be located easily and quickly in HOW 4 by using a four-step process:

1. Find the chapter you need by turning to the list of contents shown on the outside back cover.
2. Turn to the Solution Finder at the beginning of that chapter by using the tabs that appear on the outside edge of the pages.
3. Locate the information you need in the Solution Finder. Each main topic is listed alphabetically followed by subsections of that topic and their rule numbers.
4. Turn to the appropriate section within the chapter by referring to the page guide references (the rule numbers shown at the top right corner of the odd-numbered pages).

If information cannot be located through surveying the contents listed on the back cover, use the comprehensive index at the end of the book to find the appropriate section. Then use the tabs on the outside edge of the pages to locate the appropriate chapter and the page guides to find the specific section.

Contents

1 Punctuation *1*

2 Hyphenating and Dividing Words *55*

3 Capitalization *67*

4 Numbers *85*

5 Abbreviations and Contractions *101*

6 Literary and Artistic Titles *117*

7 Words Often Misused and Confused *123*

8 Grammar and Usage *157*

9 Address Format and Forms of Address *183*

10 Business Letters and Memorandums *199*

11 Reports, Manuscripts, and Minutes *249*

12 Mail, Telegrams, and Cablegrams *283*

Appendix A Terminology Used in the Automated Office *293*

Appendix B Secretarial Shortcuts *301*

Index *316*

Punctuation

Ampersand   *1–1d, 1–66*

Apostrophe

   Contractions   1–56a
   Plurals   1–56b
   Possessives   1–55

Asterisk   *1–63*

Brackets

   *Placement with other punctuation
      marks   1–62*
   Usage   1–61

Colon

   Capitalization with   1–28
   Enumerated items   1–23
   Explanatory sentences   1–24
   Listed items   1–23
   *Placement with other punctuation
      marks   1–27*
   Quotations, long   1–25
   Salutations   1–26a
   Special-purpose uses   1–26
   When not to use   1–23b

Comma

   Abbreviations after names   1–4d
   Addresses, street   1–6a
   Adjectives, independent   1–8
   Appositives   1–4
   Cities   1–6b
   Clarity, punctuation for   1–14
   *Contrasting, limiting, and opposing
      expressions   1–12*
   *Coordinating conjunctions   1–7,
      1–18b*
   Dates   1–5a-b
   Direct address   1–3

   Etc.   1–1c
   Independent adjectives   1–8
   Introductory clauses   1–9
   Introductory phrases   1–2f, 1–10
   Nonrestrictive clauses   1–11a-d
   Nonrestrictive phrases   1–11e
   Numerals   1–16
   Omitted words   1–13
   Parenthetical expressions   1–2
   *Placement with other punctuation
      marks   1–15d, 1–60e*
   Quotations, short   1–15
   Restrictive clauses   1–11a-c
   Restrictive phrases   1–11e
   Series   1–1
   States   1–6b
   Time zones   1–5c

Dash

   Format of dash   1–32
   *Hesitations in verbal reports
      1–30*
   Parenthetical elements   1–29
      Abrupt thoughts   1–29b
      Afterthoughts   1–29e
      Containing commas   1–29a
      Emphatic thoughts   1–29b
      Examples   1–29d
      Explanations   1–29d
      Summaries   1–29c
   *Placement with other punctuation
      marks   1–32*
   Sources of quotations   1–31

Diagonal   *1–64*

Ellipsis   *1–38, 1–52*

Exclamation Point

   *Placement with other punctuation
      marks   1–46*
   Usage   1–45

Parentheses

Enumerated items   *1–59*
Nonessential expressions   *1–57*
Numerals enclosed in   *1–58*
Placement with other punctuation
   marks   *1–60*

Period

Abbreviations   *1–35a*
Decimals   *1–37*
Ellipses   *1–38, 1–52*
Emphasis, for   *1–38*
Format   *1–39*
Independent phrases   *1–34*
Indirect question   *1–33*
Initials   *1–35b*
Omissions, to show   *1–38*
Outlines   *1–36*
Placement with other punctuation
   marks   *1–39c-d*
Polite requests   *1–33, 1–41e*
Sentences   *1–33*

Question Mark

Direct questions   *1–40*
Expressions of doubt   *1–42*
Placement with other punctuation
   marks   *1–44*
Polite requests   *1–41e*
Series of questions   *1–43*
Statements with questions   *1–41*

Quotation Marks

Capitalization with   *1–53*
Definitions of words and
   expressions   *1–48b*
Direct quotations   *1–47*
Ellipses   *1–38, 1–52*
Omissions in quoted material
   1–52
Placement with other punctuation
   marks   *1–54*
Quotations within quotations *1–50*
Quoted paragraphs   *1–51*
Short quoted expressions   *1–48*
Titles, literary and artistic   *1–49*
Words marked or
   stamped   *1–48c*

Semicolon

Enumerations   *1–21*
Explanations   *1–21*
Independent clauses   *1–17,
   1–18, 1–19*
   Coordinating conjunctions,
      with   *1–18*
   Coordinating conjunctions,
      without   *1–17*
   Transitional words, with   *1–19*
Placement with other punctuation
   marks   *1–22*
Series   *1–20*
   Complete thoughts   *1–20*
   Containing commas   *1–20*

Underscore   *1–4e, 1–48b, 1–49,
1–65*

Comma

1–1. Series

a. In a sentence containing three or more equally ranked elements (words, phrases, or short clauses), place a comma after each item as well as before the conjunction *(and, or, nor)*. (See Section 1–1d for exception to this rule.)

words

Our branch office advertised for an accountant, a secretary, and a clerk-typist.

phrases

A new office manager was hired to supervise office services, improve the filing system, and conduct studies of office procedures.

short clauses

I signed the contract, Karen Jones mailed it, and Ralph Harris initiated computer installation procedures.

b. Commas are not used when items in a series are all joined by conjunctions.

words

Neither jewelry *nor* cash *nor* appliances were stolen from the store.

phrases

For several years we have employed custodians to clean the building *and* gardeners to maintain the grounds *and* special crews to perform painting and electrical maintenance.

c. Although generally avoided, *etc.* is sometimes used to indicate "and so forth" at the end of a series. If it is used, *etc.* is set off by commas; it is never preceded by the word *and.*

within a sentence

Staples, paper clips, fasteners, rubber bands, etc., were placed on our last supplies order.

end of sentence

We plan to visit all our branch offices this year--New York, Los Angeles, San Francisco, Chicago, etc.

d. A comma is not used before an ampersand (&) in an organizational name unless the organization officially uses the comma in its name.

no comma

Her first interview is with Gates, Hamilton & Gates.

comma

Augner, Haight, Liggett, & Phelan is a new accounting firm in the Chicago area.

1-2. Parenthetical Expressions

a. Transitional words and phrases that are considered unnecessary for the grammatical completeness of a sentence and that *interrupt its natural flow* are set off with commas. A partial list of such parenthetical expressions follows:

according to our records	however	obviously
accordingly	in addition	of course
after all	incidentally	on the contrary
all in all	in conclusion	on the other hand
all things considered	indeed	on the whole
also	in fact	otherwise
as a matter of fact	in general	perhaps
as a result	in my opinion	periodically
as a rule	in other words	secondly
at any rate	instead	so
at the same time	in summary	that is
besides	in the first place	then
between you and me	in the meantime	therefore
by the way	likewise	thus
consequently	moreover	too
even so	namely	under the circumstances
finally	needless to say	unfortunately
for example	nevertheless	what is more
fortunately	no	without a doubt
furthermore	no doubt	yes
hence		

beginning of sentence

Needless to say, he is planning to attend the meeting.

end of sentence

The store will be closed over the Labor Day weekend, *without a doubt.*

within a sentence

A large crowd, *nevertheless,* attended the exhibit.

b. Sometimes words and phrases used as parenthetical expressions *do not* interrupt the flow of a sentence. In such cases no commas are used with the expression.

beginning of sentence

Perhaps the package will arrive in Los Angeles by Monday.

end of sentence

My boss is planning a trip to New York City *too.*

within a sentence

She was *indeed* concerned about the omissions in the financial analysis.

c. Exclamations at the beginning of a sentence are parenthetical expressions that require a comma.

Oh, what a surprise to see Mrs. Hilton at the Christmas party!

Ah, it will not be easy to transfer these holdings into liquid assets!

d. Enumerations or explanations used as parenthetical expressions *within a sentence* are set off by commas, dashes, or parentheses. Use commas when the enumerated or explanatory information has no internal commas; use dashes or parentheses when the information contains commas within it or when the information is not closely related to the rest of the sentence.

commas

Only one company, *namely, Consolidated Enterprises,* bid on the contract.

dashes

He had invited several relatives--*namely, Aunt Meredith, Cousin Elma, and Uncle Ben*--to attend the company picnic.

parentheses

Our new vice president toured several cities *(Cleveland, Columbus, and Toledo)* to find a suitable plant site.

e. A parenthetical expression introducing an enumeration or explanation *after a complete thought* may be set off with either (1) commas or (2) a semicolon and a comma. If the enumeration or explanation itself is a complete thought or contains internal commas, use a semicolon and a comma. Otherwise, use just commas.

commas

We are expecting two exceptionally large orders next week, *namely,* from Reed's Department Store and Payco.

There are several ways we can cut our expenses during the next quarter, *for example,* by reducing our advertising budget.

semicolon and comma

This customer ordered new furniture for her living room; *namely,* a sofa, two chairs, and a cocktail table.

Your insurance does not cover all hazards; *i.e.,* any losses resulting from earthquake damage are not recoverable.

f. Short introductory prepositional phrases essential to the meaning of the sentence should not be mistaken for parenthetical expressions. These phrases answer specifically questions such as when, where, why, or how. Introductory prepositional phrases containing fewer than five words (but not containing a verb form) flow smoothly into the sentence and are *not* followed by a comma.

when?

In the future please place your orders with our Eastern Washington office.

At your convenience please return the enclosed form.

where?

At the conference we met agents from two of our branch offices.

In this case we are able to grant only a partial refund of the purchase price.

how?

In this way you will be able to cut your travel costs by 20 percent.

On your own you can prepare for this difficult examination.

why?

For that reason we have turned over your account to our attorney for collection

On this basis we are unable to employ any additional personnel.

g. Parenthetical expressions used as adverbs do not require commas.

However brilliant his work may be, Mr. Rogers will not be promoted until his disposition improves.

Obviously concerned with Ms. Jones's illness, the supervisor phoned her home.

Too many managers were absent yesterday.

1–3. Direct Address

Nouns of direct address are set off by commas. Capitalize only proper nouns or personal and professional titles used in direct address.

beginning of sentence

Ladies and gentlemen, it is a pleasure to address you this evening.

Mrs. Phelps, you are the winner of a Thanksgiving turkey.

within a sentence

Will you please, *Dr. Jones,* send us your check for $50 by March 30.

The book you have ordered, *Professor,* is presently out of stock.

end of sentence

You are certainly a competent secretary, *Ms. Boyer.*

You also should be concerned about this issue, *fellow American.*

1–4. Appositives

a. Appositives rename or explain previously mentioned nouns or pronouns and are usually set off by commas.

within a sentence

All the reports were submitted to Mr. Hartford, *our sales manager,* for approval.

end of sentence

She had reservations on the 5:30 p.m. flight, *the last flight to San Francisco that day.*

b. Restrictive appositives—appositives that are *needed to identify* (which one or what kind) the person or thing explained or renamed—are not set off by commas.

necessary for identification

The book *Secretarial Shortcuts* will be released next week.

Your student *Larry Green* has an appointment to see you tomorrow.

Manufacturers *like us* find themselves in financial difficulty today.

unnecessary for identification

His latest book, *College English,* was released last December.

Your best student, *Ann Freeman,* has an appointment to see you next week.

Small appliance manufacturers, *like us,* are in financial difficulty today.

c. One-word appositives or those forming parts of proper names do not require commas.

one-word appositives

My sister *Ellen* has the leading role in the school play.

You must obtain approval from our head nurse *Bertha.*

I *myself* plan to attend the organizational meeting in Memphis.

proper name

The novel dealt with the life of Richard *the Lionhearted.*

d. Abbreviations, Roman numerals, and college degrees written after individual names are set off by commas. Abbreviations after company names are also set off by commas. However, Roman numerals and the abbreviations *Inc.,* *Ltd., Jr.,* and *Sr.* are not placed in commas if a particular company or individual elects to omit them.

abbreviations with commas after individual and company names

Mr. Lowell T. Harrison, *Jr.,* has just been promoted to exccutive vice president.

Our firm will be represented by Alan Moskley, *Esq.**

Caroline R. Ryan, *Ph.D.,* is the author of *Executive Decision Making.*

Hargrave & Lyons, *Inc.,* was awarded the equipment contract.

Roman numeral with commas after name of individual

Donald J. Ellington, *III,* has just been appointed Secretary of State.

college degree after name of individual

Marilyn Drengson, *Doctor of Divinity,* will deliver the main graduation address.

omission of commas

Clothiers *Ltd.* is one of the largest jobbers on the West Coast.

Please send copies of the contract to David Warburton *Jr.* and the other names listed in the attached letter.

Only Robert T. Link *II* has access to the safety deposit box.

e. Words or expressions referred to simply as words or expressions should be underscored or placed in quotation marks rather than set off by commas.

underscored

The word <u>convenience</u> is often misspelled in business letters.

quotation marks

The phrase "Thanking you in advance" is an outdated expression that should be avoided in business letters.

1–5. Dates and Time Zones

a. Dates containing combinations of weekday, calendar date, and year require commas. Place a comma *after each element* used unless, of course, the element concludes a sentence. Commas are not used with a calendar date expressed alone.

calendar date expressed alone

On *February 28* our books were audited by the Internal Revenue Service.

---

*Courtesy titles are not used with the term *Esq.*

I

calendar date and year

On *February 28, 1986,* our books were audited by the Internal Revenue Service.

weekday and calendar date

On *Tuesday, February 28,* our books were audited by the Internal Revenue Service.

weekday, calendar date, and year

On *Tuesday, February 28, 1986,* our books were audited by the Internal Revenue Service.

b. Expressions of month and year may be written with or without commas as long as consistency is maintained. Remember, though, that a comma must be used after the year if one is used before it, unless the year appears at the end of the sentence.

with commas

In *March, 1988,* we will release our new line of products.

without commas

In *March 1988* we will release our new line of products.

c. Set off by commas any time zones used with clock times.

Our flight will leave Denver at 9:35 a.m., *MST,* and arrive in New York at 3:18 p.m., *EST.*

Your message arrived in San Diego at 8:40 a.m., *PDT.*

1–6. Addresses

a. Elements within an address are separated by commas.

name and complete address

Please send the check to *Ms. Harriet Buckley, 14832 Ventura Boulevard, Encino, California 91316,* after May 1.

complete address only

Mr. Livingston may be reached at *740 Gayley Avenue, Los Angeles, California 90025.*

b. Use commas to set off a state following the name of a city. Remember to use the second comma after the state name when it appears in the middle of a sentence.

within a sentence

The letter was sent to Kansas City, *Missouri,* in error.

end of sentence

On our tour we will visit Boston, *Massachusetts.*

1–7. **Coordinating Conjunctions**

a.   Place a comma before a coordinating conjunction *(and, but, or, nor)* that separates two independent clauses in a compound sentence. No comma is used if both clauses are not totally independent and could not stand alone as separate sentences. (See Section 1–18 for use of semicolon instead of comma.)

two independent clauses

Several salespeople will reach their goals this month, and they will earn a bonus trip to Philadelphia.

There are still 43 orders to fill, but we will close for vacation as scheduled.

I have not purchased any new appliances within the past month, nor have I purchased any new furniture during the last year.

no second independent clause

I hope to complete this project by Wednesday but cannot mail it to the district office until Friday.

We are aware that sales have increased in your district and that another salesperson should be assigned to your territory.

b.   In imperative sentences the subject *you* is understood. Separate with a comma two independent clauses, whether one or both are in the imperative form.

Ship the books to me at Eastern High School, but send the bill to the bookstore manager of Grant High School.

Please call Dr. Greenberg's office tomorrow morning, and his nurse will let you know what time the doctor is expected to finish surgery.

c.   When a simple adverb, introductory phrase, or dependent clause precedes and applies equally to two clauses, these clauses are not independent. Consequently, no comma is used between them.

simple adverb

Please call the doctor's office tomorrow morning and arrange to have your appointment changed to next week. (The adverb *please* modifies both *call* and *arrange.* Therefore, the two clauses are not independent of each other and no comma is used.)

introductory phrase

During the next month the board will visit several sites in Memphis and they will make a decision regarding the location of the new branch office.
(During the next month applies equally to both clauses. Consequently, they are not independent and are not separated by a comma.)

11

dependent clauses

If Mr. Howard calls, ask him for his address and send the brochure to him. (Subject *you* is understood in both clauses. *If Mr. Howard calls* applies to both clauses. Therefore, they are not independent and no punctuation mark is used.)

As soon as we receive your response, we will notify our distributor and he will ship your order immediately. (In this case *As soon as we receive your response* applies to both clauses; therefore, no punctuation mark is needed between the last two clauses.)

d. Omit the comma in short compound sentences connected by *and.*

Sharpen the pencils and return them immediately.

Do it now and you will be rewarded.

She demonstrated and we watched.

Give me your address and I will send you a catalog.

1–8. Independent Adjectives

Use commas to separate two or more independent adjectives that modify a noun. No commas are needed, though, when the first adjective modifies the second adjective and the noun as a unit. To identify independent adjectives, (1) reverse the adjectives, (2) read the adjectives independently, and (3) read the sentence with the word *and* between the adjectives. If the sentence makes sense and means the same thing with the adjectives read in these ways, then commas should be placed between them.

independent adjectives

He enclosed a *stamped, addressed* envelope.

The president had surrounded herself with *efficient, intelligent* assistants.

We received a *long, demanding, discourteous* letter from your company.

first adjective modifies second adjective and noun

The posters were lettered in *large bold print.*

He received several *attractive business offers.*

1–9. Introductory Clauses

a. An introductory dependent clause is separated from the rest of the sentence by a comma. Dependent clauses contain a subject and a verb and usually begin with one of the words listed below.

as ⎫		after	provided	until
if ⎬ are most common		although	since	whenever
when ⎭		because	so	while
		before	unless	

When Mr. Jones inherited $10,000, he invested the money in mutual funds.

So that we may reach a decision by March 14, please submit the papers immediately.

b. A shortened form of an introductory clause is separated from the rest of the sentence by a comma.

If so, the delivery of these materials will be delayed. (If that is so, ...)

As agreed, he will be dismissed. (As we have agreed, ...)

Whatever the reason, I would like to have the error corrected immediately. (Whatever the reason may be, ...)

c. Occasionally an introductory clause may be preceded by another introductory expression. In these cases place a comma only after the introductory clause.

Mrs. Jones said that *when this account is paid,* we will reinstate their credit privileges.

I hope that *before you file your income tax return,* you will check with our tax attorneys on this issue.

d. When an introductory clause is followed by two main clauses, place a comma only after the introductory clause.

When Jerold answers the telephone, he speaks clearly and he answers all questions courteously.

If you wish employment with our company, fill out the enclosed application form and mail it in the enclosed envelope.

1–10. Introductory Phrases

a. An introductory infinitive phrase (a verb preceded by *to*) is followed by a comma.

To arrive at an immediate decision, Mr. Holmes called a meeting of the stockholders.

To carry out the original plans, Miss Hyde hired two additional employees.

b. An introductory participial phrase (a verb form used as an adjective) is followed by a comma.

Hoping to obtain several large orders, Mr. Irwin embarked upon a selective advertising campaign.

Concerned about the sudden decrease in sales, Ms. Alexander flew to the West Coast.

c. An introductory prepositional phrase (a group of words that includes a preposition and an object) is separated from the rest of the sentence by a comma if it contains a verb form *or* five or more words. After an introductory prepositional phrase that contains no verb form and fewer than five words, use a comma only if the comma is necessary for clarity. A partial list of prepositions used to begin introductory prepositional phrases follows:

about	among	behind	during	on	until
above	around	below	for	over	up
after	at	between	from	through	upon
along	before	by	in	under	with

verb form

Upon receiving the papers, Swift & Company filed suit against its former parent company.

five or more words

During the past few days of litigation, concessions were made by both sides.

no verb form and fewer than five words

In the magazine article several new medical discoveries were discussed.

comma necessary for clarity

After this class, discussion will continue in Conference Room 14.

d. An introductory phrase that is preceded by another introductory expression is treated as if the opening introductory expression were not included.

infinitive phrase

Mr. Wilson explained that *to meet our production deadline,* we would have to work overtime the remainder of the week.

participial phrase

Mrs. Winston expressed concern over the poor telephone techniques used by our receptionist; and *speaking clearly and distinctly,* she demonstrated how Miss Davis should handle incoming calls.

prepositional phrase, fewer than five words

We were notified that *on Monday* we will resume our regular schedule.

prepositional phrase, five or more words

I hope that *in view of the urgency of the situation,* we will obtain the cooperation of our staff.

e. Any phrase that represents the subject or is part of the predicate is not followed by a comma.

infinitive phrase

To arrive at an immediate decision was Mr. Reed's intent.

participial phrase

Helping his employees prepare for advancement is not one of Mr. Green's attributes.

prepositional phrase

During the past few days of litigation came several unexpected concessions.

1–11. Restrictive and Nonrestrictive Phrases and Clauses

Restrictive phrases and clauses modify and contribute substantially to the main idea of a sentence and are essential to its meaning. They tell who, what, or which one and are not set off with commas.

Nonrestrictive phrases and clauses add an additional idea and do not significantly change or contribute to the main idea of the sentence. They are unessential word groups; that is, they are not needed by the main clause to tell who, what, or which one. Set off nonrestrictive phrases and clauses from the rest of the sentence with commas.

a. Relative clauses (those beginning with *who, whose, whom, which,* or *that*) are either restrictive (no comma) or nonrestrictive (comma required).

restrictive and essential to meaning

Office employees *who can type and take shorthand* can obtain well-paying jobs. (Tells which kind of office employees.)

nonrestrictive and not essential to meaning

Ms. Kennedy, *who can type and take shorthand,* can obtain a well-paying job. (Additional idea.)

In the first example the clause "who can type and take shorthand" limits the type of office employee who "can obtain well-paying jobs." In the second example "who can type and take shorthand" is of no assistance in identifying Ms. Kennedy but is merely an additional idea. Therefore, this is a nonrestrictive clause and is set off by commas.

restrictive and essential to meaning

All students *who are enrolled in history classes* will take part in organizing World Affairs Day. (Tells which students.)

nonrestrictive and not essential to meaning

Joseph, *who is enrolled in a history class,* will take part in organizing World Affairs Day. (Additional idea.)

b. Careful writers will use *that* for restrictive clauses (no comma) and *which* for nonrestrictive clauses (comma required).

15

restrictive

He has written a new book *that will be released next December.*

nonrestrictive

Her new book, *which was scheduled for spring publication,* will be released next December.

c. Dependent adverbial clauses (ones that begin with words such as *if, as, when, since, because,* etc.) that follow the main clause may be restrictive (no comma) or nonrestrictive (comma required). Restrictive clauses (1) answer such questions as when, why, how, or whether or (2) limit the main idea of the sentence. Nonrestrictive clauses, however, add an additional idea that does not alter the meaning of the main clause.

restrictive and essential to meaning

We will ship your order *as soon as your account is approved.* (Tells when.)

The company has doubled its monthly sales *since the advertising campaign started.* (Tells when.)

Please send us this information by March 1 *so that we may bring your records up-to-date.* (Tells why.)

Our company president retired last month *because his doctor recommended a six-month leave of absence.* (Tells why.)

We cannot install the additional equipment you requested *unless we receive an authorization from your main office.* (Limits main idea.)

You may order additional merchandise at the advertised sale prices *as long as we receive your order by March 31.* (Limits main idea.)

nonrestrictive and not essential to meaning

He has written his letter of resignation, *although I do not believe he will submit it.* (Additional idea.)

She will continue with her plans for introducing a new product, *whatever the competition might be.* (Additional idea.)

Several executives will tour our new South Haven plant, *where we will be hiring several hundred new employees.* (Additional idea.)

d. A dependent clause used parenthetically within a sentence is nonrestrictive and is set off with commas.

Sales figures for last year, *as you can see from the financial reports,* were nearly 10 percent higher than we had projected.

On Tuesday morning, *when you arrive for the meeting,* please give the manuscript to my secretary.

e. Participial, infinitive, or prepositional phrases within a sentence may be restrictive (no comma) or nonrestrictive (comma required).

participial restrictive

All employees *planning to attend the picnic* must sign up by July 1. (Tells which ones.)

participial nonrestrictive

The entire accounting staff, *planning to attend the picnic,* arranged for car pools. (Additional idea.)

infinitive restrictive

We are planning *to attend the company picnic* on July 1. (Tells what.)

infinitive nonrestrictive

The picnic will be held on July 4, *to mention only one company social function.* (Additional idea.)

prepositional restrictive

The announcements *for the company picnic* will be ready June 15. (Tells what.)

prepositional nonrestrictive

We are planning, *in response to requests,* an annual company picnic. (Additional idea.)

1–12. Contrasting, Limiting, and Opposing Expressions

Contrasting, limiting, or opposing expressions are set off with commas. Words often used to introduce these expressions are *not, never, but, seldom,* and *yet.*

contrasting expression

She had considered selling her stocks, *not her real estate,* to increase her liquid assets.

limiting expression

The association will give us four tickets, *but only for members of our sales staff.*

opposing expression

The sooner we are able to contact our investors in Chicago, *the sooner* we will be able to finance this new project.

The more money you can invest, the *greater the return you can expect.*

1–13. Omitted Words

Commas are often used to indicate the omission of words when the context of the sentence makes the omitted words clearly understood.

I

Four new secretaries were hired in the Accounting Department; three, in the Policy Issue Department. (Three *new secretaries were hired* in the Policy Issue Department.)

Last week Mr. Higgins dictated three complete reports; this week, two complete reports. (This week *Mr. Higgins dictated* two complete reports.)

Our A-100 contract expired on March 10; the A-107 contract, March 23; and the A-116, March 31. (The A-107 contract *expired on* March 23, and the A-116 *contract expired on* March 31.)

1–14. Punctuation for Clarity

a. Two identical verbs that appear together in a sentence are separated by a comma.

Whoever *wins, wins* a trip to Miami.

Whatever *occurs, occurs* with the knowledge of the president.

Whoever *travels, travels* at his own risk.

b. Words repeated for emphasis are separated by a comma.

Many, many years ago this company was founded by Mr. Bernard Harris.

It has been a *long, long* time since one of our vice presidents visited the West Coast.

c. A word or phrase that could be read incorrectly with the words that follow is set off by a comma.

Ever since, she has been employed by the Hirschell Corporation of Boston.

The week before, the corporation expanded its operations to Brazil.

d. A name written in inverted form is separated by a comma between the last name and the first name.

Irwin, Carl   Luers, Barbara R.

1–15. Short Quotations

a. A short quoted sentence is set off from the rest of the sentence by a comma. When the quoted sentence is broken into two parts, commas are required before and after the interjected thought.

beginning quotation

"All employees will receive two days' vacation after the contract is completed," said Mr. Jones.

interrupted quotation

"All employees will receive two days' vacation," said Mr. Jones, *"after the contract is completed."*

ending quotation

Mr. Jones said, *"All employees will receive two days' vacation after the contract is completed."*

b. Unless the quotation is interrupted, do not use commas when the quoted sentence is a question or an exclamation.

question

"When will the vacation period begin?" asked Ms. Snow.

interrupted question

"When," asked Ms. Snow, *"will the vacation period begin?"*

exclamation

"What a wonderful opportunity you have given our staff!" exclaimed Mr. Stevens.

interrupted exclamation

"What a wonderful opportunity," exclaimed Mr. Stevens, *"you have given our staff!"*

c. No comma is needed to set off a quotation or part of a quotation that is woven into a complete sentence or one that is not a complete thought.

woven into sentence

The chairperson operated on the premise that *"A stitch in time saves nine."*

John is reported to have said that *". . . no one will be able to take a vacation until June."*

incomplete sentence

Please mark this package *"Fragile."*

The personnel manager advised me *"to submit my application as soon as possible."*

He merely answered *"yes"* to all the questions.

d. When a comma and a quotation mark fall at the same point in a sentence, place the comma inside the closing quotation mark. Periods are also placed inside the closing quotation mark.

"Please arrive at the airport by 9 p.m.," requested Mrs. Chambers.

Her last magazine article, *"Western Travel,"* appeared in the <u>Automotive Digest</u>.

John said, *"Be sure to mail your report by June 11."*

e. For placement of question marks and exclamation points with closing quotation marks, see Section 1–44a, b.

1–16. Numerals

a. Numerals of more than three digits require commas.

1,320	1,293,070
51,890	23,092,946
963,481	

b. Two independent figures appearing consecutively in a sentence are separated by a comma.

Two consecutive numbers that act as adjectives modifying the same noun are not separated by a comma. Instead, express one number in figures and the other one in word form. Generally express the first number in word form and the second one in figure form. However, if the second number can be expressed in *fewer words* than the first one, place the first number in figure form and the second one in word form.

independent figures

Of this *$23,000, $12,000* is secured by real property.

During *1985, $76,000* worth of sales were financed through this plan.

two numbers modifying a noun

I will need *thirty 12-inch* rulers for my accounting class.

Each package contains *twelve 2-inch* nails.

Be sure to order *twenty-four 100-watt* bulbs for the lamps in the doctors' waiting rooms.

When you are at the post office, please purchase a roll of *100 twenty-cent* stamps.

The prescription was for *250 ten-milligram* tablets.

When the carton fell, *27 forty-watt* bulbs were broken.

c. Commas are omitted in years, house numbers, zip codes, telephone numbers, decimal fractions, metric measurements, and any word-numeral combinations. In metric measurements use a space to separate all numerals containing *more than four* digits.

years

1984   1838

house number

9732 Porter Street

zip code

Northridge, CA 91324

telephone number

(212) 482-9768

decimal fraction

.2873

metric measurements

1200 kilometers *(but)* 10 200 kilometers

word-numeral combinations

Serial No. 83621   page 1276   Room 1890

d.   Volume numbers and page references are separated by commas.

Please refer to Volume XI, page 9.

The article appeared in Volume X, July 1983, page 23.

e.   Measurements (such as weights, capacities, dimensions, etc.) are treated as single elements and are not interrupted by commas.

weight

Their new baby weighed *8 pounds 7 ounces.*

dimension

He is 5 *feet* 10 *inches* tall.

time period

Our flight time was estimated to be *2 hours 40 minutes.*

Semicolon

1–17.   Independent Clauses Without Coordinating Conjunctions

a.   A semicolon is used between two or more closely related independent clauses (complete thoughts that could stand alone as separate sentences) that are not connected with a coordinating conjunction *(and, or, but, nor).*

two independent clauses

Several orders were delayed in the Dallas office last month; Ms. Williams will check into our shipping procedures there.

Plan to attend the next American Management Association meeting; it will benefit you greatly.

three independent clauses

Mr. Horowitz drafted the contract specifications last week; Mr. Aames consulted the firm's attorneys on Monday; Mr. Dotson signed and mailed the company's offer on Wednesday.

b. Short and closely related independent clauses may be separated by commas.

two short independent clauses

She collated, I stapled.

three short independent clauses

The vase teetered, it fell, it broke.

I came, I saw, I conquered.

1–18. Independent Clauses With Coordinating Conjunctions

a. Two independent clauses linked by a coordinating conjunction are normally separated with a comma. If either or both clauses contain one or more commas, however, they should generally be separated by a semicolon.

no comma within clauses

She planned to attend the Chicago meeting, but several important matters interfered with her plans.

commas in one clause

Several new orders were recently placed through the Miami office; and Ms. Frisby, our merchandising director, was pleased with the progress of this new office.

commas in both clauses

You, of course, need not attend the committee meeting; but I believe it would be helpful, Mr. Plotkin, if you read over the minutes before addressing the Board of Directors.

b. A comma may be used before a coordinating conjunction that separates two *short* independent clauses containing internal commas.

Yes, Mr. Dale, we have on hand your current order, but it will be shipped only after your account is brought up-to-date.

We were pleased with the results of the survey, and you will, of course, receive a copy of the summary.

Yes, you may mail in your monthly payment, or you may take it to one of our fast, convenient pay stations.

1–19. Independent Clauses With Transitional Expressions

Two independent clauses (complete thoughts) separated by a transitional expression require a semicolon. A partial list of common transitional expressions follows. In addition, those words and phrases listed in Section 1–2 may be considered transitional expressions when they separate two closely related complete thoughts.

accordingly	indeed	notwithstanding	still
besides	in fact	on the contrary	then
consequently	in other words	on the other hand	therefore
furthermore	likewise	otherwise	thus
hence	moreover	so	yet
however	nevertheless		

A comma is used after a transitional expression of more than one syllable or where a strong pause is needed after a one-syllable expression.

transitional expression with one syllable

It will be difficult for the library staff to obtain a budget increase; *thus* it will not be possible to order all the books requested.

transitional expression containing more than one syllable

New catalogs will be shipped to our customers the first week in February; *therefore,* we can expect a 20 percent sales increase for the months of February, March, and April.

1–20. Series Containing Commas or Complete Thoughts

a. Items in a series are usually separated by commas. When, however, one or more of the elements contain a comma, use semicolons to separate the items.

Representatives from Boston, Massachusetts; Los Angeles, California; and Denver, Colorado, were not present at the conference.

Among those present at the convention were Mr. Harmon Fieldcrest, president of Fieldcrest Steel Industries; Dr. Garland Hansen, research director for the University of Wisconsin; Mrs. Joyce Morton, vice president of Wisconsin State Bank; and Ms. Georgia Fillmore, secretary-treasurer of CRA Consultants, Inc.

b. Three or more independent clauses (complete thoughts) comprising a series are separated by semicolons. Only very short clauses are separated by commas.

I

short clauses

It rained, it hailed, and it snowed.

long clauses

Nearly 7,000 circulars were mailed to prospective clients in 1978; over 15,000 circulars were mailed in 1983; and next year we plan to mail over 10,000 new brochures as well as 20,000 circulars.

long clauses with commas

Mr. John Harris, our company president, will arrive Saturday; Mrs. Olga Williams, one of our vice presidents, will arrive Monday; and Ms. Carol Watson, our company treasurer, will arrive Tuesday.

1–21. Enumerations and Explanations

a. When words or phrases that introduce enumerations or explanations follow an independent clause (complete thought), a semicolon or comma is used before the introductory expression and a comma is used after it. If the words following the expression contain commas or form another complete thought, use a semicolon before the expression. If not, use a comma. Some common introductory expressions follow.

such as	for instance	that is (i.e.)
for example (e.g.)	namely (viz.)	that is to say

semicolon and comma

Many factors have contributed to the sharp increase in production costs during the last three months; *namely,* price increases in raw materials, wage increases for electrical workers, and overtime salaries for the entire production staff.

To open its Syracuse office, Caldwell Industries advertised for a number of new employees; *that is to say,* not all the staff members were willing to transfer to the new location.

commas

You may wish to call Ms. Hendrix for further advice, *for example,* to inquire which filing system would be more efficient for your office.

b. Enumerations or explanations used as parenthetical expressions within a sentence are not set off by semicolons. Use commas when the enumerated or explanatory information has no internal commas; use dashes or parentheses when the information contains internal punctuation.

commas

Your accounting procedures, *for example, posting customer deposits,* can be streamlined with our new computer system.

dashes

Because of current economic conditions, we must find new vendors for some of our audiovisual equipment--*e.g., cassette tape recorders, video playback units, and carousel projectors*--to stay within our budget allocations.

parentheses

Your recommendations *(namely, increasing our staff, improving our hiring procedures, and revamping our testing program)* were approved unanimously by the board.

c. Enumerations or explanations without introductory expressions are preceded by a colon, not a semicolon.

Several new items were introduced in this popular line: gloves, scarves, and hosiery.

The following people were present at the sales managers' meeting: Roberta Adams, Horace Brubaker, Philip Haledon, and Susan McCloskey.

1–22. Semicolon Placement

Always place the semicolon outside closing quotation marks and parentheses.

quotation marks

Last month Mr. Harrison promised, "I will mail you a check the 1st of next month"; yet we have received no money or explanation from him.

parentheses

Several of our staff from the Accounting Department were out ill (with the flu); consequently, the end-of-the-month reports will be a week late in reaching the home office.

Colon

1–23. Formally Enumerated or Listed Items

a. Use a colon after an independent clause (complete thought) that introduces a formal listing or an enumeration of items. Words commonly used in introductory independent clauses include "the following," "as follows," "these," and "thus." Sometimes, however, the introduction is implied rather than stated directly. Use a colon following both direct and implied introductions.

In determining whether to use a colon or semicolon for introducing enumerated items, use the colon when the enumeration is not preceded by a transitional introductory expression such as *namely, e.g., for example, that is,* or *i.e.* If an introductory expression immediately precedes the listing, use a semicolon before the expression and a comma after it. (See Section 1–21a for examples.)

I

direct introduction

Mrs. Robinson ordered *the following* furniture and equipment for her offices: three desks, six chairs, two sofas, two electronic typewriters, and one personal computer.

These rules should be observed for a successful job interview:

1. Dress appropriately.
2. Appear interested in the company and the job.
3. Answer questions courteously.
4. Thank the interviewers for their time.

implied introduction

Several kinds of microcomputers were on display: IBM, DEC, Apple, Commodore, TRS, and Atari.

b. In three situations the colon is not used to introduce listings of items: (1) when an intervening sentence separates the introductory sentence and the enumerated items, (2) when the enumerated items are introduced by a *being* verb, and (3) when the listing is immediately preceded by a preposition or an enumerating expression.

no colon: intervening sentence

The following new silverware patterns will be available January 1. They will be introduced to our dealers next month.

Fantasia   Sunburst
Apollo   Moonglow

no colon: listing after "being" verb

The words most commonly misspelled *were* "convenience," "occasionally," "commodity," "consequently," and "accommodate."

no colon: listing after preposition

Sales meetings are scheduled *for* January 3, February 4, March 7, and April 9.

no colon: listing after enumerating expression

Please order some additional supplies; *namely,* bond paper, legal-sized envelopes, and shorthand dictation pads.

1–24. Explanatory Sentences

Separate two sentences with a colon when the second sentence explains, illustrates, or supplements the first.

explains

During the next three months, we will gross approximately 50 percent of our annual sales: major toy purchases occur during September, October, and November.

illustrates

Our new advertising campaign will be directed to buyers of economy cars: we will stress gas mileage, maintenance costs, and reliability.

supplements

Several new customers complained about the delay in receiving their charge account plates: they wished to have them in time to complete their holiday shopping.

1–25. Long Quotations

Long one-sentence quotations and quotations of two or more sentences are introduced by a colon.

long one-sentence quotation

Miss Alison Williams, personnel manager of Higgins Corporation, reported: "Graduates from the University of Southern California's School of Business have been placed in a number of our divisions, and they have risen to middle-management positions within a three-year period."

quotation of two or more sentences

One item of importance was noted from the board minutes of November 16:

Two new products, which will revolutionize word processing, will be introduced on July 1. Trade journal publicity and direct-mail advertising will be the major vehicles for distributing information about these products. Efforts by the sales staff for January and February will be directed specifically at marketing the Model AB 1781 and the Model AB 2782 communication networks.

1–26. Special-Purpose Uses for Colon

a. In business letters a colon is placed after the salutation when the mixed punctuation format (see Section 10–19) is used.

Dear Bill: Dear Ms. Corrigan: Gentlemen:

b. Use the colon to separate hours and minutes in expressions of time.

We will arrive at *8:30 a.m.* on Tuesday, March 24.

At *12:15 p.m.* Ms. Hardesty is scheduled to address the Compton Chamber of Commerce.

I

    c.   In expressing ratios, use the colon to represent the word *to.*

       The label instructions recommend proportions of *4:1.*

       The union members voted *2:1* against accepting the new contract.

    d.   The colon is often used to separate items in literary references.

       between place of publication and publisher

       Hoffer, Charles R. *The Understanding of Music.* Belmont, Calif.: Wadsworth Publishing Company, Inc., 1982, 483 pp.

       between titles and subtitles

       William C. Himstreet and Wayne Murlin Baty, *Business Communications: Principles and Methods,* 7th ed. (Boston: Kent Publishing Company, 1984), p. 151.

       biblical citations

       As an introduction to his sermon, the minister quoted Psalm *23:1* (Chapter 23, verse 1).

1–27. Colon Placement

    a.   In *typewritten* copy leave two blank spaces after a colon.

       May I please have the following documents by next week: copies of the rental agreement, the returned check, and the 30-day notice to move.

    b.   Place the colon outside closing quotation marks and parentheses.

       closing quotation mark

       Several staff members have already read her latest article, "Closing the Sale Effectively":   they had received advance copies last week.

       closing parenthesis

       Several contractors were being considered for the new project (Mountain Hills):   Wyeth and Sons, Burnside Developers, and Hartman Associates.

1–28. Capitalization With Colons

    a.   When a colon is used to introduce a horizontal listing of items, the initial letter after the colon is not capitalized unless it begins a proper noun.

       lowercase

       Place the following items in the tray: the original invoice, the duplicate invoice, and the shipping copy.

proper noun capitalized

Four employees were promoted last week: Teresa Caruana, Ina Geller, Gary Oliver, and Daniel Streebing.

b.   Do not capitalize the first letter after a colon when the second sentence explains or supplements the first unless the letter begins a proper noun.

lowercase

Your account has been temporarily closed: outstanding bills for $327 still remain unpaid.

proper noun capitalized

The $1,000 award was given to Mary Ellen Guffey: Dr. Guffey's essay was the most original one submitted.

c.   Capitalize the first word after a colon when the colon introduces a formal rule or principle stated as a complete sentence.

You should be able to apply the following rule in typing all your business correspondence: Always place commas and periods inside closing quotation marks.

Mr. Wilson emphasized the importance of strict adherence to the following policy: In case of absence all employees must notify their immediate supervisors by 8:30 a.m. that day.

d.   When two or more sentences follow a colon, capitalize the initial letter of each sentence.

Several suggestions emerged from the discussion: To begin with, an engineering firm should be consulted to determine the extent of damage to the property. Then a building contractor should be contacted for estimates to repair the damage. Finally, financial institutions should be surveyed to obtain the best terms for reconstructing the property.

e.   Capitalize the initial letter of material introduced by short words such as *Note, Attention,* or *For Sale.*

Warning: All cars parked illegally will be towed away at owners' expense.

Caution: Please hold children by hand.

f.   Capitalize the initial word of quoted material that follows a colon.

Mr. Rosen informed the board of expansion plans for this year: "Property has been purchased on the corner of Tampa and Nordhoff at a cost of $180,000. Construction of our new branch office will begin early this spring, and we can plan to open this office in July or August."

Dash

1–29. Parenthetical Elements

    a.   Parenthetical elements are usually set off from the rest of the sentence by commas. When the parenthetical element contains internal commas, however, substitute dashes (or parentheses) for the separating commas. Use dashes when the parenthetical element requires emphasis. In typed material a dash is formed by typing two hyphens with no space before, between, or after; in printed material a dash appears as a solid line.

       Last month Miss Owens--with the hope of increasing sales, recruiting new employees, and establishing sources of supply--made several trips to the East Coast.

       Three state dignitaries--Governor Hanson Williams, Attorney General Steven Mills, and Secretary Willard Robinson--attended the opening session of the convention.

    b.   To achieve greater separation, abrupt parenthetical elements or those requiring emphasis may be separated from the rest of the sentence by dashes instead of commas.

       abrupt parenthetical element

       Her only concern--notwithstanding her interest in job security--was finding employment in an organization where opportunities for advancement were numerous.

       emphatic parenthetical element

       Several orders were rerouted to the Milwaukee office--not to the Salt Lake City branch.

    c.   Dashes may be used to set off a brief summary or an appositive from the rest of the sentence.

       summary

       Thanksgiving, Christmas, and New Year's Day--these are the only holidays the store will be closed.

       appositive

       Additional heavy-duty equipment--bulldozers and graders--was needed to complete the project.

    d.   For emphasis use a dash in place of a comma or a semicolon to introduce an example or explanation.

example requiring emphasis

Insurance coverage adequate five years ago may no longer fulfill the purpose for which it was designed--for example, if current inflationary trends continue, fire and theft insurance may not cover the replacement costs of the insured properties.

explanation requiring emphasis

Our sales of greeting cards have increased 25 percent since 1983--namely, from $100,000 to $125,000.

e. Afterthoughts or side thoughts generated from the text, but not necessarily part of it, may be separated from the rest of the sentence by dashes.

side thought

All members of our staff were invited to the conference on simplifying communication procedures--only Ms. Harris was unable to attend the session.

afterthought

Mrs. Wilson had planned to finish the correspondence this afternoon--at least John thought she had planned to do it then.

1-30. Hesitations in Verbal Reports

Use dashes to indicate hesitations, falterings, or stammering in reports of conversations, testimonies, or speeches.

Miss Tomlin: Yes, Mr. President--we expect perhaps a--oh--35 percent increase in sales during the next year.

Mr. Schatz: Well--perhaps a new inventory-control system will solve some of the current problems.

1-31. Source of Quotations

A dash is placed before the source of a quotation when the source is listed after the quotation.

"We can expect a great decrease in our unemployment rate during the next ten months."

--H. J. Scott

"The difference between the right word and the almost right word is the difference between lightning and the lightning bug."

--Mark Twain

1–32. Format and Placement of Dash

a. Form the dash by typing consecutively two hyphens; leave no space before, after, or between the hyphens. A dash never begins a new line, but it may appear at the end of a line.

end of line

Our new contract negotiations--after reaching an impasse on December 20-- were resumed on January 5.

within line

Several influential community organizations--the Kiwanis Club, the Chamber of Commerce, and the Rotary Club--sponsored Mr. Harrison Strong for the vacant seat on the board of education.

b. The only punctuation mark that may precede an opening dash is a period in an abbreviation. Closing dashes may be preceded by a period in an abbre- viation, a question mark, or an exclamation point.

opening dash after abbreviation

Prices quoted on all Eastern furniture were f.o.b.--freight charges from Pennsylvania to Los Angeles amounted to $834.

closing dash after question mark

A new kind of after-dinner mint--do you know which one I mean?--was introduced by the Walter Candy Company last month.

Period

1–33. End of Sentence

Place a period at the end of a declarative sentence, an imperative statement or command, an indirect question, and a polite request. Polite requests end with a period even though they may appear to have the format of a question. A polite request (1) asks the reader to perform a specific action and (2) is answered by the reader's compliance or noncompliance with the request.

declarative sentence

Several new products were introduced to the stockholders at the February 5 meeting.

imperative statement

Answer the telephone before the third ring.

indirect question

She asked who would be attending the conference scheduled for next week.

1–34. End of Independent Phrase

Independent phrases, those phrases representing implied complete thoughts not directly connected with the following thought, are concluded with a period.

Now, to get to the point. Will you be able to accept responsibility for conducting a sales campaign during June?

Yes, for the most part. Our salespeople have increased their sales since the new incentive program was initiated.

1–35. Abbreviations and Initials

a. An abbreviation is usually concluded with a period. However, after abbreviations for business and governmental organizations, radio and television stations, federal agencies, and certain professional designations (CLU, CPA, CPS, PLS), the periods are omitted. (See Section 1–39a for spacing following the period.)

period after abbreviation

Fletcher, Hagan, Ross, and Company, *Inc.,* released several new stock issues.

periods after abbreviations

Mr. Haynes requested that all orders be sent on a *c.o.d.* basis.

no periods with certain abbreviations

I hope the educational project director for *NASA* will be able to address our convention.

Did you purchase additional *IBM* stock?

b. Place a period after an initial.

Ms. Charlene *P.* Holt accepted the invitation to address the convention participants.

We have tried for several days to contact *A. F.* Elliot.

1–36. Outlines

a. Use periods after letters and numbers in outlines, except those enclosed in parentheses.

I

```
I.    . . . . .
   A.   . . . . .
   B.   . . . . .
      1.  . . . . .
      2.  . . . . .
         a.  . . . . .
         b.  . . . . .
            (1)  . . . . .
            (2)  . . . . .
               (a)  . . . . .
               (b)  . . . . .
II.   . . . . .
```

b. Use periods after complete sentences in outlines and listings. No punctuation mark is placed after an incomplete thought.

periods—complete sentences

A. Two new processes were developed as a result of the experiments.
   1. Lamination of fiberglass to wooden surfaces contributes to vessel buoyancy.
   2. Sealing of surfaces prevents excessive moisture absorption.

no periods—incomplete sentences

A. New Processes
   1. Lamination of fiberglass to wooden surfaces
   2. Sealing of surfaces

1–37. Decimals

Periods are used to signify decimals.

It was hard to believe that *34.7* percent of the students failed the final examination.

Last year Mr. Phoenix paid $120 for the 2,000 sales announcements; this year he paid *$145.50* for the same kind and number.

1–38. Emphasis and Omission

An ellipsis (a series of three periods with a space before, between, and after the series) is used for emphasis in advertising material or for showing omissions in quoted material. In showing omissions, indicate the completion of a thought with an additional period. (See Section 1–52 for further information on the use of ellipses.)

emphasis

Place your order today . . . for relief from tension headaches . . . for ending miserable aches and pains . . . for a happier, tension-free you.

omission

The president read from the consulting company's report: "Basically, operations should be conducted according to the attached plan. . . . Several new operations personnel should . . . implement the recommended procedures."

1–39. Period Format

a. No space is placed between a decimal point and a number or after a period within an abbreviation. However, within a sentence one space follows an initial or the concluding period in an abbreviation. In typewritten copy allow two spaces after a period at the end of a sentence.

decimal—no space

Since 1982 costs of manufacturing materials have risen *18.5* percent.

period within abbreviation—no space

Be sure to ship the order *c.o.d.*

initial—one space

John *R.* Gardner was elected chairman of the committee.

abbreviation within sentence—one space

Dr. Sussman has scheduled *Mrs.* Johnson for surgery at 9 *a.m.* in Encino Hospital.

end of sentence—two spaces

Please begin transcribing your notes after the morning session.   I believe the committee wishes to have the minutes by tomorrow morning.

b. Use only one period to end a sentence, even though the sentence may end with an abbreviation.

She is scheduled to arrive between 9 and 10 a.m.

Mr. Kirk's mail is to be forwarded to his Washington, D.C., address: 1938 South Harvard Street, N.W.

c. A period is always placed inside the closing quotation mark.

Ms. Allison promptly replied, "No funding requests will be honored after July 1."

Joseph was pleased with your magazine article, "New Ideas for Home Builders."

d. A period is placed inside the closing parenthesis when the words in parentheses are a complete sentence. When words in parentheses are not a complete thought and are part of another sentence, place the period outside the closing parenthesis.

complete sentence in parentheses

Several executives left the company after the merger. (They were disappointed with the leadership of the new company.)

incomplete sentence in parentheses

Only three items were discontinued after the consulting analysts completed their investigation (last March).

Question Mark

1–40. Direct Questions

Conclude a direct question that requires an answer with a question mark.

How many times have you tried to contact Miss Wilson?

Of all the people at the board meeting, how many would you estimate were antagonistic toward the salary proposal?

1–41. Statements With Questions

a. When a sentence contains a statement followed by a direct question, conclude the sentence with a question mark. Separate the statement from the question with a comma, dash, or colon, depending upon the nature of the statement.

question mark with comma

I would recommend that we contact at least three other vendors before selecting a permanent source of supply, wouldn't you agree?

question mark with dash

They were satisfied with the report--weren't they?

question mark with colon

Consider the following question: how do you view the profit picture for next year?

b. A statement that is meant as a question is concluded with a question mark.

You still expect to leave for Cleveland tomorrow morning?

The conference has been delayed until April?

c. Conclude a statement that contains a short, direct question with a question mark.

It was Mr. Stevens--or was it Mrs. Harrison--who requested the stationery?

You have filed your income tax return, have you not, for the last taxable year?

d. A period, rather than a question mark, is placed after an indirect question.

Mr. Holcomb asked when we expected our Albany office to release the information.

Ms. Holdridge inquired as to the possibility of placing several students in our Accounting Department as trainees in a cooperative work-experience program.

e. Polite requests phrased as questions are followed by periods rather than question marks because they are considered to be commands. A polite request (1) asks the reader to perform a specific action and (2) is answered by having the reader either take or ignore the action requested instead of responding with a "yes" or "no." Both components *must* be present for a period to be used; otherwise, a question mark is correct.

polite request requiring period

Will you please send us three copies of your latest financial report.

May I please have this information by the end of the month.

Won't you take a few minutes now to fill in the enclosed questionnaire and return it in the self-addressed envelope.

May we count on your support with a "yes" vote on Proposition 11.

direct question requiring question mark

Would you be willing to address envelopes for the Senator's reelection campaign? (Requires "yes" or "no" answer.)

May we have your support in the future? (Does not require reader to return a "yes" or "no" answer, but no *specific* action is requested.)

Wouldn't you like to be the proud owner of a new Supra 28 personal computer? (Does not require reader to return a "yes" or "no" answer, but no *specific* action is requested.)

May I compliment you on your outstanding performance in meeting this year's sales quota? (No "yes" or "no" answer required; however, no *specific* action requested.)

1–42. Expressions of Doubt

Doubt in expressing statements of fact may be signified by enclosing a question mark in parentheses.

His last visit to the East Coast was in 1982(?).

She earns $1,700(?) a month.

1–43. Series of Questions

When a sentence contains a series of questions, place a question mark at the end of each element. Only the initial letter of the sentence is capitalized unless an element begins with a proper noun or is a complete thought. Leave one space after a question mark that appears within a sentence.

series of incomplete questions

What are the primary responsibilities of the president? of the executive vice president? of the treasurer?

Who requested the report--the vice president? the secretary? the treasurer?

series of proper noun questions

Will the new flight routes stop in San Diego? Los Angeles? San Francisco?

series of independent questions

Several important issues were discussed at the conference last week: What style trends will be popular during the next decade? What comfort demands will the public make on furniture manufacturers? How much will price influence consumer furniture purchases?

1–44. Question Mark Placement and Format

a. Question marks may be placed either inside or outside the closing quotation mark or parenthesis. When a complete question is contained within the quotation or parenthetical remark, place the question mark inside the closing quotation mark or parenthesis. If the entire sentence, not just the quotation or parenthetical remark, comprises the question, place the question mark outside the closing quotation mark or parenthesis. Use only one concluding mark at the end of a sentence.

complete question contained in parentheses

We received official notification last week *(did your notice arrive yet?)* that we must vacate our offices by the 1st of the month.

The committee informed me that J. Wilson Edwards has been appointed manager of the Phoenix office. *(Did you approve this appointment?)*

complete question contained in quotation marks

"Will the entire original cast be present for the opening night in Philadelphia?" asked a local reporter.

The Governor asked, "Who is in charge of this committee?"

question encompasses entire sentence

Can you let us know your decision by March 21 (earlier if possible)?

Have you finished reading the article "Hidden Magic"?

b. If the entire sentence and the quotation are both questions, use only the first question mark—the one appearing inside the closing quotation mark.

Did the president ask, "When will the directors hold their next meeting?"

c. In typewritten copy leave one space after a question mark that appears within a sentence and two spaces after a question mark that appears at the end of a sentence.

one space

Shall I place these supplies on the desk? in the cabinet? in the storeroom?

two spaces

What time shall we leave for the airport?   When is your flight scheduled to depart?   What time do you expect to arrive in Atlanta?

Exclamation Point

1–45.

Use of Exclamation Point

To express a high degree of emotion, use an exclamation point after a word, phrase, clause, or sentence.

word

What! You mean the materials will not arrive until next week?

phrase

How beautiful! The designer certainly used a great deal of color and imagination in creating this pattern.

clause

If he comes! He'd better come, or Mr. Harrison will get a new assistant.

sentence

So, she finally answered my question!

1–46. Exclamation Point Placement and Format

a. If the typewriter does not have an exclamation point key, form the exclamation point by typing the apostrophe, back-spacing, and then typing a period. Double-space after the exclamation point before beginning the next sentence.

b. The exclamation point should be used sparingly in business correspondence, and one exclamation point directly following another should be avoided. Instead, use commas, periods, or question marks to complete an exclamatory thought.

exclamation with comma

Oh, it will be impossible for us to meet the contract deadline!

exclamation with period

No! Mr. Jones has not resigned.

exclamation with question mark

What! You expected the completed analysis last week?

c. Exclamation points may be placed before or after the closing quotation mark or parenthesis. When a complete exclamatory remark is a quotation or is enclosed in parentheses, place the exclamation point inside the closing quotation mark or parenthesis. If the entire sentence, not just the quotation or parenthetical element, comprises the exclamatory expression, place the exclamation point outside the closing quotation mark or parenthesis. Use only one concluding mark at the end of a sentence.

complete exclamatory expression in quotation marks

One of the employees shouted, *"Break down the door!"*

complete exclamatory expression in parentheses

He obtained the help of several advisors *(what a mistake that was!)* to assist him in selecting the project subcontractors.

Management was shocked at the employees' reactions to the new process. *(Only 4 percent of the staff agreed to follow the new procedures!)*

exclamatory expression encompasses entire sentence

If you wish to take advantage of these bargains, you will have to act now (today)!

I cannot believe Marie Huffinger's statement, "Only 3 percent of the merchandise was returned"!

Quotation Marks

1–47. Direct Quotations

Place direct quotations, the exact wording used by a writer or speaker, within quotation marks. Quotation marks are not used for indirect quotations that do not use the exact wording of the reference.

direct quotation

"The economy cannot help slowing down by next year," said Dr. Roger Watson, a renowned economist.

indirect quotation

Donna Roberts, our production manager, said that our manufacturing costs per unit will increase at least 30 percent within the next year.

1–48. Short Expressions

a. When short expressions—such as words used in humor, technical words used in a nontechnical way, or slang words—need to be emphasized or clarified for the reader, they are placed in quotation marks. These same words are often shown in italics when they appear in print.

slang words

My secretary was certainly "on the ball" when she discovered the error in the contract.

technical words used in nontechnical way

Mr. Rollins announced that "all systems are go" for the new space exploration project.

b. Place in quotation marks the definitions of words or expressions. Underscore the word or expression defined.

defined word

According to some economists, a <u>recession</u> is actually a "little depression."

defined expression

The French term <u>faux pas</u> means "a social blunder."

c. References to words marked or stamped are placed in quotation marks.

Be sure to mark all packages "Glass--Handle With Care."

The envelope was stamped "Addressee Unknown, Return to Sender."

1–49. Titles

Titles of various kinds of literary or artistic works such as magazine or newspaper articles, chapters of books, movies, television shows, plays, poems, lectures, songs, and themes are placed within quotation marks. Names of books, magazines, pamphlets, and newspapers, however, are underscored or typed in all capital letters.

chapter and book title

The chapter "Principles of Office Organization" contained in <u>Office Management and Automation</u> was helpful in implementing our office reorganization.

movie title

Disney's "Cinderella" has been a favorite of children for many years.

lecture title

Her lecture, "Combating Inflationary Trends," was very well attended.

song title

We arrived at the musical just in time to hear "With a Little Bit of Luck."

1–50. Quotations Within Quotations

Use single quotation marks to signify a quotation within a quotation. Single quotation marks are typed by using the apostrophe key.

The report stated, "According to the U.S. Chamber of Commerce, 'The problem of air and water pollution must be solved within the next decade if our cities are to survive.' "

1–51. Quoted Paragraphs

a. When a quoted paragraph contains three or fewer lines and consists of two or more sentences, place quotation marks at the beginning of the first sentence and at the end of the last sentence.

Mr. Williams wrote: "My wife became ill on Monday and was taken to the hospital. Therefore, I will not be able to attend the meeting."

b. When a quotation contains four lines or more, indent from both margins and single-space the quoted material in a separate paragraph. No quotation marks are used with the quotation. Introduce the quotation with a colon.

The speaker brought out the importance of management communication when she made the following statement:

> To exercise the function of leadership, there must be effective communication. If a leader cannot communicate, there is no leader because information cannot pass between the two groups. For instance, in management it is not possible to delegate duties and authority without effective communication.

1–52. Ellipses

An ellipsis (a series of three periods with a space before, between, and after the series) is used to show an intentional omission of quoted material. If the omission occurs at the end of a sentence, use an ellipsis, leave a space, and then place the closing punctuation mark for the sentence. If one or more sentences have been omitted, first place the closing punctuation mark immediately after the last word; then follow with an ellipsis to show the omission.

omission within sentence

The new sign was worded to discourage nonresidents from parking in the private lot: "Violators will be towed . . . cars will be released only upon payment of a $50 fine."

end-of-sentence omission

The guarantee reads: "All repairs that do not come under the warranty will be made at less than 30 percent of the regular cost . . . ."

"How many miles is the home office from our various branch offices; i.e., Houston, Dallas, Oklahoma City, . . . ?"

one or more sentences omitted

"Please ship our foreign orders by September 1. . . . Our European distributors must have their merchandise by October 1." (Double-space after final period in ellipsis before beginning the next sentence.)

"Will you be able to attend the conference in Baltimore? . . . We will need to set up our display booths on September 9." (Double-space after final period in ellipsis before beginning next sentence.)

1-53. Capitalization With Quotation Marks

a. Capitalize the first word of a complete sentence enclosed in quotation marks.

"Please call me before 10 a.m. tomorrow," requested Mrs. Edwards.

Andrew replied, "Yes, I will be able to attend the conference on Monday."

b. Capitalize incomplete thoughts enclosed in quotation marks only if the quoted words themselves are capitalized. Quoted expressions preceded by "stamped" or "marked" are usually capitalized.

capitalized

His check was returned from the bank marked "Insufficient Funds."

"Handle With Care" was stamped on the package.

not capitalized

Mrs. Atkins asked us to spend "as little time as possible" on this project.

1-54. Quotation Mark Placement

a. Periods and commas are always placed inside the closing quotation mark; semicolons and colons, outside the closing quotation mark.

period

The purchase requisition reads, "Cancel this order if the merchandise cannot reach us by the 1st of the month."

comma

"Our operating costs must be lowered," said Mr. Collins.

semicolon

The consultant's report stated, "A thorough analysis of the company's data processing system should be made"; however, no steps have been taken to initiate such an analysis.

colon

Miss Cox recommended the following vacation policy "unless a better one can be found":   (1) Employees should select their vacation time on the basis of seniority and (2) conflicts should be resolved by the employees themselves, whenever possible.

b.   When a complete question or exclamation is contained within the quotation, place the question mark or exclamation point inside the closing quotation mark. If the entire sentence comprises the question or exclamation, then place the appropriate mark outside the closing quotation mark. If both the quotation and the entire sentence are questions, use only the first question mark.

complete question within quotation

He asked, "Where are the annual reports filed?"

entire sentence comprises question

Do you have a copy of her latest article, "Air Pollution Control"?

complete exclamation within quotation

"Do not," exclaimed Mr. Rey, "leave the lights burning all night again!"

entire sentence comprises exclamation

Our new sales manager is a real "go-getter"!

question within a question

Did Mr. Heinze inquire, "What time will our flight depart?"

Apostrophe

1–55.   Possessives

a.   When a noun, singular or plural, does not end with a pronounced *s*, add an apostrophe and *s ('s)* to form the possessive case.

singular noun

Yes, I found the request on my *secretary's* desk.

Lisa's father owns the company.

plural noun

Women's fashions are much more colorful this year.

This garment is made from *sheep's* wool.

b. When a noun, singular or plural, ends with a pronounced *s,* generally add an apostrophe *(')* to form the possessive case. However, an apostrophe and *s* *('s)* may be added to singular nouns ending in a pronounced *s* if an additional *s* sound is also pronounced.

singular noun

Mrs. Simons' attendance record has been perfect during the last five years.

Ask *Mr. Jones'* secretary for a copy of the report.

plural noun

Customers' accounts must be reviewed every 90 days.

The Simonses' home was burglarized earlier this week.

singular noun with additional "s" sound

We have been invited to our *boss's* home for dinner on April 15.

This *class's* grades are unusually low.

c. Possessives are generally formed on nouns that represent people or animals (animate objects) or nouns relating to time, distance, value, or celestial bodies. For other types of nouns (inanimate objects), show possession by an *of* phrase.

animate possessive

The *employees'* picnic is scheduled for next Saturday.

Our *company's* declining profits eventually caused bankruptcy.

time possessive

This *year's* profit and loss statement showed a gain of nearly 12 percent.

Enclosed is a check for three *months'* rent.

value possessive

She ordered several thousand *dollars'* worth of paper.

You owe me 50 *cents'* change.

celestial possessive

During the summer months the *sun's* rays can be extremely harmful if one is not careful.

Is *Mars'* atmosphere suitable for human survival?

distance possessive

He came within a *hair's* breadth of hitting the parked car.

The thief rushed by within an *arm's* length.

inanimate possessive

The *terms of the loan* were extended another six months.

Who broke the *base of the pot*?

d. Form the possessive of compound nouns by having the last word show possession.

She was designated her *father-in-law's* beneficiary.

Our next Christmas party will be held at the *chairman of the board's* home.

My two *sisters-in-law's* business is doing well.

e. When two or more nouns have joint possession, only the last noun shows possession. When the nouns represent individual ownership, however, each noun must show possession.

joint possession

Bill and Sheryl's new secretary has worked at ABCO Corporation for three years. (Bill and Sheryl share the same secretary—joint possession.)

The Harrises and the Bradys' new boat was damaged in the storm. (The Harrises and the Bradys own the same boat—joint possession.)

individual possession

Mary's and Henry's new secretaries had worked in the clerical pool for over a year. (Mary and Henry have different secretaries—individual possession.)

The Phillipses' and the Gonzalezes' houses are on the same street. (The Phillipses and the Gonzalezes live in different houses—individual possession.)

f. The possessive of indefinite pronouns such as *anyone, everyone, someone, anybody, everybody, somebody,* and *nobody* is formed by using the same rules that apply to possessive nouns.

It is *anyone's* guess when we will be able to resume production.

Somebody's car is blocking the entrance to the parking lot.

g. The possessive forms of personal or relative pronouns (such as *its, theirs, whose,* or *yours*) do not include apostrophes. These pronouns are often confused with verb contractions, all of which contain apostrophes.

possessive pronoun

I met Ralph, *whose* father has a large account with our organization.

Although the company had *its* greatest sales volume last year, it still failed to show a profit.

contraction

I met Sara, *who's* going to apply for a job with our firm.

It's impossible to read his handwriting.

h. Possessives of abbreviations are formed by using the same rules that apply to possessive nouns.

noun not ending with "s"

The *CPA's* report was comprehensive.

NASA's new space project is scheduled for a 1987 launching.

noun ending with "s"

Barker Bros.' annual sale will be held next week.

All *R.N.s'* badges are to be turned in at the end of each shift.

You may wish to follow the *IRS's* advice in this instance. (Use *'s* instead of *'* because of extra pronounced syllable.)

i. Use the possessive case of a noun or pronoun before a gerund (an *-ing* verb used as a noun).

noun

Don's accounting of the convention expenses was incomplete.

pronoun

We would appreciate *your* returning the enclosed form by March 31.

j. Sometimes an explanatory expression, instead of the noun it modifies, shows possession. When this form of writing sounds awkward, show possession by using an *of* phrase.

apostrophe

It was Ms. Madden, our *office manager's,* idea to hold the meeting.

"of" phrase

It was the idea *of our office manager,* Ms. Madden, to hold the meeting.

k. Many organizations with plural possessives in their names have omitted the apostrophe; organizations with singular possessives have tended to retain the apostrophe. The precise format used by the organization itself should be followed.

I

plural possessive

We have just been granted a loan from the *Farmers* Bank and Trust Company.

singular possessive

The contract was issued to *Linton's* Manufacturing Company.

l. Sometimes the possessed item is not explicitly stated in a sentence, but it is understood or clearly implied. In such cases the ownership word still uses an apostrophe to show possession.

This year the holiday office party will be at *Sandy's*.

Be sure to meet me at the *doctor's* by 2 p.m.

The wallet found in the corridor was Mr. *Lopez's*.

Deliver this floral arrangement to the *Briggses'*.

1–56. Additional Uses

a. Use the apostrophe to form contractions.

single-word contraction

acknowledged   *ack'd*

two-word contraction

is not   *isn't*

b. For clarity the apostrophe is used to form the plural of all lowercase letters and the capital letters *A, I, M,* and *U.*

plural of lowercase letter

Be sure to dot your *i's* and cross your *t's*.

plural of letters "A," "I," "M," and "U"

Mr. Craig's daughter received three *A's* on her report card.

Parentheses

1–57. Nonessential Expressions

Parentheses are used to set off and subordinate nonessential expressions that would otherwise confuse the reader because (1) they give supplementary information that has no direct bearing on the main idea or (2) they call for an abrupt change in thought. References and directions are examples of expressions that are often enclosed in parentheses.

abrupt change in thought

I wrote to Mr. Furstman (I tried to call him, but there was no answer) and asked him to contact us before October 4.

reference

All major repairs must first be cleared through proper channels. (See Bulletin 8 dated March 2.)

directions

Please reproduce 100 copies of this form by tomorrow. (Center the material and use yellow paper.)

1–58. Numerals

Numerals in legal, business, and professional documents are often shown in parentheses to confirm a spelled-out figure.

All work is guaranteed for ninety (90) days.

Compensation for services rendered will not exceed three thousand dollars ($3,000).

1–59. Enumerated Items

Enclose numbers or letters in parentheses when they are used to enumerate lists of items within a sentence.

numbers

I need the following information for the current year: (1) the number of people hired, (2) the number of people retired, and (3) the number of people terminated.

letters

Please send us the following information: (a) current salary trends, (b) unemployment statistics, and (c) placement requests.

1–60. Parentheses Placement

a. Words, phrases, and clauses enclosed in parentheses in the middle of a sentence function as part of the sentence in applying rules of punctuation and capitalization.

word

We will fly to Oakland *(California)* for our annual convention.

phrase

Ms. Haven will gross nearly $800,000 *(as compared to a $500,000 average)* in sales this year.

clause

Our new manager *(several members of our staff met him last week)* will conduct a communications seminar in the spring.

b. When a period is used to close a sentence that ends with an incomplete thought enclosed in parentheses, place the period outside the closing parenthesis.

According to our latest reports, this procedure violates state laws (Minnesota and Wyoming).

Several members of the committee will meet in Kansas City this weekend (if possible).

c. When a period is used to close a sentence that ends with a complete thought enclosed in parentheses, the two elements are treated separately. Place a period at the end of both thoughts, with the final period appearing inside the closing parenthesis.

Yes, your order is on its way. (I mentioned this fact to your secretary yesterday.)

Several members of our staff attended the ATLW conference this year. (It was held in Hawaii.)

d. If a word, phrase, or clause shown in parentheses requires a question mark or exclamation point, use such a mark of punctuation only if the sentence ends with a *different mark.*

parenthetical question

Our new manager (do you know Marsha Karl?) will arrive in Los Angeles tomorrow.

Were you informed that our new price list (has your copy arrived yet) will go into effect on October 1?

parenthetical exclamation

Have you heard about the enormous price increases (I can scarcely believe them!) in single-family homes?

Prices in this tourist town are high (unusually high)!

e. Place commas, semicolons, and colons outside the closing parenthesis.

comma

If you plan to attend the company party (on May 16), please send your reservations to Terry Thomsen by Monday, May 12.

semicolon

His report dealt with the importance of our country's major transportation systems (railroads, inland waterways, motor trucks, pipe lines, air transportation, express, and parcel post); therefore, little emphasis was given to rising transportation costs.

colon

On February 15 Ms. Pangonis will introduce two new product lines (in our women's fashion department): the Sportswoman Series and the Sun and Surf Coordinates.

Brackets

1–61. Use of Brackets

Brackets are generally used to insert remarks or set off editorial corrections in material written by someone else. In addition, use brackets to enclose the term *sic* (meaning *thus* or *so)* to show that an error in quoted material appeared in the original document.

In his report Mr. Gilmer stated: "With new equipment to speed up the production process [*he did not specify what new equipment was needed*], substantial savings can be mad [*sic*] in both material and labor costs."

1–62. Brackets Placement

The placement of other punctuation marks with brackets follows the same principles outlined for parentheses in Section 1–60.

Asterisk

1–63. Use of Asterisk

When a footnote needs to be called to the reader's attention, use an asterisk. The asterisk generally follows other punctuation marks, except when it is used with a dash or with a complete thought enclosed in parentheses.

after most punctuation marks

A government report states, "Air traffic is expected to double in the next decade."*

before parenthesis or dash

Very good results have been obtained by companies that have hired outside consultants to develop cost-cutting procedures. (Several articles attesting to this fact have recently appeared in professional journals.*)

We are studying the works of Ray Bradbury*--one of today's leading science fiction writers.

Diagonal

1-64. Use of Diagonal

Use a diagonal (also called a "solidus," "slash," or "virgule") between (1) letters in some abbreviations, (2) numerals in fractions, and (3) the expression *and/ or* to indicate the terms are interchangeable. No space is left before or after the diagonal.

abbreviation

Please address the envelope: Mrs. Adeline Price, *c/o* George Martin, Display Manager, Wilson Disc Company, 1141 Western Avenue, Los Angeles, California 90024.

fraction

Costs have increased *1/2* percent since last week.

and/or

Authorizations for future purchases may be obtained from Ms. Jorgensen *and/or* Mr. Kline.

Underscore

1-65. Use of the Underscore

The underscore is used to emphasize such items as headings; words that would normally be italicized in print; and titles of books, magazines, newspapers, or pamphlets. Continuous lines, with no spacing between words, are used for underscoring. Except for periods with abbreviations, punctuation marks immediately following underlined material are not underlined.

word italicized in print

He always misspells the word <u>convenience</u>.

magazine title

According to an article in <u>Business Week</u>, most movies are currently being filmed outside the United States.

abbreviation

Be sure to place <u>a.m.</u> in lowercase letters.

Ampersand

1–66.   Use of the Ampersand

The ampersand (&), a symbol that represents the word *and,* is primarily used when it is part of the official name of some business organizations.

ampersand in company name

Johnson & Johnson was the subcontractor for the project.

use of "and" in company name

All merger talks with Merritt *and* Sons have been delayed until the end of our fiscal period.

Hyphenating and Dividing Words

Hyphenating and Dividing Words Solution Finder

2

Dividing Words

Rules for word division   2–7
   Compound words   2–7a
   Double letters   2–7c
   Hyphenated words   2–7a
   Prefixes   2–7b
   Suffixes   2–7b
   Vowels   2–7d, e
Word divisions to avoid   2–6
   Line endings   2–6d, e
   Proper nouns   2–6c
   Small words   2–6a
   Two-letter prefixes   2–6b
Word groups   2–8
   Addresses   2–8c, d
   Dashes, with   2–8f
   Dates   2–5e, 2–8a
   Lists within sentences   2–8e
   Names and titles   2–8b
   Numerals and descriptive
     units   2–5e
Words not to be divided   2–5
   Abbreviations   2–5d
   Contractions   2–5f
   Last words   2–5h
   Line endings   2–5g
   Numerals   2–5f
   One-syllable words   2–5a
   Single-letter syllables   2–5b
   Two-letter suffixes   2–5c
   Word-and-number groups
     2–5e

Hyphenating Words

Adjectives   2–2
   Colors   2–2g
   Comparatives   2–2f
   Compound nouns used as
     adjectives   2–2c
   Dollar amounts   2–2i, 2–4d
   Fractions used as compound
     adjectives   2–4c
   ly adverbs combined with
     adjectives   2–2e
   Numbers and nouns used as
     compound adjectives
     2–4d
   Percentages   2–2i
   Permanent compounds
     2–2b,c,f
   Proper nouns used as
     adjectives   2–2d
   Series of hyphenated
     adjectives   2–2h
   Superlatives   2–2f
   Temporary compounds   2–2a
Adverbs   2–2e
Nouns   2–1
Numbers   2–4
   Compound numbers   2–4a, b
   Fractions   2–4c
   Hyphen to represent
     "through"   2–4e
   Numbers used as
     adjectives   2–2i, 2–4d
Prefixes   2–3
Verbs   2–1

Hyphenating Words

2–1. Compound Nouns and Verbs

2

Often two or more words act as single-thought units. Nouns and verbs in this category may be written as separate words, written as single words, or hyphenated. Consult an up-to-date dictionary to determine the exact form of compound verbs and nouns.*

separate words, nouns

sales tax   work force   notary public   editor in chief

single words, nouns

bookcase   checkbook   lawsuit   heavyweight

hyphenated words, nouns

light-year   brother-in-law   stand-in   trade-off

single words, verbs

to uphold   to typewrite   to downgrade   to landscape

hyphenated words, verbs

to tape-record   to air-condition   to triple-space   to free-lance

2–2. Compound Adjectives

a. When two or more words appearing before a noun or pronoun act as a single-thought modifier, these words are hyphenated and function as a compound adjective. Such groups of words not shown in the dictionary are known as *temporary compounds.* These same word groups are not hyphenated, however, if they appear after the nouns or pronouns they modify.

temporary compound before noun or pronoun

Capture that *never-to-be-forgotten* moment with pictures by Mardell!

The Holtzes are interested in purchasing a *four-bedroom* home.

The Walters' *7-pound-12-ounce* son was born yesterday at 5 a.m.

We did not believe the Senator's opponent would resort to such *low-level* tactics.

All *city-owned* property is exempt from these state taxes.

A *well-established* firm has been retained to represent our interests.

All vehicles are expected to abide by the *55-mile-an-hour* speed limit on this freeway.

---

*All spellings and hyphenations used in this manual are based upon *Webster's Ninth New Collegiate Dictionary* (Springfield, Mass.: Merriam-Webster Inc., 1983).

The mayor's *not-too-cordial* attitude toward the press was evident.

temporary compound following noun or pronoun

Your wedding should be a day that is *never to be forgotten.*

The Holtzes' new home has *four bedrooms.*

The Watsons' baby weighed *7 pounds 12 ounces* at birth.

Who would believe that our opponent's tactics could be so *low level!*

None of the properties on this block are *city owned.*

This firm has been *well established* in the Chicago area for nearly thirty years.

The speed limit on this highway is *55 miles an hour.*

The greetings from Mr. Simms this morning were certainly *not too cordial.*

b. Some compound adjectives are shown hyphenated in the dictionary. These permanent compounds are hyphenated whether they appear before or after the nouns or pronouns they modify.

permanent compound before noun or pronoun

up-to-date reports   small-scale operation
well-known reporters   hands-off policy
part-time employment   machine-readable text
snow-white clouds   no-fault insurance
smooth-tongued salesperson   public-spirited citizens

permanent compound following noun or pronoun

None of these files are *up-to-date.*

If your job is *part-time*, please fill out the enclosed form.

These clothing brands are *well-known* throughout the country.

Most addresses on envelopes from major corporations are *machine-readable.*

You cannot deny that this community is *public-spirited.*

c. Some compounds used as single adjectives are so well-known that they have become compound nouns and are shown as such in the dictionary. In these cases the hyphen is no longer used to indicate a single thought unit.

charge account customer   *word processing* center
high school teacher   *gold mine* stocks
data processing equipment   *life insurance* policy
income tax return   *money market* account
department store personnel   *data base* management
mobile home sales   *early bird* special
real estate commission   *finance company* records

d. When two separate proper nouns are combined as a single adjective before another noun or a pronoun, these proper nouns are hyphenated. The components of a single proper noun, however, are not hyphenated when they are used as an adjective.

separate proper nouns used as an adjective

This morning's issue of the newspaper carried several articles on *Sino-American* relations.

Your *Chicago-New York* flight has been delayed until tomorrow.

single proper nouns used as an adjective

We have been negotiating with an *East Coast* firm for the last three months.

How many *University of Nebraska* alumni have you been able to locate in Salt Lake City?

e. Adverbs ending in *ly* that are combined with adjectives to form a single modifier are not hyphenated.

I understand that your suggestion was the most *hotly debated* issue discussed at the conference.

Ms. Stevens is an *exceptionally gifted* nuclear physicist.

f. When the first word of a compound modifier is a comparative or a superlative ending in *er* or *est*, the compound is usually not hyphenated. Only comparatives and superlatives used in permanent compounds (those shown in the dictionary) are followed by a hyphen.

temporary compounds

Only a *smaller sized* drill can be used for this project.

You have already purchased the *slowest paced* reading program we have available.

permanent compounds

John Seymour's *best-selling* novel is available in all our bookstores.

The children from *better-off* families were dressed in more expensive clothing.

g. Two separate colors stated in a compound modifier are hyphenated. Other adjectives, however, used in conjunction with colors are not hyphenated unless the combination is a permanent compound shown in the dictionary.

two separate colors

This *blue-green* fabric was selected for upholstering the sofas in the hotel lobby.

The artist used *red-orange* hues effectively in portraying the Hawaiian sunset.

adjective combined with color

The *bluish green* water magnified the size of the iridescent, colorful fish.

The *bright red* flag can easily be seen from a distance.

Ask all our salesmen to wear *dark gray* suits to the exhibition.

The *emerald green* cover of your new book stands out quite visibly.

Place these artists' prints against a *snow-white* background to accentuate their deep color contrasts.

h. When a series of hyphenated adjectives has a common ending, use suspending hyphens.

All construction bids for this hillside are based on *two- and three-level* family dwellings.

Please order a supply of *1/16- and 1/8-inch* drills.

i. Dollar amounts in the millions and billions and percentages are *not* hyphenated when they function as compound adjectives.

You will receive a *10 percent* discount on all orders placed before October 1.

There will be a *½ percent* increase in state sales tax effective July 1.

How will the President deal with the projected *$1 billion* decline in the Gross National Product?

Nearly *2.5 million* people in the United States use our soap.

2-3. Prefixes

a. Words beginning with *ex* (meaning "former") and *self* are usually hyphenated. Words beginning with *pre, re**, and *non* are generally not hyphenated, and those beginning with *co* and *vice* may or may not be hyphenated. Use your dictionary to check the hyphenation of words with these beginnings.

"ex" and "self"

The *ex-baseball* hero is now in the real estate business.

Our *ex-chairman* still has all the committee records in his files.

She is very *self-confident* about her work.

Employee *self-satisfaction* contributes to morale and productivity.

"pre," "re," "non"

All our diapers are *prefolded.*

---

*The word *re-direct*, meaning "to direct again," and the word *re-create*, meaning "to create again," are exceptions to this rule.

Where will the *preemployment* interviews be held?

Please *recheck* all the total columns carefully.

Please have the tires on the truck *realigned.*

Tuition reimbursements will not be made to *nonaccredited* educational institutions.

Please initiate legal proceedings against Phillips Bros. for *nonpayment* of its account.

"co"

co-edition	coauthor
co-owner	coed
co-organizer	copilot

"vice"

vice-chancellor	vice admiral
vice-consul	vice president

b. When a prefix is added to a proper noun, place a hyphen between the prefix and the proper noun.

We found that many firms operating today date back to *pre-Civil War* times.

If you cannot promise a *mid-September* delivery date, cancel the order.

To some people a 4th of July without fireworks would be *un-American.*

2–4. Numbers

a. Compound numbers from *21* to *99* are hyphenated when they appear in word form.

Ninety-six responses to the questionnaire have been returned so far, but *twenty-four* are still missing.

b. In numbers over 100, elements other than compound numbers are not hyphenated.

The lessee shall pay a sum of *Two Thousand Eight Hundred Seventy-five Dollars* ($2,875) to the lessor.

c. Simple fractions are expressed in word form. These fractions are hyphenated only when they function as compound adjectives.

simple fraction
Nearly *two thirds* of our employees voted to ratify the new contract.

Can you believe that over *three fourths* of the computers purchased last year were personal computers?

compound adjective

Our company wishes to purchase a *one-fourth* interest in the new shopping mall planned for the Pinehurst area.

A *two-thirds* majority vote is needed to pass this proposition, which will appear on the November ballot.

d. When a number and a noun function as a single unit in describing another noun (compound adjective), separate the words in the compound adjective with a hyphen. Only in percentages and dollar amounts in the millions and billions are the hyphens omitted.

hyphen—compound adjective

We have a *three-year* lease on this building.

Our freeways have a *55-mile-an-hour* speed limit.

She was charged a *25-cent* toll for using the speedway.

He just started a *$1,500-a-month* job.

The Joneses' *7-pound-8-ounce* baby girl was born on December 25.

no hyphen—percentage

We have had a *25 percent* sales increase during the past year.

no hyphen—dollar amount in the millions

Ridgewood, Inc., announced a *$3 million* profit for the year.

e. The hyphen may be used to replace the terms *to* or *through* between two numerals.

Your vacation will be July *3-18* this year.

Refer to pages *70-75* for further instructions.

Dividing Words

The division of words at the end of a typewritten line should be avoided where possible because complete words are easier to understand, easier to read and neater in appearance. Sometimes, however, word divisions at the end of a line cannot be avoided because not to do so would result in awkward line lengths and unbalanced paragraph constructions.

Certain rules need to be observed to divide words correctly at the end of a line. Some of these rules should be adhered to strictly; others are flexible in their application.

2–5. When Not to Divide Words

Certain words may not be divided under any circumstances:

a. Do not divide one-syllable or one-syllable "ed" words.

2

one-syllable words

straight   threats   thought   through   bread

one-syllable "ed" words

changed   weighed   planned   striped   shipped

b. Do not set off a single-letter syllable at either the beginning or the end of a word.

beginning of a word

a warded   e nough   i dentity   o mitted   u niform

end of a word

radi o   bacteri a   health y   photocop y

c. Do not set off a two-letter syllable at the end of a word.

present ed   compa ny   month ly
build er   week ly   debt or

d. Unless a hyphen already appears within an abbreviation, do not divide capitalized abbreviations or abbreviations of academic degrees.

not divided

UNESCO   U.S.A.   UCLA   Ph.D.

may be divided

AFL-CIO   KMET-TV   NBEA-WBEA

e. Do not divide a day of the month from the month, *a.m.* or *p.m.* from clock time,
percentages from the word *percent,* page numbers from page references, or
other such closely related word-and-number groups.

month and day

November 25   August 30   January 5

"a.m." or "p.m." from clock time

10 a.m.   2:45 p.m.   12 midnight   12 noon

percentages from the word "percent"

1 percent   43 percent   20 percent   100 percent

2

page from page references

page 23   page 241   page 1073

other word-and-number combinations

7 ounces   Room 341   Model 4A   Serial No. 437892

f.   Do not divide contractions or numerals.

contractions

wouldn't   doesn't   haven't   shouldn't

numerals

$15,487   1,240,500   3 billion   4,500 $2.5 million

g.   Do not divide the last word of more than two consecutive lines.

h.   Do not divide the last word on a page.

2–6.   When to Avoid Dividing Words

Situations may occur where end-of-the-line word divisions are undesirable. While it may not always be prudent to adhere strictly to the following rules, these should generally be observed:

a.   Avoid dividing words containing six or fewer letters.

forget   person   better   number   ratio

b.   Avoid dividing a word after a two-letter prefix.

en large   im portant   un necessary   de pendent

c.   Avoid dividing proper nouns.

Boulevard   Washington   Fernando
Corporation   Lieutenant   Mississippi

d.   Avoid dividing a word at the end of the first line of a paragraph.

e.   Avoid dividing a word that concludes the last full line of a paragraph.

2–7.   How to Divide Words

Always divide words between syllables. Use an up-to-date dictionary or a word division manual to locate the correct syllabication of words to be divided. All word divisions shown in this reference manual are based on the syllabication shown in *Webster's Ninth New Collegiate Dictionary,* the 1983 printing, published by Merriam-Webster Inc.

Words containing several syllables often require forethought to determine the appropriate place to separate the word. Use the following guidelines to determine after which syllable to divide a word:

a. Divide hyphenated and other compound words at their natural breaks.

hyphenated compound

vice-/chancellor   self-/esteem   Governor-/elect   stepping-/stone

single-word compound

common/place   hand/made   break/down   sales/person

b. Where possible, divide words after a prefix or before a suffix.

prefix

anti/body   pre/condition   mis/fortune
dis/crepancy   sub/stantiate

suffix

evasive/ness   inspira/tion   oversell/ing   unemploy/ment

c. Divide words between double letters except when the root word itself ends with a double letter and is followed by a suffix.

divided double letters

accom/modate   bul/letin   suc/cess   oscil/late   neces/sarily

double letters not divided

business/like   fulfill/ment   helpless/ness   install/ing

d. Divide words between two vowels pronounced separately.

continu/ation   gradu/ation   extenu/ating   insinu/ation

e. Divide words *after,* not before, a single vowel except when the vowel is part of a suffix.

single vowel

congratu/lations   assimi/late   bene/ficial
clari/fication   docu/ment

suffix vowel

accept/able   collaps/ible   forc/ible   collect/ible   allow/able

65

2

2–8. Where to Divide Word Groups

Certain word groups should be divided in specific places. Use the following recommendations in separating dates, names of individuals, addresses, numbered items, and copy containing dashes.

a. Divide dates between the day and the year, but *not* between the month and the day.

January 7, / 1985 *not* January / 7, 1985

April 15, / 1986 *not* April / 15, 1986

b. Full names of individuals appearing with titles are ideally divided between the first and last names or after the middle initial. However, names preceded by long titles may be separated between the title and the first name.

Mr. William / Harrison   Lieutenant / Harvey Petrowski
Dr. Robert P. / Rosenberg   Professor / Alice Martinez

c. Street addresses may be broken between the street name and the street designation (*Street, Avenue, Boulevard, Lane,* etc.). If the street name contains more than one word, the address may *also* be broken between words in the street name.

1138 Monogram / Avenue   6800 Coldwater / Canyon Avenue
849 North 73 / Street   17325 San Fernando / Mission Boulevard

d. Geographical locations in addresses are divided only between the city and state, not between the state and zip code.

Dubuque, / Iowa 52001   Poughkeepsie, / New York 12601

e. Divide a numbered or lettered list directly before the number or letter, but not directly after.

An affirmative action officer gave these reasons: (1) fewer job openings in the teaching profession, (2) enrollment declines in the student population, and (3) an increase in the mandatory retirement age for teachers.

f. A sentence with a dash may be broken after the dash, but not directly before it.

Your new policy on recruitment is excellent--
a step in the right direction.

At the end of the year--possibly in December--
we are planning to take a trip to the Orient.

Capitalization

3

Capitalization Solution Finder

Abbreviations   3–3

Academic Subjects, Courses, and Degrees

   Courses   3–7a
   Degrees
      Abbreviations   3–7c
      After person's name   3–7b, c
      General use   3–7b
   Subject areas   3–7a

Beginning Words

   Colon, words following   3–1d
   Complimentary closes   3–1c
   Enumerations   3–1d
   Outlines   3–1a
   Parentheses, words enclosed
      in   3–1e
   Phrases
      Independent   3–1a
      Quoted   3–1b
   Poetry   3–1a
   Salutations   3–1c
   Sentences
      Quoted   3–1a
      Regular   3–1a

Business Subdivisions   3–8e

   Departments   3–8e
   Divisions   3–8e

Celestial Bodies   3–12

Dates and Events

   Centuries   3–10
   Days of the week   3–10
   Decades   3–10
   Historical events   3–10
   Holidays   3–10

   Months of the year   3–10
   Religious days   3–10
   Seasons   3–10

Educational Subdivisions   3–8g

   Colleges   3–8g
   Departments   3–8g
   Divisions   3–8g
   Offices   3–8g
   Schools   3–8g

Ethnic References

   Culture   3–11
   Language   3–11
   Race   3–11

Geographical Locations

   Compass points   3–9c
   General localities or
      directions   3–9c
   Geographical terms   3–9a
   Nicknames of geographical
      localities   3–9b
   Places, names of specific   3–9a
   Regions
      General   3–9c
      Names of contrived areas
      3–9b
      Specific   3–9c
   Words derived from   3–9d

Governmental References

   Agencies   3–8f
   Bureaus   3–8f
   Departments   3–8f
   Divisions   3–8f
   General references   3–8c, d
   Names of   3–8a
   Offices   3–8f
   Shortened forms   3–8c
   "the" preceding organizational
      names   3–8b

3

Capitalization Solution Finder (continued)

Literary or Artistic Works

Artistic works   3–6a
Literary works   3–6a
Publications   3–6a
Subsections   3–6b
Typewritten reports   3–6b

Numbered or Lettered Items   3–4

Organizational Names   3–8

Proper Nouns and Adjectives

Capitalization of   3–2a
Nicknames   3–2b

Proper nouns, not capitalized
    3–2c
Trade names   3–2c

Titles

Academic degrees   3–7b, c
Academic subjects and
    courses   3–7a
Artistic works   3–6a
"elect" with titles   3–5g
"ex" with titles   3–5g
Family   3–5a
"former" with titles   3–5g
"late" with titles   3–5g
Literary works   3–6a, b
Military   3–5a–e, g
Political   3–5a–e, g
Professional   3–5a–g

3

General Format

3–1. Beginning Words

a. Capitalize the beginning words of sentences, quoted sentences, independent phrases, lines of poetry, and items in an outline.

sentence

All employees are requested to work overtime until the inventory has been completed.

quoted sentence

The guarantee states, *"Defective* parts will be replaced free of charge."

independent phrase

Now, to the important point.

poetry

By the rude bridge that arched the flood,
Their flag to the April's breeze unfurled,
Here once the embattled farmers stood,
And fired the shot heard round the world.
                                        —Emerson

outline

1. *Specific* instructions
    a. *Type* of correspondence
    b. *Number* of copies
    c. *Special* mailing notations

b. The initial letter of an incomplete quoted thought is not capitalized unless the first word (1) is a proper noun, (2) is capitalized for another rule of capitalization, or (3) is preceded by identification words such as *marked* or *stamped.*

lowercase

Mr. Reyes was directed to "take care of this situation immediately."

proper noun

Mr. Stone's curt answer was "George's car."

rule of capitalization

My favorite song in the production is "My Boy Bill."

preceded by identification words "marked" or "stamped"

This package should be stamped "Priority Mail."

Your check was returned by the bank marked "Insufficient Funds."

c. In correspondence the beginning words of the salutation and complimentary close are capitalized. Any nouns included in the salutation should be capitalized, but any intervening adjectives should not.

salutations

Dear Mr. Jones   *Gentlemen*   *My* dear *Friend*

complimentary closes

Sincerely yours   *Cordially* yours   *Yours* very truly

3

d. When the words preceding a colon introduce a complete thought that presents a rule or requires emphasis, capitalize the first word after the colon. Also, if the material following a colon consists of two or more sentences or begins an enumeration on the following line, capitalize the beginning word. Always capitalize proper nouns. In other cases do not capitalize the first word following a colon.

rule following colon

Please apply the following in typing our office correspondence: *Use* modified block format with mixed punctuation.

item of special emphasis following colon

Note: *Several* of our employees were listening to the World Series during working hours.

Wanted: *Student* to work weekends and holidays.

two or more sentences following colon

Here are two important questions to consider: Will it be economically feasible for us to enlarge our facilities at this time? Is the current market able to assimilate the increased production?

enumeration beginning on following line

Please send us copies of the following items:

1. *Lease* agreement with Property Management Associates
2. *Statement* of rental income for 1985
3. *List* of projected expenses for 1986

proper noun

Three colleges are involved in the project: *DeKalb* Community College, MiraCosta College, and the City College of New York.

first word not capitalized

We need to order the following garden supplies: *lawn* seed, liquid fertilizer, and insect spray.

Our production schedule is experiencing a two months' delay: *the* warehouse fire set us back considerably.

3

e. The first word of a complete thought contained in parentheses is not capitalized if it appears within a sentence unless the word is a proper noun. A complete thought contained in parentheses that appears immediately after a sentence is treated as a separate unit, and the first word is capitalized.

lowercase within sentence

Several minor changes *(these* were recommended by Mr. Lloyd) will be made in the final draft.

proper noun capitalized within sentence

Your recommendations (*Ms.* Williams approved all of them) will be incorporated into the marketing survey.

capitalized at end of sentence

A group of marketing students wishes to tour our main plant in Atlanta, Georgia. (*The* students will arrange for their own transportation.)

3–2. Proper Nouns and Adjectives

a. Proper nouns (words that name a particular person, place, or thing) and adjectives derived from proper nouns are capitalized. Capitalize the names of persons, places, geographic localities, streets, parks, buildings, shopping centers, developments, ships, airplanes, etc.

proper nouns

We have opened a new branch office in *Austin, Texas.*

I will meet you at the top of the *Empire State Building.*

The *Orange County Fair* will be held in *Petit Park* this year.

When will the *Brownsville Shopping Mall* be ready for occupancy?

We flew to *Florida* on a *Boeing 747* to meet our cruise ship, the *Song of Norway.*

Next month *John* and *Lisa* will take a raft down the *Colorado River.*

How much is the toll for the *Golden Gate Bridge,* which crosses *San Francisco Bay*?

adjectives derived from proper nouns

Be sure to order *Roquefort* dressing for all the salads.

The *Socratic* method is often used in debates.

Your decorator selected *Vandyke* brown carpeting for the executive offices.

How much *Canadian* money do you have in your wallet?

The use of the *Heimlich* maneuver has saved many people from choking.

According to a recent *Gallup* poll, the President's foreign policy is looked upon favorably by more than 60 percent of those Americans eligible to vote.

b. When well-known descriptive terms such as nicknames are used in place of proper nouns, they are capitalized.

My territory includes sales districts west of the *Rockies*. (Rocky Mountains)

Most of his business trips have been to the *Windy City*. (Chicago)

Old Hickory was particularly popular with the frontiersmen. (Andrew Jackson)

Several of our colleagues from the *Big Apple* will attend the convention. (New York City)

c. Sometimes proper nouns, such as widely used commercial products, acquire common noun meanings through popular usage.* As a result, they are not capitalized. Always capitalize, however, specific trade names of products. The product itself is not capitalized unless it is a coined derivation that is considered part of the trade name.

common noun meanings

Please run 200 *mimeograph* copies of this test.

Yes, *india* ink was included in the order.

Our restaurant serves *french* fries with all sandwiches.

Copies of the *braille* alphabet may be obtained from the Foundation for the Junior Blind.

This statue is made from plaster of *paris*.

How many *china* patterns does this company manufacture?

The old-fashioned *venetian* blinds in your office should be replaced with a more attractive window covering.

trade names with common noun products

Did you order a *Sony portable television set*?

Our new *Frigidaire freezer* was delivered today.

Please deliver the *Kirby vacuum* to Dr. Ianizzi's home.

The *Xerox copier* in our office enables us to copy forms on colored paper.

Does your drugstore chain carry *Kleenex tissues* exclusively?

---

*Check an up-to-date dictionary to determine which proper nouns have acquired common noun meanings and are no longer capitalized. The examples shown here are based on entries from *Webster's Ninth New Collegiate Dictionary* (Springfield, Mass.: Merriam-Webster Inc., 1983).

trade names and products capitalized

Your *Amana Radarange* will give you many years of service.

Next week we will install a *Griffin Mail-O-Meter* in our office.

Both *IBM Displaywriters* and *IBM Personal Computers* will replace our Zang word processing equipment.

Every day Mr. Rosen orders a *McDonald's Burger* for lunch.

3–3. Abbreviations

Most abbreviations are capitalized only if the words they represent are capitalized.

lowercase

Please send 5 *doz.* hammers *c.o.d.*

You may contact me any time after 5:30 *p.m.*

uppercase

She sat for the *CPS* examination last May.

Mrs. Johnson was awarded a bachelor of arts degree from *UCLA* in 1980.

3–4. Numbered or Lettered Items

Nouns followed by numerals or letters are capitalized except in the case of page, paragraph, line, size, and verse references. The word *number* is abbreviated except when it appears at the beginning of a sentence.

uppercase

A reservation was held for you on *Flight 487* to Chattanooga.

Please check *Invoice B3721* to verify that all items have been shipped.

I believe my policy, *No. 68341*, covers the injury.

Did you receive our order for your *Model 23D* china case?

lowercase

Refer to *page 3, paragraph 2,* of the contract for the schedule of project completion.

We are sold out of *size 10* in our Style 483 blazer.

"number" at beginning of sentence

Number 145–MD has been out of stock for over three months.

Titles

3–5. People

a. Capitalize the title of a person's profession, political office, rank, or family relationship when it precedes and is used directly with his or her name.

3

profession

The meeting will be conducted by *Professor* Sharon Jones.

political office

We are looking forward to meeting *Mayor* Barton Siller next Friday.

rank

All medical problems should be brought to the attention of *Major* Richard Cortez.

family relationship

When *Aunt* Olive arrives, we can be seated for dinner.

b. When a title follows a person's name, it is not capitalized except in cases pertaining to high-ranking government officials (President of the United States, Vice President of the United States, Cabinet members, governors, and members of Congress).

regular title

Carla Irwin, *comptroller* of A & I Enterprises, wrote the report.

Subpoena Jeremy Cole, *president* of AMCO Products, to appear in court on May 11.

title of high-ranking government official

George Dillon, *Senator* from Georgia, received an award for outstanding service.

Tonight at 8 p.m., EST, Ronald Reagan, *President* of the United States, will appear on national television.

c. A person's title is not capitalized when it is followed by an appositive.

I went to see the *vice president,* Don Curry.

She consulted with her *doctor,* Linda Montgomery, about the accident.

d. When a person's title is used in place of his name, it is generally not capitalized. However, in the case of direct address and in reference to high-ranking government officials (President of the United States, Vice President of the United States, Cabinet members, members of Congress, and governors), capitalize

3

the title if it replaces the name. Do not, however, capitalize common nouns such as *sir, ladies,* or *gentlemen* used in direct address.

regular title

The *auditor* indicated that our books were in order.

After the meeting the *president* directed his *executive assistant* to inform all the department managers that the *director of marketing* had resigned.

direct address

Did I pass the test, *Professor?*

Yes, *Doctor,* we have your reservation for May 8.

I believe, *ladies and gentlemen,* that all our sales personnel will meet their quotas this year.

title of high-ranking government official

It was a pleasure to meet the *Secretary of State* last week.

Please invite the *Governor* to attend the conference.

e. A person's title is always capitalized in business correspondence when it appears in the inside address, signature line, or envelope address.

Ms. Ellen Davis, *President*

Mrs. Delieu Scopesi, *Personnel Director*

f. When the title of an executive officer is used in that organization's minutes, bylaws, or rules, it is capitalized.

The *Treasurer's* report was read and approved.

The *President* will be responsible for the negotiation of all labor contracts.

g. Descriptive terms such as *ex, elect, late,* and *former* are not capitalized when they are combined with a title.

"ex"

Since *ex*-President D. J. Morgan was appointed chairman of the board, our company has prospered.

"elect"

Councilman-*elect* Norman Rittgers will be sworn in on January 2.

"late"

The *late* President Eisenhower was an avid golfer.

"former"

A copy of the report was sent to *former* President Carter.

3–6. Literary or Artistic Works

a. Capitalize the principal words in titles and subtitles of publications and other literary or artistic works such as movies, plays, songs, poems, and lectures. Articles (*a, an, the*), conjunctions (*and, but, or, nor*), and prepositions with fewer than four letters (*of, in, on, to, up,* etc.) are not capitalized unless they appear as the first or last words of the title or subtitle.

3

The titles of books, magazines, pamphlets, and newspapers are underscored or typed in all capital letters. Titles of other literary or artistic works are placed in quotation marks.

book

I learned a great deal from the book The Art of Readable Writing.

DuPont, the Autobiography of an American Enterprise will be available in June.

The best-seller Up Into the Wild Blue Yonder has sold over one million copies.

book with subtitle

The students are using Sociology: An Introduction as their basic textbook.

magazine

We have ordered the Journal of Abnormal and Social Psychology for our reference library.

play

Mr. Conway's new production, "A Comet Is Coming," will open on Broadway next week.

movie

"Snow White and the Seven Dwarfs" is scheduled for screening in neighborhood theaters next month.

b. Capitalize the main words and place in quotation marks the titles of subsections contained in books, magazines, pamphlets, or newspapers. Also capitalize the main words and place in quotation marks the titles of typewritten reports.

chapter of book

Please review carefully "Supervision of Office Personnel" in the book Office Organization and Management.

magazine article

Did you read "Word Processing Shortcuts" in the latest issue of The Executive Secretary's Journal?

newspaper column

"Jim Elwood Reports" in yesterday's <u>Vista Daily Journal</u> covered extensively the city council's feud with the mayor.

typewritten report

Here is your copy of "Research Personnel Available."

3–7. Academic Subjects, Courses, and Degrees

a. Titles of specific courses are capitalized, but the names of academic subject areas are not unless the subject area name contains a proper noun.

specific courses

How many students are enrolled in *Digital Computer Programming 43*?

Last year she took *Speech 125, Introduction to Public Debate.*

You are scheduled to teach two sections of *Survey of Business Law* next semester.

subject areas

It is important that Ms. Harris take an *accounting* class this spring.

Our college offers over 20 different *history* classes.

subject area containing proper noun

I earned an "A" in my *business English* class.

Perhaps you should take a course in *conversational French.*

b. References to academic degrees are generally not capitalized unless they are used after and in conjunction with the name of an individual.

general reference

Mr. Sorenson will be awarded a *bachelor of science* degree this June.

after person's name

Wilma P. Koskey, *Doctor of Divinity,* will deliver the opening address.

c. Capitalize abbreviations of academic degrees appearing after a person's name. Remember, though, that the *h* in *Ph.D.* appears in lowercase form.

Dan Shriver, *D.D.S.,* is an excellent dental surgeon.

We have asked Marilyn Delaney, *D.B.A.,* to be our speaker.

Make your check payable to Elbert Gann, *M.D.*

Barbara Roesner, *Ph.D.,* will join our clinic in June as a staff psychologist.

Groups, Places, Dates

3–8. Organizations

a. Principal words in the names of all organizations—business, civic, educational, governmental, labor, military, philanthropic, political, professional, religious, and social—are capitalized.

Boston Chamber of Commerce	Illinois Bar Association
Los Angeles Board of Education	Young Republican Club
Department of Motor Vehicles	National Council of Churches
Tactical Air Command	Porter Valley Country Club
United Way	Stanford Research Institute

b. When the word *the* precedes an organizational name and is officially part of the name, it must be capitalized.

We received two letters from *The* Prudential Insurance Company.

c. When the common noun element of an organization's name is used in place of the full name, it is generally not capitalized. In formal documents and in specific references to national government bodies, however, capitalize the shortened form.

general communication

All employees of the *company* are allowed ten days' sick leave a year.

The *board of education* met at its regular meeting yesterday to consider the school crisis.

Three members from our local *chamber* received Presidential appointments.

formal communication

As agent for the *Association,* I am authorized to sign the convention contracts.

On April 17, 1985, the *Company* acquired several additional holdings.

national government bodies

The bill is now before the *House.* (House of Representatives)

Three *Cabinet* members were interviewed by the press. (President's Cabinet)

When will *Congress* reconvene? (United States Congress)

d. Governmental terms such as *federal, government, nation,* and *constitution* are often used in place of their respective full names. Because they are used so often and are considered terms of general classification, they are not capitalized.

"federal"

Veterans Day is a holiday for all *federal* employees.

"government"

The *government* is concerned about inflation and its effect on the economy.

Loans such as these from the *federal government* are fully guaranteed.

"nation"

The *nation* has been able to overcome a number of crises.

"constitution"

Interpretation of the *constitution* is the Supreme Court's responsibility.

e. The title of a division or department within a business organization is usually capitalized when one employed by that organization refers to it. When reference is made to a division or department within another organization, however, the name is usually not capitalized unless it is known definitely that the name used is the official name. Always capitalize the division or department title in a return address, an inside address, a signature block, or an envelope address.

department in own organization

Please notify the *Personnel Department* when you are going to be absent from work.

This contract must be signed by two members of the *Board of Directors*.

A check for this amount must first be approved by the manager of our *Accounting Department*.

department in another organization—official title unknown

The efficiency of your *accounting department* can be increased by using our computer system.

Your *advertising department* may wish to contact one of our account executives to take advantage of this rare opportunity.

department in another organization—official title known

We will send a copy of our official findings to your *Department of Research and Development*.

Will you be able to send a member from your *Word Processing Department* to the conference?

return address, inside address, signature block, or envelope address

Mr. George Juett, Manager, *Credit Department*

f. Capitalize the names of departments, bureaus, divisions, offices, and agencies in governmental organizations.

We will forward this information to the *Department of Health and Human Services* within the next week.

Have you contacted the *Bureau of Indian Affairs* about this matter?

You may obtain photocopies of the proposed freeway route from the *Division of Highways.*

This case is under investigation by the *Office of Internal Affairs.*

3

To work for the *Federal Bureau of Investigation,* you must first receive a security clearance.

g. Capitalize the names of specific departments, divisions, and offices within educational institutions. The names of schools or colleges within universities are also capitalized.

educational departments, divisions, or offices

Each year the *Music Department* of our high school sponsors a spring music festival.

Does Professor Joyce Arntson teach in the *Social Science Division?*

All such budget requests must be submitted to the *Office of Educational Services* by June 30.

Please submit your application for admission to the *Admissions Office* by March 1.

university schools or colleges

I am presently taking courses in the *School of Business and Economics* at Kentview State University.

The major in which you are interested is offered in the *College of Letters and Sciences.*

3–9. Geographical Locations

a. The names of specific places such as states, cities, streets, mountains, valleys, parks, oceans, lakes, rivers, and harbors are capitalized. When geographical terms appear before the names of specific places or are used in plural form, they are not capitalized.

specific places

They live in *New York City.*

The magazine article outlined camping facilities on the *Colorado River.*

We visited *Yellowstone National Park* last June.

geographical term before specific place

They vacationed in the *state* of Utah last summer.

Will your tour include the *city* of London?

geographical term in plural form

The excursion will include trips on both the Mississippi and Missouri *rivers.*

Most of our discoveries have been in the San Bernardino and San Gorgonio *mountains.*

3

   b. Nicknames of geographical localities and the names of regional areas developed as a result of usage are capitalized.

geographical nickname

All our pineapples are shipped daily from the *Aloha State.* (Hawaii)

In 1984 the Olympics were held in the *City of the Angels.* (Los Angeles)

regional names

Many of our clients are from *Upper State New York.*

Police reports indicate that the *Lower East Side* has the highest crime rate in our city.

Merchants from the *Greater Los Angeles Area* have banded together to support this worthwhile project.

Many residents in the *Bay Area* are concerned about the pollution occurring in San Francisco Bay.

   c. Points of the compass are capitalized when they are used as simple or compound nouns to designate *specific regions.* Points of the compass are not capitalized, however, when they are used to indicate *direction* or *general localities.*

specific regions

Firms connected with the aerospace industry are heavily concentrated in the *West* and *Southwest.*

Our company has increased its trade in the *Far East.*

The festival was held in *East Los Angeles.*

The sales of our *Southern Region* have increased 25 percent during the past year.

Within the next month we will expand our operations into *East Texas.*

direction

The study recommended that our new plant be located just *north* of Baltimore.

Will the sale of our product be affected by the fact that birds fly *south* every winter?

My territory includes all states *west* of the Mississippi River.

By taking the *eastbound* on-ramp, you will get to the center of Madison.

general localities

The *southern* part of our state is suffering a severe drought.

Our customers from the *western* section of the city registered more complaints than any other sector.

Our delivery service is restricted to the *east* side of Miami.

Did you survey most of the *western* states?

This new weather stripping is guaranteed to protect you against the severity of *northern* winters.

d. Words derived from simple or compound nouns representing *specific regions* are capitalized.

I have often been accused of being a typical *Midwesterner.*

Southern Californians are known for their casual lifestyle.

3–10. Dates and Events

Capitalize days of the week, months of the year, holidays (including religious days), specific special events, and historical events or periods. The names of seasons, decades, and centuries are generally not capitalized.

month and day of week

Our committee will meet the first *Monday* in *March, June, September,* and *December.*

holiday

Will our store be closed on *New Year's Day* this year?

specific special event

Our company will celebrate its *Silver Anniversary* next year.

During April many employers and their secretaries observe *National Secretaries' Week.*

historical event or period

The *Apollo 10 Moon Landing* was the most dramatic event of this century.

The stock market crash of 1929 brought the *Roaring Twenties* to a dismal end.

During the *Industrial Revolution* children were often forced to work long hours under intolerable conditions.

century

Technological developments of the *twentieth century* have advanced man further than all other developments combined in man's previous history.

Many of Mr. Ryan's critics believe that he still operates his business on *nineteenth-century* principles.

season

Our greatest sale item during the *spring* is the Model 550 patio table.

decade

A number of movies involving life in the *sixties* have been released during the last year.

3–11. Ethnic References

Ethnic-related terms (references to a particular culture, language, or race) are capitalized.

language

A knowledge of both *German* and *English* is required for the job.

race

The census indicated that many *Orientals* are living in this area.

Courses in *Afro-American* history and culture are taught in many major colleges and universities throughout the United States.

culture

Cinco de Mayo is observed with many festivities in the *Mexican-American* community.

The predominant language spoken by *Latin Americans* is Spanish.

3–12. Celestial Bodies

The names of celestial bodies are generally capitalized except for the terms *earth, sun,* and *moon.* Since the capitalization of *earth* is shown in the dictionary as a secondary spelling, this term may be capitalized when it is used in conjunction with the names of other planets in its solar system.

lowercase

Television broadcasts of the *moon* landing were viewed by millions of Americans.

None of the pieces from the satellite found their way back into *earth's* atmosphere.

uppercase

We have been studying the orbital paths of *Mars* and *Earth.*

Can you pick out the *Big Dipper* among the many stars in the sky?

Numbers

4

Numbers Solution Finder

Addresses

Apartment and suite numbers
4–13c
Box and rural route numbers
4–13c
House numbers   4–13a
Street numbers   4–13b
Zip codes   4–13d
Zip + 4   4–13e

Dates   4–9

Decimals   4–5b

Fractions   4–15

General Format

Approximations   4–1c
Consecutive numbers   4–3b, c
Numbers
Above ten   4–1a
Beginning a sentence   4–1b
Ten and below   4–1a, 4–2a
Related numbers   4–2a-c,
4–4b, c
Round Numbers
Approximations   4–1c, d
Billions   4–1d, 4–2b, 4–4c
Millions   4–1d, 4–2b, 4–4c

Measures and Weights

Metric   4–7
Standard   4–6

Money   4–4

Numbers Used With

Abbreviations   4–8b
Symbols   4–8c
Words   4–8a

Ordinals   4–16

Percentages   4–5a

Plurals of Numerals   4–3e

Roman Numerals   4–17

Telephone Numbers   4–14

Time

Ages   4–12
Anniversaries   4–12
Clock   4–10
Dates   4–9
Periods of   4–11

Typing Format

Commas, use of   4–3a, b, d
Consecutive numbers   4–3b, c
Number plurals, formation of
4–3e

4

General Format

4–1. General Rules for Numbers

a. Numbers *one* through *ten* are written in words. Write numbers above *ten* in figures.

number "ten" or below

Only *seven* people attended the meeting.

number above "ten"

We received *182* complimentary letters this month.

b. A number that begins a sentence is expressed in word form. When the number cannot be written in one or two words, however, change the word order of the sentence so that the number does not begin the sentence.

number written in words

Twenty-four people responded to our advertisement for a stenographer.

sentence order rearranged

The questionnaire was answered by *260* respondents. (Not: *Two hundred sixty* [or *260*] respondents answered the questionnaire.)

c. Approximations that can be expressed in one or two words may be written in word form, or they may be written in figures. Keep in mind that figures are more emphatic.

approximation written in words

He expected over *fifty* people for the conference.

approximation written in figures

Nearly *300* people sent telegrams to the mayor.

d. Round numbers in the millions or billions are expressed in a combination of figures and words. *One million* used as an approximation is usually written in all word form.

round number

Captain Samek has flown *2 million* miles since he earned his wings.

round number with fraction

Our company manufactured *3½ billion* pens last year.

round number with decimal

Will we exceed our production quota of *1.2 million*?

"one million" as an approximation

Look to establish additional locations in cities with populations of more than *one million.*

4–2. Related Numbers

a. Numbers used similarly in the same document are considered related numbers and must be expressed in the same form. Therefore, write numbers *one* through *ten* in figures when they are used with related numbers above ten.

Of the *130* items inspected, only *2* were found to be defective.

Please send us *3* reams of bond paper, *24* shorthand notebooks, and *8* packages of carbon paper.

b. Round numbers in the millions or billions are expressed in figures when they are used with related numbers below a million or with related numbers that cannot be expressed in a combination of words and figures.

combined with number below 1 million

Our production of umbrellas rose from *970,000* to *2,000,000* this year.

combined with number over 1 million written in figures

During the past two years, our circulation has risen from nearly *3,000,000* copies to *3,875,500* copies.

c. Unrelated numbers used in the same sentence are considered individually to determine whether they should be expressed in words or figures.

unrelated numbers

Please send the *four* vice presidents *15* copies of our monthly report.

combination of related and unrelated numbers

Our warehouse inventory of *22* dishwashers, *17* refrigerators, and *8* washing machines must be distributed among our *three* stores.

4–3. Numeral Format

a. Numerals of more than three digits are pointed off by commas. Years, house numbers, telephone numbers, zip codes, serial numbers, page numbers, and decimal fractions do not have commas. Metric measurements of five or more figures are separated into groups of three by the use of a space.

commas

9,823   128,492   2,865,395

no commas

1982   Serial No. 14896-AN   1111 Figueroa Street   page 1032

.7534   (205) 987-6132   Evansville, IN 47701

space

Our dairy delivers daily over 45 000 liters of milk to homes in this city.

b. Two independent figures that appear consecutively (one after the other) in a sentence are separated by a comma.

By *1985, 52* homes had been built around the golf course.

c. When two numbers appear consecutively and both modify a following noun, use figure form for one number and word form for the other. Use word form for the one that may be expressed in the *fewest* number of words. If both numbers have an equal word count, spell out the first number and place the second one in figures.

Please purchase *130 twenty-two-cent* stamps from the post office.

The contractor plans to build *36 five-bedroom* houses on this land.

The bank has agreed to finance your purchase of a *1984 twenty-foot* mobile home.

Each package contains *twenty 3-inch* nails.

Did you order *seventy 50-watt* bulbs?

d. Separate volume numbers and page references by commas. Weights, capacities, and measures that consist of several words are treated as single units and are not separated by commas.

volume and page number

This information can be found in *Volume IV, page 289.*

measure as a single unit

Mr. Knight verified that the room length measured *28 feet 4 inches.*

capacity as a single unit

In conventional terms the capacity of the pitcher is *2 quarts 1 cup.*

e. The plural of a numeral is formed by adding *s.*

How many *7s* do you see in this serial number?

The *1900s* will be noted for man's first successes in space travel.

Figure Form

4–4. Money

a. Amounts of money $1 or over are expressed in figures. Omit the decimal and zeros in expressing whole dollar amounts, whether or not they appear with mixed dollar amounts.

money expressed in figures

We paid *$484.95* for this new typewriter.

omission of decimal and zeros

The list of purchases included items for $6.50, *$3*, $79.45, *$200*, and *$265*.

b. Amounts of money less than $1 are expressed in figures combined with the word *cents* unless they are used in conjunction with related amounts of $1 or over. Unrelated amounts of money appearing in the same sentence, however, are treated separately.

amounts less than $1

Last week the basic bus fare was increased from *60 cents* to *75 cents*.

related amounts of money

To mail the three reports, I paid *$.85, $1.40,* and *$2* in postage.

unrelated amounts of money

The tax on this *$8* item was *52 cents*.

c. Round amounts of money in millions or billions of dollars are expressed in combined word and figure form except when they are used with related dollar figures below a million or related amounts that can be expressed in figures only.

round amount

The cost of the new building was over *$12½ million*.

Nearly *$2.5 billion* in assets provides the customer confidence that has made Liberty Fed the largest savings and loan association in the country.

related to amount less than $1 million

We estimate that *$850,000* will be needed to equip the Wilmington plant and *$2,000,000* will be needed for the Van Nuys plant.

related to amount that can be expressed in figures only

Our sales decreased from *$12,450,000* last year to less than *$12,000,000* this year.

d. Amounts of money in legal documents are often expressed in words, followed by figures contained in parentheses.

The Company shall pay up to *One Thousand Dollars ($1,000)* within 90 days upon receipt of a valid release statement.

4-5. Percentages and Decimals

a. Write percentages in figures followed by the word *percent*. The percent symbol (%) is used only for statistical or technical tables or forms.

"percent" used in sentence format

Last month we were able to decrease our energy consumption by only *1 percent*.

Our travel expenses are up *8 percent* over last year's.

This year a *12½ percent* pay increase was granted to all employees.

% used in statistical tables or forms

32.5%   80%   99.9%   4.3%   6%

b. Numbers containing decimals are expressed in figures. To prevent misreading, place a zero before a decimal that does not contain a whole number or begin with a zero.

decimal with whole number

Our trucks average *12.843* miles per gallon of gasoline.

decimal beginning with 0

The part had to be made within *.002* inch of specifications.

decimal not containing whole number or beginning with 0

Only *0.4* percent of all the items manufactured this year were rejected because of defective workmanship.

4-6. Standard Weights and Measures

For quick comprehension express in figures the amount something weighs or measures. Units of weight and measure (inches, feet, yards, ounces, pounds, tons, pints, quarts, gallons, each, dozens, gross, reams, degrees, etc.), however, are written out fully in words. Abbreviations or symbols representing these units are limited to use in business forms or statistical materials.

general use

His luggage was *3 pounds 6 ounces* overweight.

Over *2 tons* of waste material leave the plant daily.

Place the *8 reams* of duplicator paper in the storeroom.

Approximately *150 square yards* of carpeting will be needed for this office.

Use *3-inch* screws for this job.

use for forms and statistical materials

4 doz.   *12 yds.*   *84°*   *9#*   *9 ft.*   *85 lb.*   *12 ea.*

4   4–7.   Metric Weights and Measures

a. The basic metric measurements consist of meters, grams, and liters. Prefixes indicating fractions and multiples of these quantities follow:

fractions

deci (1/10)   centi (1/100)   milli (1/1000)

multiples

deka ($\times$ 10)   hecto ($\times$ 100)   kilo ($\times$ 1000)

b. Express metric measurements in figures. Use a space to separate figures of five or more digits into groups of three. No space or comma is used with four-digit figures.

regular metric measures

We will be using *1.75-liter* bottles for our large-size apple juice.

Our new package of pie crust sticks weighs 11 ounces, which is equal to *311 grams* or *3.11 hectograms.*

four-digit figures

The distance to Boston is over *2000 kilometers.*

Our bakery chain ordered *1500 kilograms* of flour and *1200 kilograms* of sugar to be delivered to our bakeries throughout the country.

five-digit figures

His 5 acres is equal to approximately 2 hectares, that is, approximately *20 000 square meters.*

c. For general correspondence spell out units of measure. Abbreviate units of measure only in technical writing, on medical reports, or on business forms.

general correspondence

10 millimeters   4 liters   80 kilometers

technical writing or medical reports

60 mm   6 mg   25 km   100 cc

d. The following tables provide equivalents for metric and standard measures. Equivalents for length, weight, and capacity are shown.

Measure of Length

1 km	= 0.6214 mi. = ⅝ mi.	1 mi	– 1.609 km = ⅝ km
1 m	= 1.0936 yd.	1 yd.	= 0.9144 m (Exact)
1 m	= 39.37 in.	1 ft.	= 0.3048 m (Exact)
1 cm	= 0.3937 in. = ⅖ in.	1 in.	= 2.54 cm (Exact)

Measure of Mass (Weight)

1 ton (or tonne) (t)	= 1.1023 T	1 T	= 0.90721
1 kg	= 2.2046 lb.	1 lb	= 453.592 g
1 kg	= 1⅕ lb.	1 oz. (avdp.)	= 28.35 grams (g)
1 kg	= 35 oz.		
1 gram (g)	= 0.035 oz. (avdp.)		

Measure of Capacity

1 hectoliter (hl)	= 2.838 bushels	1 bushel	= 35.239 liters
1 liter (l)	= 0.264 liquid gal.	1 liquid gal	= 3.785 liters
1 liter (l)	= 1.057 liquid qt.	1 liquid qt.	= 0.946 liters
1 liter (l)	= 0.908 dry qt.	1 dry qt.	= 1.101 liters
1 milliliter (ml)	= 1 cm³ (cc) = 0.034 fluid oz.	1 fluid oz.	= 29.573 milliliters

4–8. Numbers Used With Words, Abbreviations, and Symbols

a. Numbers used directly with words are placed in figures. Page numbers, model numbers, policy numbers, and serial numbers are just a few of the instances in which numerals are used with words. The words preceding the numerals are usually capitalized except for *page, paragraph, line, size,* and *verse* references. (See Section 3–4.)

page number

You will find a picture of this economy unit on *page 21* of our current catalog.

model number

We ordered *Model 3* for our Information Processing Center.

policy and serial numbers

Please return your copy of *Policy 1284691D* to the home office.

Our IBM Correcting Selectric typewriter, *Serial No. 74603552,* was reported missing from the office.

b. Direct reference to the word *number* is the most common instance in which figures are used with an abbreviation. The word *number* is abbreviated in this case except when it appears at the beginning of a sentence.

We expect to replace this office furniture with your *No. 378* series.

The following checks were returned by your bank: *Nos. 487, 492, and 495.*

Numbers 381, 1209, and 1628 were the winning raffle tickets.

c. The use of symbols is generally avoided in business writing. However, for preparing invoices, charts, tables, and other business documents where space is limited, symbols are used liberally. Numbers expressed with symbols are written in figures.

2/10, N/30   8%   #455

Time

4–9. Dates

a. When the day is written after the month, use cardinal figures (1, 2, 3, etc.). Ordinal figures (1st, 2nd, 3rd, etc.) are used for expressing dates if the day precedes the month or for expressing days that stand alone.

cardinal figure

March 23, 1988, is the deadline for filing your claim.

ordinal figure

We expect payment in full by the *10th of April.*

Your reservations for the *9th* and the *24th* have been confirmed.

b. Dates used in most business correspondence are expressed in terms of month, day, and year. Dates used in military and foreign correspondence are generally expressed day, month, and year, with no intervening comma.

business correspondence

November 27, 1986

military or foreign correspondence

27 November 1986

4–10. Clock Time

a. Figures are used with either *a.m.* or *p.m.* to express the time of day. Omit the colon and zeros with even times. Either word or figure form, however, may be used with *o'clock.*

a.m. and p.m.

Our next tour of the plant will begin at *9 a.m.*

His plane was scheduled to arrive at *1 p.m.,* but the actual arrival time was *1:27 p.m.*

o'clock

We must leave here by *eight o'clock* (or *8 o'clock*) if we are to arrive at the meeting on time.

b.   Phrases such as "in the morning," "in the afternoon," or "at night" may be used with *o'clock* but not with *a.m.* or *p.m.*

4

Coffee breaks are scheduled at *ten o'clock in the morning* and at *three o'clock in the afternoon.*

c.   When exact hours of the day are expressed without *a.m., p.m.,* or *o'clock,* use word form. Either word or figure form may be used, however, when both hours and minutes are expressed.

hour

The party will begin at *eight* tonight.

hour and minutes

The meeting was not adjourned until *6:30* (or *six-thirty*).

The power went off at *9:05* (or *five after nine*) this morning.

d.   The terms *noon* and *midnight* may be used with or without the figure *12.* When these terms are used with clock times containing *a.m.* and/or *p.m.,* however, include the figure *12.*

noon

She left promptly at *noon* (or *12 noon*).

This postal station is open Saturdays from *8 a.m.* until *12 noon.*

midnight

The new shift starts at *midnight* (or *12 midnight*).

New hours for our coffee shop are from *8 a.m.* until *12 midnight* daily.

4–11.   Periods of Time

Periods of time (relating to days, weeks, months, and years) that can be expressed in one or two words are generally written in word form. However, when special emphasis is needed for time-period data relating to loan length, discount rates, interest rates, payment terms, credit terms, or other information dealing with business contracts, use figures.

general use

During the last *sixteen months,* we have shown a slight profit.

We have been in this location for *thirty-two years.*

The auto workers' strike lasted *117 days.*

business terms

This loan must be paid in full within *90 days.*

We give a 2 percent discount on all invoices paid within *10 days* upon receipt.

You have been granted a 9 percent loan for *6 months.*

4

4–12. Ages and Anniversaries

Ages and anniversaries that can be expressed in one or two words are generally written in word form. However, figures are used when an age (1) appears directly after a person's name; (2) is used in a legal or technical sense; or (3) is expressed in terms of years, months, and sometimes days.

general expression of ages and anniversaries

David will be *twenty-three* on August 9; his son John will be *three* on the same day.

The staff brought a cake as a surprise for Miss Chu's *fifty-first* birthday.

We plan to give a party for Todd upon his *twenty-fifth* anniversary with the company.

Our city will celebrate its *150th* anniversary in 1989.

age after name

Ms. Soderstrom, *47,* was promoted to office manager last week.

age used in technical or legal sense

Employees no longer must retire at the age of *65.*

The legal voting age is *18.*

At *45* you will be eligible for these reduced insurance rates.

age in years, months, and days

According to our records, the insured was *35* years *5* months and *28* days of age upon cancellation of the policy.

Addresses and Telephone Numbers

4–13. Addresses

a. House numbers are expressed in figures except for the house number *One.* No commas are used to separate digits in house numbers.

One Alpha Street

18817 Clearview Avenue

b.   Street names that are numbered *ten* or below are expressed in words. Street names numbered above *ten* are written in figures and expressed in cardinal form when separated from the house number by a compass direction. Use the ordinal form *(st, d, th)* when the street name directly follows the house number.

street name ten or below

All visitors to New York City must stroll down *Fifth* Avenue.

street name above ten—cardinal form

His new address was listed as 3624 West *59* Place.

street name above ten—ordinal form

Will you send this order to 1111 *23rd* Street.

c.   Apartment numbers, suite numbers, box numbers, and rural route numbers are expressed in figure form.

1883 Creek Avenue, Apt. *4*

Plaza Medical Building, Suite *102*

Post Office Box *1584*

Rural Route *2*

d.   Zip codes are expressed in figures (without commas) and typed a single space after the state.

sentence format

Ms. Dougherty requested that the refund be sent to her at Pasadena City College, 1570 East Colorado Boulevard, Pasadena, California *91106.*

inside address or envelope address

Mr. Arthur M. Manuel	Miss Vauncille Jones
5565½ Eighth Avenue	1073 83d Street, Apt. 2
Inglewood, CA *90305*	Glendale, CA *91202*

e.   Address lines containing zip + 4 are written in the same manner as those containing regular zip codes. The only difference is that the four extra digits are separated from the zip code by a hyphen.

sentence format

Redirect this order to Palmer Enterprises, 1586 Cicero Avenue, Chicago, Illinois *60651-4827.*

inside address or envelope address

Ms. Eleanor Chu, Personnel Director
Parke-Dunn Pharmaceutical Company
21654 Grand Boulevard
Detroit, MI *48211-1853*

4–14. Telephone Numbers

Telephone numbers are expressed in figures. When the area code is included, place it in parentheses before the number. Extension numbers, preceded by the abbreviation *Ext.,* follow telephone numbers. If the extension number concludes a sentence, use a single comma to separate it from the telephone number. However, if an extension number appears in the middle of a sentence, use commas before and after it.

telephone number

You may reach our representative at *728-1694.*

area code

Please telephone me collect at *(714) 328-5235.*

extension

You may reach me any weekday at *(617) 555-7139, Ext. 3712.*

We were requested to call *(213) 347-0551, Ext. 244,* within an hour.

Special Forms

4–15. Fractions

a. Express fractions in word form except when they are (1) long and awkward, (2) combined with whole numbers, or (3) used for technical purposes. Fractions written in word form are not hyphenated unless they are used as compound adjectives.

fraction used alone

We have already met *three fourths* of our production quota for this year.

A *two-thirds majority vote* is needed to ratify the contract.

long and awkward fraction

The study indicated that *21/200* of a second was needed for people to begin reacting in emergency situations.

fraction combined with whole number

Our new plant is located *3½* miles from here.

fraction for technical use

Our department is temporarily out of 5/8-inch round-head metal screws.

b. Fractions written in figures that are not found on the typewriter keyboard are formed by using the diagonal to separate the two parts. Leave one space between the fraction and any whole number used with the fraction. When fractions located on the keyboard are used with those not found on the keyboard, type all fractions by using the diagonal construction.

fraction not on keyboard

We shipped *7 2/3* tons of beef last week.

4

combination of fraction on keyboard with fraction not on keyboard

Our employees averaged *31 1/2* hours sick leave last year as compared to *24 3/4* hours this year.

4–16. Ordinals

Ordinal numbers (*first, second, third*, etc.) that can be written in one or two words are generally expressed in word form except (1) in dates appearing before the month or standing alone and (2) in numbered street names above *ten*.

general use

Mr. Cox was elected to represent the *Thirty-fourth* Congressional District.

Mrs. Lang was criticized for managing the company according to *nineteenth*-century policies.

dates

Our next audit is scheduled for the *1st of August.*

Your order will be shipped by the *15th* of this month.

Please complete the audit by the *1st* of the year.

numbered streets

Our new store is located at 820 West *Third* Avenue.

I plan to meet Mr. Joyce at noon on the corner of Main and *42nd* streets.

4–17. Roman Numerals

a. When typing Roman numerals for chapter or outline divisions, use capital letters to form the numbers. Also use capital letters for expressing years written in Roman numerals.

Arabic Numeral	Roman Numeral	Arabic Numeral	Roman Numeral
1	I	16	XVI
2	II	17	XVII
3	III	18	XVIII
4	IV	19	XIX
5	V	20	XX
6	VI	30	XXX
7	VII	40	XL
8	VIII	50	L
9	IX	60	LX
10	X	70	LXX
11	XI	80	LXXX
12	XII	90	XC
13	XIII	100	C
14	XIV	1,000	M
15	XV		

b. The preliminary sections of a report such as the letter of transmittal, the table of contents, and the list of tables are numbered with lowercase Roman numerals. Number the pages consecutively using *i, ii, iii, iv, v,* etc.

Abbreviations and Contractions

5

Abbreviations and Contractions Solution Finder

Abbreviations

Addresses   5–8
Business terms   5–6a, b, 5–10
Dates   5–3a, d
General abbreviations   5–6a, d
Geographical expressions   5–8e,
   5–9b, 5–10
Measures
   Metric   5–5
   Standard   5–4
Organizational names   5–2
Plurals   5–7
States and territories   5–8c,
   5–10
Telephone extensions   5–6c
Time   5–3b, c

Titles   5–1
   Academic degrees, use
      with   5–1c, 5–9b
   Courtesy   5–1a
   Personal   5–1c
   Professional   5–1b, c
Typing format   5–9
   Capitalization   5–9a
   Periods, use of   5–9b-d
   Spacing   5–9b, c

Contractions

Single words   5–11a
Verb forms   5–11b

5

Abbreviations

5–1. Titles

a. The abbreviations *Mr., Ms., Mrs.,* and *Dr.* are used for courtesy titles.

Mr. Allen Davis

Ms. Phyllis Derry

Mrs. Myra Goldstein

Dr. Lawrence Erickson

b. When civil, educational, military, and religious titles are used with the last name only, they are written out. These titles *may be* abbreviated, however, when they appear before a person's full name and brevity is required.

5

written out—last name only

Dear *Governor* Reece

written out—full name

I believe *Professor* Amelia Leslie is in charge of the project.

abbreviated—full name

Please invite *Lt. Col.* Donald Curry to the meeting.

c. When *Jr., Sr., Esq.,* or references to academic degrees or professional designations such as *M.D., Ph.D.,* or *CPA* are used following a person's name, they are abbreviated and capitalized. A comma is used before and after an abbreviation appearing in the middle of a sentence but only before an abbreviation appearing at the end of a sentence.

Abbreviations of academic degrees or professional designations are separated by periods except for the designations *CPA* (Certified Public Accountant), *CPS* (Certified Professional Secretary), *PLS* (Professional Legal Secretary), and *CLU* (Chartered Life Underwriter).

personal title

John A. Wrigley, *Jr.,* was elected to the Lynwood City Council.

Please send a copy of the report to Robert Lucio, *Esq.*

professional designation

Cynthia Armstrong, *CPA,* was present at the meeting.

The person in charge during that shift is Eric Blake, *R.N.*

academic degree

Our new president, Armen Sarafian, *Ph.D.,* met with the Board of Directors yesterday.

First fill the prescriptions written by Mary Lou Franz, *M.D.*

5–2. Organizations

a. The names of well-known business, educational, governmental, military, labor, philanthropic, professional, and other organizations or agencies may be abbreviated. No periods or spaces are used to separate the individual letters.

A & P	AMA	FCC	NBC	SAC
AAA	CBS	NAACP	NCR	TWA
AFL-CIO	FBI	NASA	NYU	UN

b. In the names of business firms, *Co., Corp., Inc., Ltd., Mfg.,* or other parts of the firm name are abbreviated only if they are abbreviated in the official name of the organization.

We ordered the parts from Corway *Mfg. Co.*

Johnson Products, *Inc.,* will receive the contract.

5–3. Dates and Time

a. Spell out the days of the week and the months of the year. However, they may be abbreviated when space is limited; for example, in a list of dates, a table, or an illustration.

The next meeting will be held on *Monday, January 18.*

Next *Tuesday, October 8,* will mark our fifth anniversary.

b. The abbreviations *a.m. (ante meridiem)* and *p.m. (post meridiem)* are used for expressing clock time. They are typed in lowercase letters separated by periods.

Would you prefer to take the flight at *8:45 a.m.* or the one at *2 p.m.*?

He arrived at *3:30 p.m.*

c. The time zones—*EST* (Eastern Standard Time), *CST* (Central Standard Time), *MST* (Mountain Standard Time), and *PST* (Pacific Standard Time)—are abbreviated. When daylight saving time is in effect, the time zones are referred to as *EDT, CDT, MDT,* and *PDT.*

According to the latest schedule, his plane will arrive in Denver at 6 p.m., *MST.*

The new schedules were based on *EDT.*

d. The abbreviations *B.C.* (before Christ) and *A.D. (anno Domini)* are sometimes used in expressing dates. Both follow the year and are typed in capital letters with periods. In formal writing, however, *A.D.* may appear before the year.

B.C.

He claims that the statue dates back to *400 B.C.*

A.D. after the year

Her thesis dealt with the rise of Christianity from *200 to 350 A.D.*

A.D. before the year

The Spanish legions, under the leadership of Galba, conquered Rome in *A.D. 68.*

5–4. Standard Units of Measure

Common units of measure such as distance, length, temperature, volume, and weight are usually spelled out. They may be abbreviated, however, when space is limited; for example, on invoices, packing slips, and other business forms. In abbreviating units of measure, place periods after one-word abbreviations. However, in abbreviations representing more than one word, omit the periods.

5

correspondence

All perishable goods shipped over *100 miles* should be kept below *40 degrees Fahrenheit.*

forms, one-word abbreviations

12 ft. 2 in. (12 feet 2 inches)   *3 lb. 2 oz.* (3 pounds 2 ounces)

forms, multiple-word abbreviations

80 wpm (80 words per minute)   *55 mph* (55 miles per hour)

5–5. Metric Units of Measure

a. In regular business correspondence metric units of measurement are generally written out. However, on business forms and tables and in scientific and technical writing, they are often abbreviated. These abbreviations are written without periods, and the same form is used for singular and plural. Common abbreviations for measurements related to distance, weight, and volume follow.

prefixes

deci	*d*	(1/10)	deka	*da*	(× 10)
centi	*c*	(1/100)	hecto	*h*	(× 100)
milli	*m*	(1/1000)	kilo	*k*	(× 1000)

common units of measure

meter	*m*	centimeter	*cm*	kilometer	*km*
gram	*g*	kilogram	*kg*	milligram	*mg*
liter	*l*	milliliter	*ml*		

square meter	*sq m*
cubic centimeter	*cc*

b. The abbreviation for *liter* is a lowercase *l*, but it is often typed with a capital *L* because the lowercase letter "l" and numeral "1" (one) on many typewriters are typed with the same key. Therefore, to avoid confusion, the capital *L* is used instead.

    1 *L* milk   *but*   1 *ml* vaccine (abbreviation is clear)

c. Temperatures in the metric system are expressed on the Celsius scale. This term is abbreviated *C*.

    37°*C*   25°*C*

d. Express abbreviations relating to kilometers per hour with a diagonal.

    The maximum speed limit on this highway is *90 km/h* (55 mph).

    Slow down to *40 km/h* (25 mph) in the school crossing zone.

5–6. Business and General Terms

a. When the word *number* is not followed by a numeral, spell it out. The abbreviation *No.*, however, is used when a numeral directly follows the term unless the term begins the sentence.

    The stock *number* of the item you requested is *No. 4–862.*

    Please ship us three *Model No. 17A* electric motors.

    Number 18–A part is no longer stocked in our warehouse.

b. Commonly abbreviated business terms and some computer languages are typed in all capital letters with no spaces or periods separating the letters. A few business terms, when used in business correspondence, however, are written in lowercase letters separated by periods.

    capital letters
    PERT   GNP   LIFO   COBOL   BASIC   APL

    lowercase letters in correspondence
    c.o.d.   f.o.b.

c. In giving telephone numbers with extensions, capitalize and abbreviate the word *extension (Ext.)*.

    You may reach me at 987-9281, *Ext.* 1201, any weekday between 10 and 11 a.m.

    Please call me collect at (714) 365-3827, *Ext.* 248.

d. Some commonly abbreviated terms are derived from foreign expressions. They are generally typed in lowercase letters and are followed by a period at the close of each abbreviated word.

foreign abbreviations

e.g. (for example)	viz. (namely)
et al. (and others)	ibid. (in the same place)
i.e. (that is)	loc. cit. (in the place cited)
etc. (and so forth)	op. cit. (in the work cited)

5–7. Plurals

No apostrophe is used to form the plural of abbreviations; most plural abbreviations are formed by adding only *s* to the singular abbreviations. However, some abbreviations are the same in both the singular and plural forms.

plural formed by adding "s"

hr., *hrs.*	IOU, *IOUs*
mgr., *mgrs.*	CPA, *CPAs*
c.o.d., *c.o.d.s*	R.N., *R.N.s*

singular and plural form identical

deg., *deg.*   ft., *ft.*   in., *in.*

5–8. Addresses and Geographical Expressions

a. For addresses in business correspondence, short terms such as *Street, Avenue,* and *Road* are spelled out. *Boulevard (Blvd.),* however, may be abbreviated if space is limited in expressing long street names.

Ms. Lila Green
462 Olive *Avenue*
Iowa City, IA 52240

Mr. James F. Campenelli
1873 San Fernando Mission *Blvd.*
San Francisco, CA 94127

b. Terms indicating direction (North, South, East, West) within an address are spelled out. Compound directions such as *N.E.,* however, are abbreviated when they are used after the name of the street.

direction before street

851 *East* Lake Street

compound direction after street

7059 Capitol Avenue, *S.W.*

c. The post office recommends that on all mailings the names of states be abbreviated by using the official zip code designations. (They are typed in capital letters with no periods or spaces.) These two-letter state abbreviations are shown on pages 114–115 and on the page opposite the inside back cover.

Since optical scanning equipment no longer requires the use of the two-letter abbreviations, the full state name or the zip code designation may be used, depending on which form more nearly balances with the other lines of the address. If both forms provide balance, use the zip code designation.

zip code designation

Mrs. Marjory Clark, PLS
Los Angeles Pierce College
6201 Winnetka Avenue
Woodland Hills, *CA* 91371

state spelled out fully

Fielder Publishing Company
9836 West Seventh Avenue
Ridgewood, *New Jersey* 07451

d. Since 1974 the post office has recommended a format for addressing envelopes that uses all capital letters, abbreviations, and no internal punctuation marks. As yet, this format has not been widely accepted for individually typed correspondence; its use has been mainly with computer-originated mail. This format is described fully in Section 10–26.

e. A period is placed after each abbreviated word in geographical abbreviations. Only with the two-letter state abbreviations recommended by the U.S. Postal Service are the periods omitted.

capital letters

U.S.A. (United States of America)   *U.K.* (United Kingdom)
U.S.S.R. (Union of Soviet Socialist   *G.B.* (Great Britain)
    Republics)

capital and lowercase letters

So. Nev. (Southern Nevada)   *Ire.* (Ireland)

post office abbreviation

MT (Montana)   *IA* (Iowa)

5–9. Abbreviation Format

a. The capitalization of abbreviations is generally governed by the format of the original word or words. Proper nouns are always capitalized while common nouns generally appear in lowercase letters. Some common noun abbreviations, however, are capitalized.

capital letters for proper nouns

His father is a member of the *AFL-CIO*.

lowercase letters for common nouns

Please send the order *c.o.d.*

capital letters for common nouns

Who will act as *MC* for Bill Himstreet's retirement banquet?

Be sure to ask the *TV* repairman to send the bill to our home address.

b. Abbreviations that appear in all capital letters are generally typed without periods or spaces. Geographic expressions, most professional designations, and academic degrees, however, are typed with periods but no spaces. Initials in a person's name are typed with both periods and spaces.

5

general rule—no periods and no spaces

We heard the news from an *NBC* reporter.

Be sure to turn your dial to *KBIG* for beautiful music.

geographical expressions—periods with no spaces

Their travel agency sponsored several trips to the *U.S.S.R.* last summer.

We will return to the *U.S.* next spring.

professional designations—periods with no spaces

Jodi Myers, *R.P.T.*, is the physical therapist who is handling this case.

Will Robert Soto, *R.N.*, be the new director of our nursing program?

academic degrees—periods with no spaces

Mr. Fujimoto was granted an *M.A.* in business last June.

Jane Hughes, *Ph.D.*, was awarded the position.

initials—periods and spaces

Please deliver this report to Ms. *J. T.* Kelly.

Only Gerald *H.* Monroe applied for the position.

c. In lowercase abbreviations a period is generally placed after each letter or group of letters representing a word, and there is no space between letters and periods in compound abbreviations. Exceptions include the abbreviations of metric measurements and compound abbreviations representing "measures per time."

general rule—periods

c.o.d. (collect on delivery)	*mgr.* (manager)
a.m. (ante meridiem)	*qt.* (quart)
ft. (foot or feet)	*amt.* (amount)

metric measurements—no periods

mm ml cm kg cc

measures per time—no periods

rpm wam wpm mph

d. If an abbreviation containing a period falls at the end of a sentence, only one period is needed. In sentences ending with question marks or exclamation marks, place the mark directly after the period.

period

The hotel clerk awakened Mr. Sykiski at *8 a.m.*

question mark

Did you send the order *c.o.d.?*

exclamation mark

The plane was three hours late in arriving in the *U.S.A.!*

5–10. Commonly Used Abbreviations

Abbreviations of Common Business Terms

Term	Abbreviation
account	acct.
accounts payable	a/p, A/P
accounts receivable	a/r, A/R
advertisement	advt., ad
affidavit	afft.
American Standard Code for Information Interchange	ASCII
amount	amt.
anno Domini	A.D.
answer	ans.
ante meridiem	a.m.
approximately	approx.
assistant	asst., ass't.
association	assn., assoc.
attention	attn.
attorney	atty.
audiovisual	AV
avenue	ave.
average	av., avg.
balance	bal.
before Christ	B.C.
bill of lading	B/L

Abbreviations of Common Business Terms (continued)

Term	Abbreviation
bill of sale	B/S
binary digit	bit
bits per second	bps
brothers	bros.
building	bldg.
bushel	bu.
by way of	via
capital	cap.
carbon copy	cc
care of	c/o
carton	ctn.
cathode-ray tube	CRT
Celsius	C
centimeter	cm
central processing unit	CPU
characters per inch	cpi
characters per second	cps
charge	chg.
collect on delivery	c.o.d., COD
commission	comm.
Common Business Oriented Language	COBOL
company	co.
computer-aided transcription	CAT
computer output microform	COM
corporation	corp.
cubic	cu.
cubic centimeter	cc
data processing	DP
department	dept.
discount	disc.
division	div.
dozen	doz., dz.
each	ea.
Electronic Computer Originated Message	E-COM
electronic data processing	EDP
enclosure	enc., encl.
esquire	esq.
expense	exp.
extension	Ext.
facsimile	FAX
Fahrenheit	F
first in, first out	FIFO
foot, feet	ft.
FORmula TRANslator	FORTRAN
forward	fwd.
free on board	f.o.b., FOB

5

Abbreviations of Common Business Terms (continued)

Term	Abbreviation
freight	frt.
gallon	gal.
garbage in, garbage out	GIGO
gram	g
gross	gr.
gross national product	GNP
hour	hr.
hundredweight	cwt.
identification data	ID
inch	in.
incorporated	inc.
insurance	ins.
intelligence quotient	IQ
interest	int.
inventory	invt.
invoice	inv.
kilogram	kg
kilometer	km
last in, first out	LIFO
limited	ltd.
lines per minute	lpn
liter	l, L
local area network	LAN
manager	mgr.
manufacturing	mfg.
master of ceremonies	MC
memorandum	memo
merchandise	mdse.
meter	m
milligram	mg
milliliter	ml
millimeter	mm
minute	min.
miscellaneous	misc.
Mister	Mr.
Misters	Messrs.
Mistress	Mrs.
month	mo.
net weight	nt. wt.
number	No.
okay	OK
optical character recognition	OCR
organization	org.
original	orig.
ounce	oz.

Abbreviations of Common Business Terms (continued)

Term	Abbreviation
overdraft	o.d., OD
package	pkg.
page, pages	p., pp.
pair	pr.
parcel post	pp., PP
pint	pt.
post meridiem	p.m.
post office	P.O.
postscript	P.S., PS
pound	lb.
president	pres.
private automatic branch exchange	PABX
private branch exchange	PBX
profit and loss	P & L, P/L
Programmable Read Only Memory	PROM
public relations	PR
purchase order	P.O., PO
quart	qt.
quarter	qtr.
quire	qr.
railway	ry.
Random Access Memory	RAM
Read Only Memory	ROM
ream, reams	rm.
received	recd.
respond, if you please	R.S.V.P., RSVP
returned	retd.
rural free delivery	RFD
secretary	sec., secy., sec'y
section	sect.
shipment	shpt.
standard operating procedure	SOP
television	TV
treasurer	treas.
vice president	V.P.
volume	vol.
week	wk.
weight	wt.
Western Union Teleprinter Exchange Service	TWX
Wide Area Telephone Service	WATS
word processing	WP
words per minute	wpm
yard	yd.
year	yr.

5

Abbreviations of States and Territories

State or Territory	Standard Abbreviation	Two-Letter Abbreviation
Alabama	Ala.	AL
Alaska	Alas.	AK
Arizona	Ariz.	AZ
Arkansas	Ark.	AR
California	Calif.	CA
Canal Zone	C.Z.	CZ
Colorado	Colo.	CO
Connecticut	Conn.	CT
Delaware	Del.	DE
District of Columbia	D.C.	DC
Florida	Fla.	FL
Georgia	Ga.	GA
Guam		GU
Hawaii		HI
Idaho		ID
Illinois	Ill.	IL
Indiana	Ind.	IN
Iowa		IA
Kansas	Kans.	KS
Kentucky	Ky.	KY
Louisiana	La.	LA
Maine		ME
Maryland	Md.	MD
Massachusetts	Mass.	MA
Michigan	Mich.	MI
Minnesota	Minn.	MN
Mississippi	Miss.	MS
Missouri	Mo.	MO
Montana	Mont.	MT
Nebraska	Nebr.	NE
Nevada	Nev.	NV
New Hampshire	N.H.	NH
New Jersey	N.J.	NJ
New Mexico	N. Mex.	NM
New York	N.Y.	NY
North Carolina	N.C.	NC
North Dakota	N. Dak.	ND
Ohio		OH
Oklahoma	Okla.	OK
Oregon	Oreg.	OR
Pennsylvania	Pa., Penna.	PA
Puerto Rico	P.R.	PR
Rhode Island	R.I.	RI
South Carolina	S.C.	SC
South Dakota	S. Dak.	SD
Tennessee	Tenn.	TN

5

Abbreviations of States and Territories (continued)

Texas	Tex.	TX
Utah		UT
Vermont	Vt.	VT
Virgin Islands	V.I.	VI
Virginia	Va.	VA
Washington	Wash.	WA
West Virginia	W. Va.	WV
Wisconsin	Wis.	WI
Wyoming	Wyo.	WY

5

Two-Letter Abbreviations for Canadian Provinces

Canadian Province	Abbreviation
Alberta	AB
British Columbia	BC
Labrador	LB
Manitoba	MB
New Brunswick	NB
Newfoundland	NF
Northwest Territories	NT
Nova Scotia	NS
Ontario	ON
Prince Edward Island	PE
Quebec	PQ
Saskatchewan	SK
Yukon Territory	YT

Contractions

5–11. Contractions

a. Contractions are similar to abbreviations in that they are shortened forms. Unlike abbreviations, however, contractions always contain an apostrophe to indicate where letters have been omitted. The use of single-word contractions is generally limited to business forms and tables. Some common single-word contractions follow:

ack'd (acknowledged)	rec't (receipt)
ass't (assistant)	sec'y (secretary)
gov't (government)	'85 (1985)
nat'l (national)	

b. A second kind of contraction occurs with verb forms. By using an apostrophe to indicate where letters have been omitted, two words may be combined into one. The use of verb contractions is generally limited to informal business writing. A sampling of commonly used verb contractions follows:

aren't	(are not)	I've	(I have)
didn't	(did not)	that's	(that is)
doesn't	(does not)	there's	(there is)
don't	(do not)	they're	(they are)
hasn't	(has not)	wasn't	(was not)
she's	(she is)	we'll	(we will)
I'll	(I will)	who's	(who is)
isn't	(is not)	won't	(will not)
it's	(it is)	wouldn't	(would not)
let's	(let us)	you're	(you are)

5

Literary and Artistic Titles

6

Literary and Artistic Titles Solution Finder

Punctuation   6–4

   Appositive expressions   6–4a
   Comma placement   6–4b
   Period placement   6–4b
   Question mark placement   6–4c

Titles

   Artistic works   6–3
     Essays   6–3
     Lectures   6–3
     Movies   6–3
     Musicals   6–3
     Operas   6–3
     Paintings   6–3
     Plays   6–3
     Poems   6–3

     Radio shows   6–3
     Sermons   6–3
     Songs   6–3
     Television shows   6–3
   Published works   6–1
     Articles, magazines   6–1c
     Books   6–1a
     Chapters, books and
       pamphlets   6–1b
     Columns, newspaper   6–1c
     Magazines   6–1a
     Newspapers   6–1a
     Pamphlets   6–1a
     Preliminary sections of
       published works   6–1d
     Subdivisions of published
       works   6–1b, c
   Unpublished works   6–2

6

Titles

6–1. Published Works

a. Underline or place in all capital letters the titles of published books, magazines, newspapers, and pamphlets. In underlined titles capitalize the first letter of the principal words in the title. Articles (*a, an, the*), conjunctions (*and, but, or, nor*), and prepositions with fewer than four letters (*of, in, on, to, for,* etc.) are not capitalized unless they appear as the first or last words of the title or as the first word of a subtitle following a colon.

book

A copy of The Random House Dictionary of the English Language arrived yesterday.

Copies of Computers and the Electronic Age are available at your local bookstore.

magazine

Have you read the latest issue of BETTER HOMES AND GARDENS?

newspaper

An article in The Wall Street Journal yesterday discussed sales trends in our industry.

pamphlet

Your Attitude Is Showing is a publication that should be distributed to our new employees.

b. Place in quotation marks the titles of chapters, sections, units, lessons, and other such subdivisions of published books or pamphlets. Capitalize the first letter of the principal words in the title.

chapter in a book

The final chapter, "Application of Word Processing Procedures," contributed immeasurably to the success of Office Systems and Management.

section in a pamphlet

Please review the section "Filling Out the Application" before you apply for a job.

c. Place in quotation marks the titles of articles, regular features, or columns in magazines and newspapers. Capitalize the first letter of the principal words in the title.

article in a magazine

Did you see "Indoor Gardening" in last month's issue of Ladies' Home Journal?

column in a newspaper

Potter's "Financial Outlook" predicted a rising stock market during the next quarter.

d. Capitalize the first letter of subdivisions such as *preface, contents, appendix,* and *index* when they refer to a specific work.

The rule for punctuating words in a series can be found in the *Appendix.*

6–2. Unpublished Works

Place the titles of unpublished manuscripts, reports, theses, and dissertations in quotation marks. Capitalize the first letter of the principal words in the title.

title of report

Copies of "Report on Progress in Areas of Public Concern" were distributed to the board members last week.

6–3. Artistic Works

Place in quotation marks the titles of movies, television and radio shows, plays, musicals, operas, poems, songs, paintings, essays, lectures, and sermons. Capitalize the first letter of the principal words in the title.

movie

"Gone With the Wind" is a movie classic that still attracts thousands.

lecture

Dr. Zimmer's dynamic presentation, "Politics and Education," was concluded with a challenge the audience could not overlook.

television series

Reruns of "The Brady Bunch" still entertain today's children.

Punctuation

6–4. Punctuation Format

a. Titles of literary and artistic works are often used in appositive expressions; that is, they are used to rename a previously mentioned noun. In cases where the title is not needed to identify the work, set it off from the rest of the sentence with commas. Where the title is needed for identification, no commas are used.

title unnecessary to determine which article

His latest article, "Marketing Changes in the Automotive Industry," recommended a startling departure from current policies.

title necessary to determine which book

The book <u>Daisies Forever</u> should soon make the best-seller list.

b. Periods and commas appearing with closing quotation marks are always placed inside.

period with closing quotation mark

Hawaii is the location of most filmings for "Magnum, P.I."

comma inside closing quotation mark

Your last article, "Computerized Accounting Procedures in the Banking Industry," was certainly helpful to me in planning our new procedures.

c. Question marks appearing in quoted titles are placed inside the closing quotation mark. If the question mark in a title appears at the end of the sentence, no other form of punctuation is required. On the other hand, if the sentence, not the title, is a question, place the question mark outside the closing quotation mark.

statement

The play "Where Is John?" opened last night.

statement

We saw the play "Where Is John?"

question

Have you seen the play "Where Is John?"

question

When will you be able to purchase tickets for "Fiddler on the Roof"?

Words Often Misused and Confused

7

Words Often Misused and Confused Solution Finder

All entries in this chapter are in alphabetical order.

A/An
A (used before a word beginning with a consonant sound or a long ū sound)—Please call *a r*epairman to fix the typewriter. *A u*nion representative met with us yesterday. An (used before a word beginning with a vowel sound other than the long ū sound)— Please make *an a*ppointment for me with Miss Carlson.

A while/Awhile
A while (an adjective-noun combination meaning "a short time")—He will be here in *a while.*
Awhile (used as an adverb meaning "for a short time")—Exercise *awhile* each day to maintain your good health.

Accede/Exceed
Accede (to agree or consent)—I will *accede* to your wishes.
Exceed (to surpass a limit)—Many accidents occur when people *exceed* the speed limit.

Accept/Except
Accept (to take or receive)—We do not *accept* second-party checks.
Except (with the exclusion of, but)—No one else *except* you knows about the proposed merger.

Access/Excess
Access (admittance or approachability)—Everyone in the office should have *access* to the files.
Excess (beyond ordinary limits; a surplus)—At the end of the day, all *excess* materials should be stored.

Ad/Add
Ad (abbreviated form of advertisement)—We filled most of our personnel needs by running an *ad* in the local newspaper.
Add (to increase by uniting or joining)—The new computer will *add* to the efficiency of the office staff.

Adapt/Adept/Adopt
Adapt (to adjust or modify)—We must *adapt* ourselves to new situations.
Adept (skilled)—She is very *adept* at taking and transcribing dictation.
Adopt (to take and follow as one's own)—We will *adopt* Mrs. Williams' proposal.

Add: see Ad.

Addict/Edict

Addict (one who is habitually or obsessively dependent; devotee)—Our clinic has noted success with the rehabilitation of drug *addicts*. Many of today's teenagers are rock music *addicts*.
Edict (order or command)—When did our manager issue this *edict?*

Addition/Edition

Addition (the process of uniting or joining)—The *addition* of more floor space is necessary to meet the increased production quotas.
Edition (a particular version of printed material)—Only the second *edition* of this book is available now.

Adept: see Adapt.

Adherence/Adherents

Adherence (a steady attachment or loyalty)—A strict *adherence* to all safety procedures is required of all personnel.
Adherents (loyal supporters or followers)—There are many *adherents* to the space program and its importance to mankind.

Adopt: see Adapt.

7

Adverse/Averse

Adverse (opposing; antagonistic)—Rising interest rates have had an *adverse* effect on real estate sales and new home developments.
Averse (unwilling; reluctant)—Carol is a valuable employee because she is not *averse* to working overtime.

Advice/Advise

Advice n. (a suggestion, an opinion, or a recommendation)—He would have avoided the problem if he had followed our *advice.*
Advise v. (to counsel or recommend)—We had to *advise* her not to sign the contract in its present form.

Affect/Effect

Affect v. (to influence)—Large pay raises throughout the country cannot help *affect* the rate of inflation. Increased costs will *affect* our pricing policies on all merchandise.
Effect v. (to bring about or cause to happen)—Our government plans to *effect* a change in the rate of inflation by tightening bank credits. The rising costs of raw materials will *effect* large price increases in May.
Effect n. (a result or consequence)—Inflation usually has a negative *effect* on our economy. The new vacation policy had no apparent *effect* on company morale.

Aid/Aide

Aid (to help or assist; assistance)—The United States *aids* many foreign countries. Your application for financial *aid* is currently being processed.
Aide (a person who assists another)—Please ask your *aide* to deliver these papers to Dr. Powell's office by Friday afternoon.

Aisle/Isle

Aisle (a passageway for inside traffic)—After the show the *aisles* of the theater were cluttered with empty popcorn containers and candy wrappers.

Isle (a piece of land surrounded by water; island)—This script centers around two teenagers marooned on a tropical *isle.*

Allowed/Aloud

Allowed (permitted)—Passengers are *allowed* 40 pounds of baggage aboard transcontinental flights.

Aloud (to speak audibly)—The message was read *aloud* so all could hear.

All ready/Already

All ready (prepared)—We are *all ready* to initiate the new procedure.

Already (by or before this time)—The time on the parking meter has *already* lapsed.

All right/Alright

All right (approving or agreeable)—It is *all right* with the company if people wish to continue working after sixty-five years of age.

Alright (an informal spelling of *all right* that is not appropriate for business writing).

All together/Altogether

All together (everyone in a group)—We must work *all together* if the company is to survive this crisis.

Altogether (wholly; entirely)—*Altogether,* 20 families signed up for the company picnic.

Allude/Elude

Allude (to mention or refer to)—As proof of Americans' concern for economy, I *allude* to the increased popularity of small cars during recent years.

Elude (to evade or escape)—The Senator has been able to *elude* severe criticism of his program by anticipating and counteracting objections.

Allusion/Delusion/Illusion

Allusion (an indirect reference)—Several *allusions* were made to Mr. Reed's apparent laziness.

Delusion (a false belief)—Many people invested heavily in these oil stocks because the company propagated the *delusion* that their wells were active producers.

Illusion (a misconception or misapprehension)—Many of us were under the *illusion* that this new equipment would reduce our staff by one half.

All ways/Always

All ways (by all methods)—We must try *all ways* possible to solve the problem.

Always (at all times; continually)—Our company is *always* on the lookout for a good secretary.

Almost/Most

Almost (an adverb meaning nearly)—Our company *almost* reached its sales quota this year.

Most (an adjective or subject complement meaning the greatest in amount or number)—Ellen Reynolds had the *most* votes in the election.

Aloud: see Allowed.

Already: see All ready.

Alright: see All right.

Altar/Alter
Altar (a structure used for worship)—The wedding flowers made the *altar* look particularly beautiful.
Alter (to change)—The plane had to *alter* its altitude to avoid hitting the mountain.

Altogether: see All together.

Always: see All ways.

Among/Between
Among (refers to more than two persons or things)—Distribute the supplies equally *among* the three departments.
Between (refers to two persons or things)—The final selection for the position is *between* Ms. McCreery and Mr. Muha.

Amount/Number
Amount (indicates mass items that cannot be counted and singular nouns)—A great *amount* of food was wasted because of the power failure.
Number (indicates items that can be counted and plural nouns)—A *number* of errors appear in this letter.

An: see A.

Anecdote/Antidote
Anecdote (a story or a brief account of an event)—We all had to laugh at Tom's *anecdote* of what happened when the waiter accidentally tripped while carrying a tray of food.
Antidote (a remedy that counteracts poison)—Dr. Martin consented to write an article about the new *antidote* he developed to counteract five different poisons.

Annual/Annul
Annual (yearly)—The *annual* report of the company will be published next week.
Annul (to void or abolish)—We had to *annul* the contract because of legal complications.

Antidote: see Anecdote.

Any one/Anyone
Any one (any one person or thing in a group [always followed by "of"])—Please hand me *any one* of those pencils.
Anyone (any person)—We will hire *anyone* who can type 40 words a minute accurately.

Any time/Anytime

Any time (an unspecified point in time)—Please let us know *any time* you have questions about our products or services. *Any time* we can be of service, just call our toll-free number and a telephone representative will assist you. You may mail your application *any time* between today and August 30.

Anytime (at any time whatever)—Drop by our offices *anytime*. For an emergency you may call Dr. Mulcahy *anytime*, day or night. During the last quarter of the year, you may take your vacation *anytime*.

Any way/Anyway

Any way (any method)—Is there *any way* we can reach you while you are on vacation?

Anyway (in any case)—Considering the low bids of our competitors, I don't believe we would have received the contract *anyway*.

Appraise/Apprise

Appraise (to estimate)—Before the merger, we hired an outside firm to *appraise* our assets.

Apprise (to inform or notify)—I will *apprise* Janet of the situation and obtain her reaction.

As/Like

As (used as a conjunction at the beginning of a clause)—I will get the material to you by Friday *as* I promised.

Like (used when the sentence requires a preposition)—I have never met anyone *like* him.

Ascent/Assent

Ascent (rising or going up)—The recent *ascent* of stock market prices is an encouraging sign.

Assent (to agree or admit as true)—Everyone at the meeting will surely *assent* to the plan.

Assistance/Assistants

Assistance (help or aid)—The project could not have been completed without your *assistance*.

Assistants (people who assist a superior)—The staffing report indicates that the general manager should have three *assistants*.

Assure/Ensure/Insure

Assure (to promise; to make a positive declaration)—I *assure* you that the loan will be paid back on time.

Ensure (to secure or make certain)—To *ensure* the timely completion of this project, please hire additional qualified personnel.

Insure (to protect against loss)—We *insure* all our facilities against earthquake damage.

Attendance/Attendants

Attendance (being present or attending)—All members of the committee must be in *attendance* before the meeting can be called to order.

Attendants (one who attends with or to others)—The *attendants* had a difficult time parking all the cars for such a large crowd.

Averse: see Adverse.

Awhile: see A while.

Bad/Badly
Bad (an adjective or subject complement used after such intransitive verbs as *feel* or *look*)—I feel *bad* that your request for a transfer cannot be granted.
Badly (an adverb)—We *badly* need more personnel if the survey is to be completed on time.

Bail/Bale
Bail (security)—*Bail* in this case was set at $1,500.
Bale (a large bundle)—One *bale* of used clothing was lost in transit.

Bare/Bear
Bare (uncovered, plain, or mere)—The paint had chipped and peeled so badly that the *bare* wood was showing. I had time to give him only the *bare* facts connected with the problem.
Bear (to carry or bring forth)—Unfortunately, he had to *bear* the brunt of the losses.

Base/Bass
Base (bottom part of something; foundation)—When did the *base* of this marble column crack?
Bass (a low-pitched sound; musical instrument having a low range)—We could use his deep *bass* voice in our quartet. Do you play the *bass* violin?

Bear: see Bare.

Beside/Besides
Beside (by the side of)—Please put the new file cabinet *beside* the one in the corner.
Besides (in addition to)—Who else *besides* Ms. Graham was awarded a bonus?

Between: see Among.

Biannual/Biennial
Biannual (occurring twice a year)—The stockholders' *biannual* meetings are held in January and August every year.
Biennial (occurring once every two years)—The society holds *biennial* elections, and officers serve for two years.

Billed/Build
Billed (charged for goods or services)—You will be *billed* on the 10th of each month.
Build (to construct)—We plan to *build* a new plant in Texas.

Bolder/Boulder
Bolder (more fearless or daring)—The board feels we need a *bolder* person as president.
Boulder (a large rock)—The damage to the tire was caused by a *boulder* in the road.

7

Born/Borne
Born (brought forth by birth; originated)—This patient was *born* on February 14, 1928. One can hardly believe that this multimillion-dollar industry was *born* in a garage less than a decade ago.
Borne (past participle of bear)—Mrs. Talbert has already *borne* six children, and she is currently expecting her seventh. Our school district has *borne* these financial burdens for over six years.

Bouillon/Bullion
Bouillon (a clear soup)—For the first course I have ordered beef *bouillon.*
Bullion (uncoined gold or silver in bars or ingots)—Mr. Reece had hidden in his home nearly $25,000 in gold *bullion.*

Boulder: see Bolder.

Breach/Breech
Breach (a violation of a law or agreement; a hole, gap, or break in a solid structure)—The judge ruled a *breach* of contract existed when the building was not finished by the date agreed upon. If contract negotiations are to continue, we must narrow the *breach* between union and management negotiators.
Breech (part of a firearm or cannon that is located behind the barrel)—They had difficulty firing the old cannon because the *breech* would not work properly.

Build: see Billed.

Bullion: see Bouillon.

Callous/Callus
Callous (insensitive; without feeling)—Everyone on the committee agreed that Mr. Bush's *callous* remark concerning Ms. Wright's attire was in poor taste.
Callus (hard, thick skin)—The new shoes caused a *callus* that did not disappear for months.

Can/May
Can (the ability to do something)—Pauline *can* type and take dictation.
May (permission)—Yes, you *may* take a day's vacation tomorrow.

Canvas/Canvass
Canvas (a firm, closely woven cloth)—Use these *canvas* coverings to protect the new cars as they arrive.
Canvass (to survey or solicit in an area)—Do you have a volunteer who will *canvass* the residences on Jersey Street?

Capital/Capitol
Capital n. (a city in which the official seat of government is located; the wealth of an individual or firm)—The *capital* of Wisconsin is Madison. Much of our *capital* is tied up in equipment.

Capital adj. (a crime punishable by death; foremost in importance)—Treason in many countries is a *capital* crime. The forthcoming election is *capital* in the minds of the board members.

Capitol n. (a building used by the U.S. Congress [always capitalized])—The Senator needs to be in the *Capitol* by 9 a.m. for the hearings.

Capitol n. (a building in which a state legislature convenes)—The *capitol* was surrounded by angry pickets waving placards.

Carat/Caret/Carrot/Karat

Carat (a unit of weight for gems)—Her engagement ring has a 2-*carat* diamond surrounded by six 20-point diamonds.

Caret (a sign similar to an inverted *v* that is placed at the bottom of a line to show where something is to be inserted)—Our editor asked us to use a *caret* to show any insertions or additions in the manuscript.

Carrot (a vegetable)—A *carrot* can be just as delicious raw as it is cooked.

Karat (a unit of weight for gold)—The chain was made of 18-*karat* gold.

Censor/Censure

Censor (to examine materials and delete objectionable matter; one who censors)—How many scenes from this movie were *censored* for television broadcasting? When will the *censor* finish reviewing the script?

Censure (to criticize or condemn; condemnation)—The city council *censured* the mayor for awarding the contract to his brother-in-law's firm. After the facts were disclosed, Senator Dillon was subjected to public *censure*.

Census/Senses

Census (an official count of a country's population)—The United States takes a *census* every ten years.

Senses (the specialized functions of sight, hearing, smell, taste, and touch)—Our client's *senses* of hearing and touch were altered as a result of the accident.

Cereal/Serial

Cereal (a breakfast food made from grain)—The diet called for a serving of wheat *cereal*.

Serial (arranged in a series)—The *serial* numbers of all our vehicles should be on file.

Choose/Chose

Choose (to select or make a choice)—We don't know whom he will *choose* for his executive secretary.

Chose (past tense of "choose")—He *chose* Ms. Randall to be his executive secretary.

Cite/Sight/Site

Cite (to quote or mention; to summon)—He can *cite* many authorities who have studied the problem. Did the officer *cite* you for speeding?

Sight (to see or take aim; a view or spectacle)—Luckily the salesperson did not *sight* Ms. Clary leaving the office. The Statue of Liberty is a frequently visited tourist *sight* in New York City.

Site (a location)—This is a perfect *site* for the housing project.

7

Coarse/Course
Coarse (rough texture)—This material is too *coarse* for our use.
Course (a particular direction or route; part of a meal; a unit of learning)—We are now committed to a *course* of action that will hopefully solve the problem. Which menu item have you selected for the main *course?* You need only three more *courses* to graduate.

Collision/Collusion
Collision (a crash)—No one was hurt in the *collision.*
Collusion (an agreement to defraud)—No one suspected them of *collusion.*

Command/Commend
Command (to order or direct; an order)—The sergeant *commanded* his troops to return to base by 0600. This dog will obey only its owner's *commands.*
Commend (to praise or flatter)—Please *commend* the staff for the fine job it did in promoting our line at the San Francisco convention.

Complement/Compliment
Complement (that which completes or makes perfect)—The color of the trim will *complement* the color of the walls.
Compliment (to praise or flatter)—Mr. Rose did *compliment* me on the fine job I had done.

Complementary/Complimentary
Complementary (serving mutually to blend, fill out, or complete)—Both these wall coverings are *complementary* to the carpeting you have selected.
Complimentary (favorable; given free)—We appreciate receiving your *complimentary* letter about the service you received in our Fifth Avenue store. To receive a *complimentary* copy of this textbook, merely fill out and return the enclosed postcard.

Confidant/Confident
Confidant (a trusted friend)—He has been his closest *confidant* for years.
Confident (sure of oneself)—Mrs. Allan was *confident* she would get the position.

Conscience/Conscious
Conscience (the faculty of knowing right from wrong)—In the last analysis, it was his *conscience* that made him release the funds.
Conscious (aware or mentally awake)—Yes, we are *conscious* of the fact that a new product similar to ours is on the market. Most of our patients are *conscious* during this type of surgery.

Console/Consul
Console (a cabinet)—The stereo was so popular because of its attractive *console.*
Consul (an official representing a foreign country)—Travel information can often be obtained by contacting the *consul* of the country one wishes to visit.

Continual/Continuous
Continual (a regular or frequent occurrence)—These *continual* telephone calls are disrupting my regular routine.
Continuous (without interruption or cessation)—The *continuous* humming of the new air conditioner is disturbing to everyone in the office.

7

Cooperation/Corporation

Cooperation (working together)—The full *cooperation* of all employees is needed to reduce our high rate of absenteeism.
Corporation (one type of business organization)—We are looking into the possibility of forming a *corporation*.

Corespondent/Correspondence/Correspondents

Corespondent (person named as guilty of adultery with the defendant in a divorce suit)—Who was named as *corespondent* in this divorce case?
Correspondence (letters or other written communications)—Our last *correspondence* from Mr. Flores was on October 14.
Correspondents (letter writers or news reporters)—Be sure to have *correspondents* answer these customers' letters within the next three days. Our African *correspondents* report that several countries are now having severe food shortages.

Corporation: see Cooperation.

Corps/Corpse

Corps (a body of persons having a common activity or occupation)—A *corps* of students have been soliciting funds for the stadium lights. Representatives from the Marine *Corps* will visit our campus next week.
Corpse (a dead body)—The identity of the *corpse* is still unknown.

Correspondence: see Corespondent.

Correspondent: see Corespondent.

Council/Counsel

Council (a governing body)—We will present the proposal to the *council* in the morning.
Counsel (to give advice; advice)—Our staff *counsels* at least eight students each day. He received good *counsel* from his advisors.

Course: see Coarse.

Credible/Creditable

Credible (believable or reliable)—The reason she gave for her long absence was a *credible* one.
Creditable (bringing honor or praise)—The new time-saving device developed by Ms. Cohen is a *creditable* feat of which she can be proud.

Decent/Descent/Dissent

Decent (in good taste; proper)—The *decent* thing would have been for the salesperson to apologize.
Descent (moving downward; ancestry)—The view of the city was breathtaking as the plane started its *descent* into the airport. Mr. Sirakides is of Greek *descent*.
Dissent (to differ or disagree)—There was no *dissent* among the council members concerning the resolution to expand our parking facilities.

Defer/Differ

Defer (to put off or delay)—They decided to *defer* the project until next spring.
Differ (to vary or disagree)—Doctors *differ* in their opinions as to the best treatment for this particular virus.

Deference/Difference

Deference (yielding to someone else's wishes)—In *deference* to the shoppers' requests, the store remained open until 9 p.m. during the summer months.
Difference (state of being different; dissimilarity)—There is little *difference* between the two products.

Delusion: see Allusion.

Deprecate/Depreciate

Deprecate (to disapprove or downgrade)—His speech did nothing but *deprecate* the present zoning system.
Depreciate (to lessen the value)—We will *depreciate* this new equipment over a ten-year period.

Descent: see Decent.

Desert/Dessert

Desert (an arid, barren land area)—Palm Springs was once a *desert* area occupied only by California Indians.
Dessert (a sweet course served at the end of a meal)—Apple pie and ice cream is a traditional American *dessert*.

Device/Devise

Device (an invention or mechanism)—The *device* worked perfectly during the demonstration.
Devise (to think out or plan)—It was not easy to *devise* an overtime plan that would be equitable for everyone.

Dew/Do/Due

Dew (drops of moisture)—The heavy morning *dew* caused her to delay the flight.
Do (to perform or bring about)—We must *do* everything possible to ship the order by June 17.
Due (immediately payable)—All payments are *due* by the 10th of each month.

Differ: see Defer.

Difference: see Deference.

Disapprove/Disprove

Disapprove (to withhold approval)—The boss will *disapprove* any plan that is not properly justified.
Disprove (to prove false)—We must *disprove* the rumor that we are cutting back production next month.

Disburse/Disperse

Disburse (to pay out; to distribute methodically)—A new system has been devised to *disburse* commissions more rapidly. The property will be *disbursed* according to the provisions outlined in Mr. Simons' will.

Disperse (to scatter; to cause to become spread widely)—Those factories that *disperse* pollutants will be subject to heavy fines beginning January 1. Please *disperse* this information to our branch offices immediately.

Disprove: see Disapprove.

Dissent: see Decent.

Do: see Dew.

Done/Dun

Done (past participle of *do*)—Our company has not *done* any further research in this area.

Dun (to make persistent demands for payment; a variable drab color averaging a neutral brownish gray)—Whose responsibility is it to *dun* slow-paying customers? One of our tasks is to repaint these *dun*-colored walls to achieve a more pleasant atmosphere.

Due: see Dew.

Dun: see Done.

Edict: see Addict.

Edition: see Addition.

Effect: see Affect.

Elicit/Illicit

Elicit (to draw out or bring forth)—The speaker had a difficult time trying to *elicit* responses from the audience.

Illicit (unlawful)—He was cited for *illicit* business practices.

Elude: see Allude.

Emigrate/Immigrate

Emigrate (to move from a country)—The Johnsons *emigrated* from Norway in 1972.

Immigrate (to enter a country)—How many Canadians were permitted to *immigrate* to the United States last year?

Eminent/Imminent

Eminent (prominent; distinguished)—Mr. Mendez is an *eminent* authority on labor relations.

Imminent (impending; likely to occur)—There is *imminent* danger of equipment breakdown unless periodic service checks are made.

Ensure: see Assure.

Envelop/Envelope
Envelop (to wrap, surround, or conceal)—The chief said his fire fighters would *envelop* the fire by morning.
Envelope (a container for a letter)—Please send me your answer in the return *envelope* provided for your convenience.

Every day/Everyday
Every day (each day)—I will call you *every day* and give you a status report on the new project.
Everyday (ordinary)—Sales meetings are an *everyday* occurrence in this office.

Every one/Everyone
Every one (each person or thing in a group [Always followed by "of"])—*Every one* of our secretaries can operate our word processing equipment.
Everyone (all people in a group)—*Everyone* is expected to be on time for the stockholders' meeting.

Exceed: see Accede.

Except: see Accept.

Excess: see Access.

Executioner/Executor
Executioner (one who puts to death)—The *executioner*-style murders still remain unsolved.
Executor (person appointed to carry out the provisions of a will)—Whom have you named as *executor* of your will?

Expand/Expend
Expand (to enlarge)—The plan to *expand* our storage facilities was approved.
Expend (to use up or pay out)—We must be careful not to *expend* too much time on minor problems.

Expansive/Expensive
Expansive (capable of expanding; extensive)—An *expansive* commercial development is planned for this area.
Expensive (costly)—The consultant's recommendations were too *expensive* to implement.

Expend: see Expand.

Expensive: see Expansive.

Explicit/Implicit

Explicit (expressed clearly)—The letter gives *explicit* instructions for assembling the new machine.
Implicit (implied)—By reading between the lines, one can discern an *implicit* appeal for additional funds.

Extant/Extent

Extant (currently or actually existing)—Please provide me with a three-year budget for all *extant* and projected programs.
Extent (range, scope, or magnitude)—Unfortunately, we will be unable to assess the *extent* of the damage until next week.

Facetious/Factious

Facetious (humorous or witty, often in an inappropriate manner)—His seemingly *facetious* remark contained a kernel of truth.
Factious (creating faction or dissension)—A series of *factious* disputes eventually led to the dissolution of the partnership.

Factitious/Fictitious

Factitious (artificial)—One manufacturer created a *factitious* demand for copper alloy by spreading rumors of shortages.
Fictitious (nonexistent; imaginary; false)—Many people believe that the reported UFO sightings are *fictitious.*

7

Fair/Fare

Fair (marked by impartiality and honesty; an exhibition; mediocre)—Further legislation was passed recently to enforce *fair* employment practices. Our annual county *fair* is usually held the first week in September. He did a *fair* job.
Fare (get along or succeed; price charged to transport a person)—Our company did not *fare* well in its last bidding competition. How much is the first-class airline *fare* from Chicago to New York?

Farther/Further

Farther (a greater distance)—The trip to the plant is *farther* than I thought.
Further (additional; to help forward)—Refer to my July 8 memo for *further* details.

Feat/Fete

Feat (an act of skill, endurance, or ingenuity)—Under stress human beings have been known to perform *feats* beyond their normal capabilities.
Fete (to honor or commemorate; a large elaborate party)—A large banquet is being planned to *fete* our company president upon his retirement in September. The *fete* to honor our company president will be held on May 19.

Fewer/Less

Fewer (used with items that can be counted and plural nouns)—We had *fewer* sales this month.
Less (used with mass items that cannot be counted and singular nouns)—You will get by with *less* work if you follow my suggestions.

Fictitious: see Factitious.

Finally/Finely
Finally (in the end)—The missing part was *finally* delivered.
Finely (elegantly or delicately)—We all admired the *finely* embroidered tapestry.

Flagrant/Fragrant
Flagrant (glaring; scandalous)—His behavior was a *flagrant* violation of company rules.
Fragrant (sweet smelling)—She received a *fragrant* bouquet of flowers from the staff.

Flair/Flare
Flair (a natural talent or aptitude)—Mrs. Pastis has a *flair* for making people feel at ease when they enter the office.
Flare (to blaze up or spread out)—The gusty winds could easily cause the fire to *flare* out of control.

Flaunt/Flout
Flaunt (to make a gaudy or defiant display)—Although everyone knows Ms. Paige is very wealthy, she does not *flaunt* her wealth.
Flout (to mock or show contempt for)—As a new driver, the young man continued to *flout* the posted speed limit.

7

Flew/Flu/Flue
Flew (past tense of *fly*)—The plane *flew* to the West Coast in record time.
Flu (abbreviated form of *influenza*)—Over 30 percent of our employees are absent because of the *flu.*
Flue (a duct in a chimney)—Unless the *flue* is open, smoke cannot escape through the chimney.

Flout: see Flaunt.

Flu: see Flew.

Flue: see Flew.

Formally/Formerly
Formally (in a formal manner)—At our next meeting you will be *formally* initiated into the organization.
Formerly (in the past)—She was *formerly* the president of a large community college.

Former/Latter
Former (first of two things or belonging to an earlier time)—As a *former* employee, Grace Noonan is always welcome at our yearly company picnic.
Latter (second of two things or nearer to the end)—Of the two proposals the *latter* one seems to be more economical.

Forth/Fourth
Forth (forward)—The speaker asked that his illustrations be brought *forth*.
Fourth (a numeric term)—The *fourth* member of our group never arrived.

Fragrant: see Flagrant.

Further: see Farther.

Good/Well
Good (an adjective that describes a noun or pronoun)—Mr. Collins writes *good* letters.
Well (an adverb that describes a verb, an adjective, or another adverb; a person's well being and health)—Miss Farley takes dictation very *well*. My secretary did not look *well* today.

Grate/Great
Grate (to reduce to small particles by rubbing on something rough; to cause irritation; a frame of parallels or crossed bars blocking a passage)—In the future please use a food processor to *grate* the cheese for our pizzas. His continual talking could *grate* on anyone's nerves. Be sure to place a *grate* over this excavation when you have finished.
Great (large in size; numerous; eminent or distinguished)—From the cruise ship we often sight a *great* white shark. A *great* many people have expressed an interest in purchasing our Model No. 47A video recorder. Many *great* performers from stage and screen will be present at our annual benefit.

7

Guarantee/Guaranty
Guarantee (assurance of the quality or length of service of a product; an assurance for the fulfillment of a condition)—The car has a one-year or 20,000-mile *guarantee*. I *guarantee* that your children will enjoy immensely the adventures Disneyland has to offer.
Guaranty (an assurance to pay the debt of another in case of default)—John Fletcher's car loan will be approved as soon as we receive his parents' signed *guaranty*.

He/Him/Himself
He (the subject of a clause or a complement pronoun)—*He* is the one I interviewed for the job. It was *he* who asked for an appointment.
Him (a direct object, an indirect object, or an object of a preposition)—The president asked *him* to head the project. Mrs. Roberts gave *him* the results of the study yesterday. The choice is between you and *him*.
Himself (a reflexive pronoun used to emphasize or refer back to the subject)—He *himself* had to solve the problem. Bud addressed the envelope to *himself*.

Hear/Here
Hear (to perceive by the ear)—Yes, I can *hear* you clearly.
Here (in this place or at this point)—Install the telephone *here*.

Her/Herself/She

Her (a direct object, an indirect object, or an object of a preposition)—When Paulette arrived, Mr. Shultz asked *her* for the information. Barbara offered *her* a chair. The check is for *her.*

Herself (a reflexive pronoun used to emphasize or refer back to the subject)—Wendy *herself* wrote and dictated the entire audit report. Lois often talks to *herself.*

She (the subject of a clause or a complement pronoun)—*She* went to lunch about 15 minutes ago. It was *she* who typed the memorandum.

Here: see Hear.

Herself: see Her.

Hew/Hue

Hew (to cut with blows of a heavy cutting instrument)—Which famous faces have been *hewed* on Mt. Rushmore?

Hue (color or gradation of color; aspect)—The *hues* of the rainbow glistened in the sunlight. Persons from every political *hue* criticized the President for not informing the American public of his actions.

Him: see He.

Himself: see He.

Hoard/Horde

Hoard (to store or accumulate for future use)—Please do not *hoard* supplies.

Horde (a multitude)—A *horde* of people were waiting for the doors to open.

Holy/Wholly

Holy (sacred)—This place is considered *holy* by some people.

Wholly (completely)—Do you agree *wholly* with the committee's recommendations?

Horde: see Hoard.

Hue: see Hew.

Human/Humane

Human (characteristic of man)—Please remember that all of us are guilty of possessing *human* frailties.

Humane (marked by compassion, sympathy, or consideration)—The treatment of elderly people in this convalescent home is certainly less than *humane.*

Hypercritical/Hypocritical

Hypercritical (excessively critical)—Many believed him to be *hypercritical* of new employees.

Hypocritical (falsely pretending)—No one likes *hypocritical* people.

I/Me/Myself

I (a subject of a clause or a complement pronoun)—*I* finished the report last night. It was *I* who took the message.

Me (a direct object, an indirect object, or an object of a preposition)—They phoned *me* this morning. She gave *me* the report to edit. None of this material is for *me*.

Myself (a reflective pronoun used to emphasize or refer back to the subject)—I wrote the entire report *myself*. I can blame only *myself* for losing this sale.

Ideal/Idle/Idol

Ideal (perfect; model)—Your proposal outlines an *ideal* solution to the problem.

Idle (doing nothing)—The production line was *idle* for almost a week.

Idol (an object for religious worship; a revered person or thing)—One of the church *idols* had been vandalized. Money is often the *idol* of ambitious, greedy people.

Illicit: see Elicit.

Illusion: see Allusion.

Immigrate: see Emigrate.

Imminent: see Eminent.

Implicit: see Explicit.

Imply/Infer

Imply (to suggest without stating)—Does that statement *imply* that I have made a mistake?

Infer (to reach a conclusion)—We must *infer* from the survey results that our advertising campaign was ineffective in this area.

Incidence/Incidents

Incidence (occurrence)—There has never been an *incidence* of theft within the company.

Incidents (events or episodes)—Four *incidents* occurred in which injuries resulted from faulty equipment.

Incite/Insight

Incite (to urge on or provoke action)—The speaker attempted to *incite* the audience to take action.

Insight (keen understanding)—His *insight* into the situation prevented a serious problem.

Indigenous/Indigent/Indignant

Indigenous (native of a particular region)—I believe that this metal is *indigenous* only to the Northwest.

Indigent (poor; needy)—My parents were *indigent* farmers.

Indignant (insulting; angry)—You should learn how to deal with *indignant* customers.

Infer: see Imply.

Ingenious/Ingenuous
Ingenious (marked by originality, resourcefulness, and cleverness)—This *ingenious* plan could save our company thousands of dollars annually.
Ingenuous (showing innocent or childlike simplicity; natural)—Mr. Warren's *ingenuous* smile and warm personality have contributed immeasurably to his successful political career.

Insight: see Incite.

Insure: see Assure.

Interstate/Intrastate
Interstate (between states)—Since expanding operations to New Jersey, we are now involved in *interstate* commerce.
Intrastate (within a state)—This firm, an Illinois corporation, is primarily concerned with *intrastate* product sales.

Isle: see Aisle.

Its/It's
Its (possessive form of *it*)—The company had *its* stockholders' meeting last week.
It's (contraction of *it is*)—*It's* a fact that our office is first in sales.

Karat: see Carat.

Later/Latter
Later (after the proper time)—The shipment arrived *later* than we had anticipated.
Latter (the second thing of two things mentioned)—Your *latter* suggestion is more likely to be adopted. [See also **Former**.]

Lay/Lie
Lay (to put or place; a transitive verb that needs an object to complete its meaning; *lay, laid, laid,* and *laying* are the principal parts of this verb)—Please *lay* the message on my desk. I *laid* the message on your desk. I have *laid* several messages on your desk. We are *laying* the foundation for the new building today.
Lie (to recline; an intransitive verb that does not have an object; *lie, lay, lain,* and *lying* are the principal parts of this verb)—May I *lie* down? He *lay* in bed for two weeks recuperating from his accident. These papers have *lain* on your desk since Monday. She is *lying* down.

Lean/Lien
Lean (to rest against; to be inclined toward; not fat)—Do not *lean* against these railings. I believe the employees *lean* toward the first contract proposal. We use only first-quality *lean* ground beef in our hamburgers.
Lien (a legal right or claim to property)—If he refuses to pay, we will be forced to obtain a *lien* on the property.

Leased/Least

leased (rented property for a specified time period)—The building has been *leased* for three years.

Least (smallest; slightest; lowest)—This month we had the *least* profit for this year.

Less: see Fewer.

Lessee/Lesser/Lessor

Lessee (one to whom a lease is given)—As specified in the lease agreement, the *lessee* must pay a monthly rent to the landlord.

Lesser (smaller or less important)—Although the decision was not wholly satisfactory, it was the *lesser* of the two evils.

Lessor (one who grants the lease)—The *lessor* for all our company cars is Allied Car Rental Service.

Lessen/Lesson

Lessen (to make smaller)—She recommended we *lessen* our efforts in the manufacturing area.

Lesson (a unit of study; something from which one learns)—The experience was a good *lesson* in how miscommunication can cause problems.

Lesser: see Lessee.

Lessor: see Lessee.

Levee/Levy

Levee (the bank of a river or a boat landing)—The river overflowed the *levee*.

Levy (an order for payment)—To pay for the flood damage, the governor ordered a 1 percent *levy* on gasoline sales.

Liable/Libel

Liable (legally responsible; obligated)—The court ruled that the company was *liable* for the accident.

Libel (a false or damaging written statement about another)—He refused to include the statement in his article because he feared he would be sued for *libel*.

Lie: see Lay.

Lien: see Lean.

Lightening/Lightning

Lightening (illuminating or brightening; lessening or alleviating)—Please select colors that will result in *lightening* the reception area. Only by *lightening* her work load can we expect to retain Ms. Burton.

Lightning (the flashing of light produced by atmospheric electricity)—During the storm *lightning* flashes streaked across the sky.

7

Like: see As.

Local/Locale
Local (limited to a particular district)—Only persons living in the *local* area were interviewed.
Locale (a particular location)—This parcel is an ideal *locale* for the new plant.

Loose/Lose
Loose (not fastened, tight, or shut up)—A *loose* connection was the probable cause of the power failure.
Lose (to fail to keep; to mislay)—Please be careful not to *lose* this statement.

Magnate/Magnet
Magnate (a powerful or influential person)—As the first *magnate* of the auto industry, Henry Ford changed the lifestyle of many Americans.
Magnet (something or someone that has the ability to attract)—It was much easier to pick up the spilled paper clips with a *magnet.*

Marital/Marshal/Martial
Marital (pertaining to marriage)—Use *"marital* bliss" for the primary sales theme in your advertising copy.
Marshal (a military rank; the head of a ceremony)—He was asked to act as honorary *marshal* of the parade.
Martial (warlike; military)—A band played *martial* music at the concert.

May: see Can.

May be/Maybe
May be (a verb form)—This *may be* the last year we will be able to expand.
Maybe (an adverb meaning "perhaps")—*Maybe* the new carpeting will reduce the noise level in the office.

Me: see I.

Medal/Meddle
Medal (a metal disk; an award in the form of a metal disk)—He should receive a *medal* for his efforts.
Meddle (to interfere)—It was an argument in which he dared not *meddle.*

Miner/Minor
Miner (a person who works in a mine)—He listed his last job as that of coal *miner.*
Minor (a lesser thing; person under legal age)—It proved to be a *minor* matter. Please post a sign that reads "No *minors* allowed."

Mode/Mood
Mode (style or preferred method)—What *mode* of transportation will you use to reach the airport?
Mood (feeling or disposition)—Before you ask Mr. Smith for a salary increase, be sure he is in a good *mood.*

7

Moral/Morale

Moral (pertaining to right and wrong; ethical)—She made the decision on a *moral* rather than on a practical basis.

Morale (a mental condition)—The announcement of a pay raise boosted the employee *morale*.

Morning/Mourning

Morning (the time from sunrise to noon)—Can you come by my office Friday *morning?*
Mourning (a period of time during which signs of grief are shown)—Please allow the family to observe this period of *mourning* without any interruptions concerning business matters.

Most: see Almost.

Mourning: see Morning.

Myself: see I.

Naval/Navel

Naval (relating to a navy)—Last week Mr. Marsh's son accepted an assignment with *naval* intelligence.

Navel (a depression in the middle of the abdomen)—One of our new style of jeans, Style 565, is cut below the *navel.*

Number: see Amount.

Ordinance/Ordnance

Ordinance (a local regulation)—The city passed an *ordinance* banning excessive noise after 10 p.m.

Ordnance (military weapons)—We should know by the end of the month whether we will receive the army *ordnance* contract.

Overdo/Overdue

Overdo (to exaggerate)—Exercise is healthful if one does not *overdo* it.

Overdue (late)—Your payment is 15 days *overdue.*

Pair/Pare/Pear

Pair (two of a kind; made of two corresponding parts)—The *pair* of gloves I bought for her birthday was too small.

Pare (to reduce in size or trim)—I hope you can *pare* this budget at least 15 percent.

Pear (a fruit)—He always eats a *pear* for breakfast.

Passed/Past

Passed v. (past tense or past participle of *pass,* meaning "to go by" or "circulate")—She *passed* around the announcement to everyone in the office.

Past n. (time gone by or ended)—Our weak profit picture is all in the *past.*

7

145

Patience/Patients
Patience (calm perseverance)—It took great *patience* on her part to type the report without error.
Patients (people undergoing medical treatment)—I am one of Dr. Taylor's *patients*.

Peace/Piece
Peace (truce; tranquillity)—Since she began the project, she has not had one moment's *peace*.
Piece (a part of limited quantity)—Each of us had a *piece* of the birthday cake.

Peal/Peel
Peal (a loud sound or succession of sounds)—The bells *pealed* from the church tower.
Peel (skin or rind; to remove by stripping)—Do any of these recipes require the use of *lemon peel*? Ask the customer to *peel* off the mailing label and affix it to the enclosed postcard.

Pear: see Pair.

Peel: see Peal.

7

Peer/Pier
Peer (one belonging to same societal group; gaze)—Teenagers often imitate the behavior of their *peer* group. Do customers often *peer* into the shop window?
Pier (a structure extending into navigable water)—No fishing is allowed from this *pier*.

Persecute/Prosecute
Persecute (to harass persistently)—He is the type of person who wouldn't hesitate to *persecute* a colleague if it would be to his advantage.
Prosecute (to start legal proceedings against someone)—We are not sure whether or not the district attorney will *prosecute* the case.

Personal/Personnel
Personal (private; individual)—She is his *personal* secretary.
Personnel (employees)—All *personnel* are requested to work overtime until the inventory has been completed.

Perspective/Prospective
Perspective (a mental picture or outlook)—His *perspective* is distorted by greed.
Prospective (likely; expected)—We interviewed several *prospective* secretaries last week.

Piece: see Peace.

Pier: see Peer.

Plaintiff/Plaintive

Plaintiff (one who commences a lawsuit to obtain a remedy for an injury to his rights)—Who is the attorney for the *plaintiff*?

Plaintive (expressive of suffering or woe)—In a *plaintive* voice Virginia explained how the gunmen executed the robbery.

Populace/Populous

Populace (masses; population)—The winning candidate must have the support of the *populace*. After the earthquake the *populace* of Evansville was evacuated.

Populous (densely populated)—At present we have restaurants only in *populous* areas.

Pore/Pour

Pore (to read studiously or attentively; a minute opening in a membrane)—How long did the auditors *pore* over these books? Hot water will open the *pores* of your skin, and cold water will close them.

Pour (to dispense from a container; to move with a continuous flow)—Please ask the waiters to *pour* the water before the guests are seated. Even before the game ends, spectators will begin to *pour* out of the stadium.

Practicable/Practical

Practicable (an idea or plan that in theory seems to be feasible or usable)—The plan to build a car that runs on electricity seems to be a *practicable* one.

Practical (an idea or plan that is feasible or usable because it has been successfully tried or proved by past experience)—Once gasoline prices began to rise, more people found small cars to be the *practical* solution to higher transportation costs.

7

Pray/Prey

Pray (to make a request in a humble manner; to address God)—I *pray* that these bureaucrats will listen to my request. Children may not be required to *pray* in public schools.

Prey (victim; to have an injurious or destructive effect)—Do not become *prey* for the quick-rich schemes of such con artists. Ms. Rice should not let this experience *prey* on her thoughts constantly.

Precede/Proceed

Precede (to go before)—Mrs. Andrews' presentation will *precede* the main speaker's address.

Proceed (to go forward or continue)—Please *proceed* with your analysis of the financial statements.

Precedence/Precedents

Precedence (priority)—Please give *precedence* to Mr. Wilson's application for funds.

Precedents (things done or said that can be used as an example)—There are no *precedents* for this particular case.

Prey: see Pray.

Principal/Principle

Principal n. (a capital sum; a school official)—Both the *principal* and interest on the balance of the loan are due next month. As *principal* of Lindberg High School, Mrs. Brereton was proud that so many of its students continued on to college.
Principal adj. (highest in importance)—The *principal* reason we changed our promotion procedures was to encourage all employees to upgrade themselves within the company.
Principle n. (an accepted rule of action; a basic truth or belief)—Her knowledge of accounting *principles* is questionable. Our country was founded on the *principle* that all men are created equal.

Proceed: see Precede.

Propose/Purpose

Propose (to suggest)—I *propose* that we borrow the money for the new equipment.
Purpose (a desired result)—The *purpose* of this meeting is to discuss ways in which sales can be increased.

Prosecute: see Persecute.

Prospective: see Perspective.

Purpose: see Propose.

Quiet/Quite

Quiet (peaceful; free from noise)—The *quiet* operation of this typewriter is one of its main sales features.
Quite (completely or actually)—The salespeople seem to be *quite* satisfied with the new commission plan.

Raise/Raze/Rise

Raise (to lift something up, increase in amount, gather together, or bring into existence; a transitive verb that needs an object to complete its meaning; *raise, raised, raised,* and *raising* are the principal parts of this verb)—Please do not *raise* your voice. We *raised* $200 for Ms. Morgan's retirement gift. He has *raised* our quota 30 percent during the last month. We are *raising* the money for his gift.
Raze (to destroy to the ground)—When does your company plan to *raze* this old warehouse?
Rise (to go up or increase in value; an intransitive verb that does not have an object; *rise, rose, risen,* and *rising* are the principal parts of this verb)—One should *rise* when her honor enters the courtroom. The rocket *rose* 30,000 feet before it exploded. Our sales have *risen* for the third month in a row. Production is *rising* steadily since the new equipment has been installed.

Real/Really

Real (an adjective meaning "great in amount or number")—The new word processing machine was a *real* help in getting out our monthly statements.
Really (an adverb meaning "actually" or "truly")—Wilma Carroll *really* needed her vacation after the tax season was over.

Reality/Realty

Reality (that which is real; that which exists)—Our problem began when the manager would not face *reality* in negotiating with the employees.

Realty (real estate)—The last *realty* company that tried to sell my property could not find an interested buyer.

Receipt/Recipe

Receipt (a written acknowledgment for receiving goods or money)—No refunds can be made without a *receipt.*

Recipe (a set of instructions)—He has always kept secret the *recipe* for his delicious spaghetti sauce.

Residence/Residents

Residence (a dwelling)—This house has been her *residence* for the past twenty years.

Residents (people who reside in a dwelling)—One of the *residents* complained that the heater in her apartment does not work.

Respectably/Respectfully/Respectively

Respectably (in a correct or decent manner)—The vagrant was dressed *respectably* for his court appearance.

Respectfully (used in the body or complimentary close of a letter to show high regard or respect for the reader)—We *respectfully* submit that the contract calls for all work to be completed by April 1.

Respectively (each in turn or in order)—Janice Jackson, John Zelinsky, and Al Turnbull were first, second, and third prize winners, *respectively.*

Rise: see Raise.

Rote/Rout/Route

Rote (mechanical or repetitious learning)—All of us had to learn the multiplication tables by *rote.*

Rout (a disorderly assembly or disastrous defeat)—The game turned into a *rout* after the opposing team scored 30 points in the first quarter.

Route (a course taken in traveling from one point to another)—Most of our delivery *routes* had to be changed after they were studied by efficiency experts.

Scene/Seen

Scene (a place of an occurrence; an exhibition of anger)—The police arrived at the *scene* shortly after the guard telephoned them. How would you handle a hostile customer who was creating a *scene*?

Seen (past participle of *to see*)—I have not *seen* our sales manager for three days.

Senses: see Census.

Serial: see Cereal.

Set/Sit

Set (to place or make solid; a transitive verb that generally needs an object to complete its meaning; *set, set, set,* and *setting* are the principal parts of this verb)—Please *set* the calculator on my desk. He *set* the clocks ahead for daylight saving time. I have *set* the times for your appointments this week. We are *setting* higher sales quotas this year.

Sit (to be seated or occupy a seat; an intransitive verb that does not have an object; *sit, sat, sat,* and *sitting* are the principal parts of this verb)—*Sit* here, Ms. Brown. I *sat* for an hour awaiting his return. He has *sat* in that chair all day watching television. If anyone calls, tell him I am *sitting* in on a meeting of all department heads.

Sew/So/Sow

Sew (to fasten by stitches with thread)—I can't find anyone who will *sew* a button on my coat.

So (in a way indicated; to that degree; therefore)—She was *so* upset over the incident that she accidentally tore the paper.

Sow (to scatter seed)—This machine can *sow* more seed than any 15 farmhands.

Shall/Will

Shall (used in formal writing when the first person is employed)—I *shall* give your request the utmost consideration. We *shall* begin legal proceedings on November 1.

Will (used with all three persons except in formal writing)—I *will* call you tomorrow. You *will* receive your refund when you return the merchandise. He *will* finish the project on time unless he runs into bad weather conditions.

She: see Her.

Shear/Sheer

Shear (to cut, strip, or remove)—We had to *shear* off the bolts before we could remove the wheel.

Sheer (transparently thin; utterly; a steep incline)—None of these *sheer* fabrics are suitable for the kind of draperies we have in mind. This conference was a *sheer* waste of time. Did any of the prisoners attempt to scale the *sheer* cliffs?

Shone/Shown

Shone (past tense and past participle of *shine*)—If only the flashing red lights had *shone* through the dense fog, the accident might have been avoided.

Shown (past participle of *show*)—The filmstrip displaying our new products has been *shown* to the salespeople.

Should/Would

Should (used in formal writing when the first person is employed)—We *should* like you to return the completed application by Friday.

Would (used with all three persons except in formal writing)—I *would* like a copy of that report. She said she *would* be happy to work overtime if the report isn't finished by 5 p.m.

Shown: see Shone.

Sight: see Cite.

Sit: see Set.

Site: see Cite.

So: see Sew.

Soar/Sore
Soar (to fly aloft or about; to rise or increase dramatically)—These miniature aircraft are built to *soar* in the sky without motor or battery power. News of the merger will cause our stock prices to *soar.*
Sore (painfully sensitive)—If you overdo an exercise program, your muscles will become *sore.*

Sole/Soul
Sole (the undersurface of a foot; being the only one)—Distribute your weight evenly between the *sole* and the heel of your foot. John is the *sole* heir to his father's fortune.
Soul (the immaterial essence of an individual; exemplification of personification)—Most contemporary religions believe that the *soul* of an individual continues on after his physical death. Mr. Perry is the *soul* of honesty and integrity.

7

Some/Somewhat
Some (an adjective meaning "an indefinite amount")—The report revealed that we will have to make *some* changes when we move into our new facility.
Somewhat (an adverb meaning "to some degree")—Most people feel that our proposed budget is *somewhat* optimistic.

Some time/Sometime
Some time (a period of time)—It took *some time* for us to get used to coming to work an hour earlier.
Sometime (an indefinite time)—Your order should be delivered *sometime* next week.

Somewhat: see Some.

Sore: see Soar.

Soul: see Sole.

Sow: see Sew.

Staid/Stayed
Staid (sedate; composed)—A more *staid* individual is needed to fill this position.
Stayed (past tense and past participle of *stay*)—She *stayed* long after closing time to finish the report.

Stationary/Stationery
Stationary (not moving)—The table would not remain *stationary* while I typed.
Stationery (writing material)—Mr. Troy wants this letter typed on his personal *stationery*.

Statue/Stature/Statute
Statue (a carved or molded image of someone or something)—Meet me in front of the *statue* of Lincoln.
Stature (the height of an object; status gained by attainment)—The *stature* alone of the pyramids is overwhelming. She is a person of great *stature* within the community.
Statute (law enacted by legislature)—There is a *statute* in this state that prohibits gambling in any form.

Stayed: see Staid.

Suit/Suite
Suit (an action filed in court; a set of garments)—A & Z Computer Corporation has already filed *suit* against Compco for patent infringements. Be sure to wear a three-piece gray business *suit* for the interview.
Suite (a group of things forming a unit; a set)—Were you able to reserve a hotel *suite* for the week of March 25 at the Americana Hotel? (refers to a group of rooms) How many pieces are featured in this bedroom *suite*? (refers to pieces of furniture in a set)

7

Sure/Surely
Sure (an adjective or subject complement meaning "certain" or "positive")—Nancy was *sure* she had made the right decision.
Surely (an adverb meaning "certainly" or "undoubtedly")—The employees believed that they would *surely* get a raise this year.

Tare/Tear/Tier
Tare (the weight of goods after the weight of the container is deducted)—The *tare* cost of our merchandise has increased over 15 percent in one year.
Tear (to pull apart or rip)—The customer complained about a *tear* in the sweater she had purchased.
Tier (things placed one above the other)—Our season tickets are on the third *tier* of the stadium.

Than/Then
Than (a conjunction used to show comparison)—Miss Espinoza has more experience *than* I in writing contract proposals.
Then (an adverb meaning "at that time")—After a letter has been typed, it should *then* be proofread carefully before it is removed from the typewriter.

That/Which
That (introduces a restrictive or essential subordinate clause)—Mr. O'Connell said *that* this order must be shipped today. All animals *that* are found wandering in the streets will be impounded. This is the telephone *that* has been out of order since this morning.
Which (introduces a nonrestrictive or nonessential subordinate clause)—The security people recommend we acquire a watchdog, *which* would be kept inside the plant at night. Our new credit system, *which* will be installed next week, will cost over $50,000.

Their/There/They're

Their (the possessive form of *they*)—It was *their* recommendation that we install the new computer system.

There (at that place or at that point)—Please be *there* promptly at ten o'clock in the morning.

They're (contraction of *they are*)—Although most of the secretaries are new employees, *they're* exceptionally familiar with our operations.

Them/They

Them (a direct object, an indirect object, or an object of a preposition)—I asked *them* to please wait outside. I sent *them* a bill last week. I waited for *them* all morning.

They (subject of a clause or a complement pronoun)—*They* are meeting this afternoon. It was *they* who painted the office.

Then: see Than.

There: see Their.

They: see Them.

They're: see Their.

7

Threw/Through

Threw (past tense of *throw*)—Mr. Samuels accidentally *threw* away the report on equipment purchases.

Through (in one end and out the other; movement within a large expanse; during the period of; as a consequence of)—It will be a pleasure to give you a tour *through* the plant. The messenger pigeons flew gracefully *through* the air. This sale will be in progress *through* June. You may order this software at a 15 percent discount from June 15 *through* June 30. We have retained this account *through* your diligent efforts.

Tier: see Tare.

To/Too/Two

To (a preposition; the sign of an infinitive)—She wanted *to* see for herself the condition of the plant cafeteria.

Too (an adverb meaning "also" or "to an excessive extent")—I was there *too*. Because the office was *too* noisy, I had a difficult time hearing you on the telephone.

Two (a number)—There was just too much work for the *two* of us to finish by five o'clock.

Us/We

Us (a direct object, an indirect object, or an object of a preposition)—The vice president took *us* on a tour of the plant. The manager gave *us* a copy of the report. This party was planned for *us*.

We (the subject of a clause or a complement pronoun)—*We* have to catch a plane at 3 p.m. It was *we* who had to solve this problem.

Vain/Van/Vane/Vein

Vain (unduly proud or conceited)—Tom would be more popular with his fellow workers if he were not so *vain.*

Van (a covered truck)—Our *van* has a variety of uses within the company.

Vane (a thin plate used to show wind direction)—The weather *vane* indicated that the wind was coming from a westward direction.

Vein (a tubular vessel that carries blood to the heart)—She had difficulty finding a *vein* from which to obtain a blood sample.

Vary/Very

Vary (to change)—The new office manager said she would not request us to *vary* any procedures at the present time.

Very (extremely)—These figures are *very* difficult to type accurately.

Vein: see Vain.

Vice/Vise

Vice (immoral habit; personal fault)—Cigar smoking is his only *vice.*

Vise (a clamp; to hold or squeeze)—He shook my hand with a *vise*-like grip.

Waiver/Waver

Waiver (the relinquishment of a claim)—Please sign this *waiver* releasing the company from any responsibility for the injury.

Waver (to shake or fluctuate)—I believe he is beginning to *waver* concerning my request for an early vacation.

We: see Us.

Weather/Whether

Weather (the state of the atmosphere; to bear up against)—Today's *weather* forecast predicted a cold, rainy day. We are glad to learn that you were able to *weather* the high rate of employee turnover during the summer months.

Whether (an introduction of alternatives)—We will not know until next week *whether* or not our company will be awarded the contracts.

Well: see Good.

Whether: see Weather.

Which: see That.

Who/Whom

Who (the subject of a subordinate clause or a complement pronoun)—I was the one *who* asked you to attend. I cannot tell you *who* it was at the door.

Whom (a direct object, an indirect object, or an object of a preposition)—*Whom* have you hired as my assistant? He sent *whom* the book? Here is the address of the person with *whom* we met for legal assistance. [See Section 8–3h for a further explanation of how to use *who* and *whom*].

Wholly: see Holy.

Whom: see Who.

Who's/Whose
Who's (a contraction of *who is*)—Please let me know *who's* taking over for her during August.
Whose (possessive form of *who*)—He is the fellow *whose* position was abolished.

Will: see Shall.

Would: see Should.

Your/You're
Your (possessive form of *you*)—*Your* secretary told me that you would invite the mayor to the reception.
You're (contraction of *you are*)—So *you're* the one who has been trying to reach me.

7

Grammar and Usage

8

Grammar and Usage Solution Finder

Adjectives

"A" and "An," use of   8–9
Absolute adjectives   8–10f
Comparison   8–10
   Irregular   8–10d
   More than two persons, places,
      or things   8–10a
   One-syllable adjectives
      8–10b
   Regular   8–10a-c
   Three-syllable adjectives
      8–10c
   Two persons, places, or things
      8–10a
   Two-syllable adjectives
      8–10c
   Within group   8–10e
Compound   8–13
Function of   8–8
Independent   8–11
Linking verbs, used with   8–12
"Other" and "else," used with
   8–10e

Adverbs

Adverbs vs. Adjectives   8–16
Comparison   8–15
Double negatives   8–17
Form of   8–14a-c
Function of   8–14

Conjunctions

"As . . . as"   8–21c
"As" vs. "like"   8–22
"Either . . . or"   8–21a
"Neither . . . nor"   8–21a
"Not only . . . but also"   8–21b
Pairs, used in   8–21a, b
"So . . . as"   8–21c

Nouns

Plurals, formation of   8–1
   Abbreviations composed of
      initials   8–1j

Alphabetic letters   8–1j
Compound nouns   8–1i
"F," words ending in   8–1d
"Fe," words ending in   8–1d
Foreign nouns   8–11
Hyphenated nouns   8–1i
Irregular   8–1g
Names used with titles   8–1k
Nouns always plural   8–1h
Nouns always singular   8–1h
Numerals   8–1j
"O," words ending in   8–1c
Proper nouns   8–1e
Regular   8–1a
Same form in singular and
   plural   8–1h
Titles used with names   8–1k
Words used as words   8–1j
"Y," words ending in   8–1b
Possessives, formation of   8–2
   Compound nouns   8–2d
   Distance   8–2g
   General rules   8–2a, b, i
   Gerund, before a   8–2e
   Inanimate objects   8–2h
   Individual ownership   8–2c
   Joint ownership   8–2c
   Time   8–2f

Prepositions

Certain words, used with   8–19
"In," "between," "among"   8–18
Phrases, in   8–20

Pronouns

Agreement with verb   8–3i
Apposition, used in   8–3f
Case   8–3
   Objective   8–3b, e, f, h
   Possessive   8–3c, d, h
   Subjective   8–3a, e, f, h
Emphatic   8–3g
Gerund, before a   8–3d
Reflexive   8–3g
"Who," "Whoever," "Whom,"
   "Whomever," "Whose"   8–3h

8

Grammar and Usage Solution Finder (continued)

Verbs

"A number" subjects   8–7g
Agreement, subject and verb
   8–7
Collective nouns   8–7j
Compound subjects   8–7c, d
Indefinite pronouns   8–7e
Infinitives split   8–7i
Irregular   8–5
"Lay" and "lie," use of   8–6

Portions preceding a verb   8–7f
Pronoun agreement, subject and
   verb   8–7b
Regular   8–4
Relative pronoun clauses
   8–7k, l
Singular subjects joined by and
   8–7d
Subjunctive mood   8–7h
"The number" subjects   8–7g
"There" preceding a verb   8–7f

8

Nouns*

8–1. Noun Plurals**

a. Most nouns form their plurals by adding *s*. However, nouns ending in *s*, *sh*, *ch*, *x*, or *z* form their plurals by adding *es*.

nouns adding "s"

account	accounts
executive	executives
letter	letters

nouns adding "es"

business	businesses
wish	wishes
branch	branches
tax	taxes
buzz	buzzes

b. Common nouns ending in *y* form the plural in one of two ways. If the letter preceding the *y* is a vowel, just add *s*. However, if the letter preceding the *y* is a consonant, drop the *y* and add *ies*.

"y" preceded by a vowel

attorney	attorneys
money	moneys
valley	valleys

"y" preceded by a consonant

company	companies
secretary	secretaries
reply	replies

c. Musical terms ending in *o* form the plural by adding *s*. Other common nouns ending in *o* may form the plural by adding *s* or *es*; the correct plural forms are shown in the dictionary.

musical terms

sopranos	concertos	cellos	solos	pianos

common nouns ending in "os"

zeros	mementos	dynamos	portfolios	ratios

---

*The rules and spellings in this chapter are based on *Webster's Ninth New Collegiate Dictionary* (Springfield, Mass.: Merriam-Webster Inc., 1983).

**Noun plurals, other than those regular ones ending in *s* or *es*, are shown in the dictionary immediately after the singular form of the word.

common nouns ending in "oes"

cargoes   heroes   potatoes   embargoes   vetoes

d. Nouns ending in *ff* form the plural by adding *s*. Nouns ending in just *f* or *fe* may add *s*, or they may drop the *f* or *fe* and add *ves*. The plurals of those nouns taking the irregular form by adding *ves* are shown in the dictionary. If the dictionary does not show the plural form, just add *s*.

plural nouns ending in "ffs"

sheriff	sheriffs	plaintiff	plaintiffs
cliff	cliffs	bailiff	bailiffs

plural nouns ending in "fs" or "fes"

proof	proofs	belief	beliefs	roof	roofs
safe	sates	chief	chiefs	strife	strifes

plural nouns ending in "ves"

wife	wives	shelf	shelves	knife	knives
half	halves	thief	thieves	self	selves

e. The plurals of proper nouns are formed by adding *s or es*. Those proper nouns ending in *s*, *sh*, *ch*, *x*, or *z* form the plural by adding *es*. All others form the plural by adding *s*.

8

proper noun plurals ending in "es"

Winters	Winterses	Rodriguez	Rodriguezes
Bush	Bushes	Bendix	Bendixes
Finch	Finches		

proper noun plurals ending in "s"

Halby	Halbys	Wolf	Wolfs	Russo	Russos
Dixon	Dixons	Kelly	Kellys	Griffin	Griffins

f. Many nouns of foreign origin have both an English plural and a foreign plural. Consult your dictionary and use the one that appears first.

foreign nouns with English plurals

memorandum	memorandums	formula	formulas
index	indexes	appendix	appendixes

foreign nouns with foreign plurals

alumna	alumnae	analysis	analyses
alumnus	alumni	basis	bases
stimulus	stimuli	crisis	crises
terminus	termini	criterion	criteria
curriculum	curricula	medium	media
datum	data	stadium	stadia

g. Some nouns form their plurals by changing letters within the word or adding letters other than *s* or *es*. These irregular plurals are shown in the dictionary.

tooth	teeth	mouse	mice
man	men	foot	feet
child	children	woman	women

h. Some nouns have the same form in both the singular and plural. Other nouns are always singular, and others are always plural.

nouns with same singular and plural form

fish	politics	Chinese	moose
scissors	measles	Japanese	cod
gross	series	corps	vermin
Vietnamese	species	sheep	odds
headquarters	deer	salmon	mumps

nouns always singular

news	mathematics	economics (course)
genetics	aeronautics	statistics (course)

nouns always plural

earnings	proceeds	pants	winnings
cattle	thanks	belongings	credentials

i. Hyphenated or open compound nouns containing a main word form their plurals on the main words. Those hyphenated compounds not containing a main word and compound nouns consisting of only one word form the plural at the end.

plural formed on main word

personnel manager*s*	sister*s*-in-law
leave*s* of absence	notarie*s* public
lieutenant colonel*s*	vice-principal*s*
attorney*s* at law	editor*s* in chief

plural formed at end

follow-up*s*	trade-in*s*
go-between*s*	stand-in*s*
teaspoonful*s*	bookshel*ves*
workm*en*	stockholder*s*

j. The plurals of numerals, most capital letters, words referred to as words, and abbreviations composed of initials are formed by adding *s* or *es*. For clarity, though, all isolated lowercase letters and the capital letters *A, I, M,* and *U* are made plural by adding an apostrophe before the *s*.

plural formed with "s" or "es"

It is difficult to distinguish between your *1s* and your *7s*.

Can you list the five *Cs* of good letter writing?

Ms. Smith, our new copy editor, does not use her *whiches* and *thats* correctly.

On the last ballot the *noes* outnumbered the *yeses*.

Mr. Wilson wants this assignment completed without any further *if, ands,* or *buts*.

Make a list of *dos* and *don'ts* for the care and maintenance of this equipment.

There are two vacancies for *R.N.s* on our team.

How many of your graduates became *CPAs* last year?

All our *c.o.d.s* still need to be sent out.

Type the *"a.m.s"* and *"p.m.s"* in lowercase letters.

plural formed with an apostrophe and "s"

We were asked to watch our *p's* and *q's* while the dignitaries were in the building.

To improve your penmanship, be sure to dot your *i's* and cross your *t's*.

Your son received three *A's* on his last grade report.

Why are the *M's* smudged on this document?

k. When referring to two or more individuals by name and title, make plural either the name or the title, but never both.

the *Messrs.* Johnson or the Mr. *Johnsons*

the *Mses.* Smith or the Ms. *Smiths*

8–2. Noun Possessives*

a. All nouns not ending with a pronounced *s*, whether single or plural, form the possessive by adding *'s*.

office of the *attorney*	*attorney*'s office
toys belonging to the *children*	*children*'s toys
books belonging to *Judy*	*Judy*'s books
lounge for *women*	*women*'s lounge
tax rate of *Illinois*	*Illinois*'s tax rate.
paycheck of *Ms. DuBois*	*Ms. DuBois*'s paycheck

(Note: *s* sound is not pronounced in *Illinois* and *DuBois*)

---

*See Section 1–55 for additional examples.

b. Nouns ending with a pronounced *s* form the possessive by simply adding an apostrophe unless an additional syllable is pronounced in the possessive form. In the latter case, *'s* is added.

no extra pronounced syllable

clothing for *girls*	*girls'* clothing
the efforts of two *cities*	two *cities'* efforts
the home belonging to the *Foxes*	the *Foxes'* home
the pen belonging to *Mr. Simons*	*Mr. Simons'* pen

extra pronounced syllable

grades of the *class*	the *class's* grades
the briefcase belonging to *Mr. Harris*	*Mr. Harris's* briefcase

c. In the case of joint ownership, possession is shown only on the last noun. Where individual ownership exists, possession is shown on each noun.

joint ownership

Mary and Alice's apartment has been newly painted.

The Rodriguezes and the Martinsons' mountain cabin closed escrow today.

Mr. Stewart and Ms. Ross's partnership agreement was drawn up over two weeks ago.

Clark and Clark's handbook is required for this class.

individual ownership

My *mother's and father's* clothes were destroyed in the fire.

Bob's and John's payroll checks were lost.

Mr. Granados' and Ms. Stone's stores are both located on Tampa Avenue in Westfield.

All *the accountants' and secretaries'* desks have been moved into the new offices.

d. The possessive form of compound nouns is shown at the end.

investments of my *father-in-law*	*father-in-law's* investments
the report for *stockholders*	the *stockholders'* report
convention of *attorneys at law*	*attorneys at law's* convention
report of the *personnel manager*	the *personnel manager's* report

e. Use the possessive form before a gerund.

We would appreciate *Lisa's helping* us with the audit.

There is no record of the *witness's being* subpoenaed.

8

f.   Use an apostrophe with the possessives of nouns that refer to time—minutes, hours, days, weeks, months, and years.

singular

peace for a *minute*	a *minute's* peace
work for a *day*	a *day's* work
delay for a *week*	a *week's* delay
notice of a *month*	a *month's* notice
mail from this *morning*	this *morning's* mail
calendar for *tomorrow*	*tomorrow's* calendar

plural

work for four *hours*	four *hours'* work
interest for two *weeks*	two *weeks'* interest
trial for three *months*	three *months'* trial
experience for five *years*	five *years'* experience

g.   Use an apostrophe with the possession of nouns that refer to distance.

He lives just a *stone's* throw from the office.

The truck missed hitting our car by just an *arm's* length.

h.   Do not form possessives for inanimate objects, except time or distance. Instead, use a simple adjective or an *of* phrase.

adjective

The *table* top is scratched. (Not: The table's top is scratched.)

The *typewriter* keys need to be cleaned. (Not: The typewriter's keys need to be cleaned.)

"of" phrase

The door *of the supply cabinet* is jammed. (Not: The supply cabinet's door is jammed.)

The stipulations *of the will* were presented by the attorney. (Not: The will's stipulations were presented by the attorney.)

i.   In some possessive constructions the item or items owned are not stated explicitly or do not directly follow the ownership word. The ownership word, however, still shows possession with an apostrophe.

The only desk to be refinished is *Mary's.*

On Tuesday we will meet at the *Culleys'* to discuss the sale of their property.

Mr. Ardigo left the *attorney's* over an hour ago.

Pronouns

8–3. Pronoun Case

a. The subjective case* pronouns are the following:

I	she	we	who
he	you	they	it

Use a subjective case pronoun (1) for the subject of a sentence, (2) for the complement of a "being" verb, and (3) after the infinitive "to be" when this verb does not have a subject.

subject of a verb

She has applied for the position.

They will arrive at 10 a.m.

complement of a "being" verb

It was *I* who answered the telephone.

The visitors could have been *they.*

infinitive "to be" without a subject

Joalene was thought to be *I.*

It had to be *we* who made the error.

b. The objective case pronouns are the following:

me	her	us	whom
him	you	them	it

The objective case is used when the pronoun is (1) the object of a verb or preposition, (2) the object of the infinitive "to be" when it has a subject, and (3) the subject or object of any other infinitive.

direct or indirect object of a verb

Mr. Reslaw will meet *her* at the airport tomorrow.

Please place *them* on my desk.

We will mail *him* these copies by Friday.

object of a preposition

When was this package sent *to us*?

Two of the customers asked *for her.*

---

*The subjective case is also known as the nominative case.

8

Between you and me, I do not believe the plan will be approved.

object of "to be" with a subject

Ms. Stapleton thought *them* to be *us.*

They expected *Mary* to be *me.*

I wanted the *candidate* to be *her.*

subject or object of an infinitive

We thought *them* to be somewhat overconfident.

Our office will not be able to mail *them* until Monday.

We expect *her* to help *us* with the decorations.

c.   The possessive case pronouns are the following:

my	mine	their	theirs
his, her	his, hers	its	its
your	yours		whose
our	ours		

All pronoun possessive case forms are written without apostrophes. They should not be confused with contractions.

possessive pronouns—no apostrophes

Its wrapping had been torn.

Is this *your* sweater?

The idea was *theirs.*

Whose briefcase was left in the conference room?

contractions—apostrophes

It's still raining very heavily here on the West Coast.

Let us know if *you're* going to the convention.

If *there's* a logical reason for the delay, please inform the passengers.

Who's in charge of ordering supplies for our personal computers?

d.   Use the possessive case immediately before a gerund.

His leaving the company was quite a surprise.

We would appreciate *your returning* the enclosed card by Friday, March 18.

e.   A pronoun after *than* or *as* may be expressed in either the subjective or objective case, depending on whether the pronoun is the subject or object of the following stated or implied verb.

subjective case

Are you as concerned about this matter as *I* am? (Stated verb *am*)

He has been with the company two years longer than *I.* (Implied verb *have*)

objective case

Our editor admires my coauthor more than he admires *me.* (Stated subject and verb *he admires*)

She works for Mr. Reece more hours than *me.* (Implied subject, verb, and preposition *she works for*)

f. Pronouns used in apposition take the same case as those nouns or pronouns with which they are in apposition.

We, Barbara and *I,* will appear in court tomorrow.

Barry told Ms. Larsen to submit her expenses to one of our accounting clerks, John or *me.*

g. Pronouns ending in *self* or *selves* emphasize or reflect a noun or pronoun used previously.

emphasizes previous noun or pronoun

Mary herself was not pleased with the results of the advertising campaign.

They themselves could not justify their exorbitant budget requests.

reflects a previous noun or pronoun

John addressed the envelope to *himself.*

They agreed to vote *themselves* monthly salary increases of $100.

h. The same rules apply to the pronouns *who, whoever, whom, whomever, and whose* as apply to the other personal pronouns. *Who* and *whoever* are used for the subjective case; *whom* and *whomever,* for the objective case; and *whose,* for the possessive case.

Isolate the clause in which the pronoun appears; and apply the rules outlined for the subjective, objective, and possessive case pronouns in Sections 8–3a, b, and c. Be sure to eliminate any extra clause that may appear in the *who, whom,* or *whose* clause and arrange the clause, if necessary, in normal subject-verb order.

subjective case—"who" or "whoever"

Mr. Gonzales is the person *who* was selected for the position. (subject of verb)

It was Ms. Graham *who* served as the seventh president of our college. (subject of verb)

I do not know *who* the caller may have been. (complement of "being" verb)

Please let me know *who* the winner is. (complement of "being" verb)

Who do you think will be appointed to the board? (Omit extra clause *do you think*.) (subject of verb)

He is a person *who* I think will be successful in the railroad industry. (Omit extra clause *I think*.) (subject of verb)

The city council will ratify the appointment of *whoever* is selected. (subject of verb)

objective case—"whom" or "whomever"

He is a person with *whom* we have done business for over twenty-five years. (object of preposition)

Whom did Mr. Williams promote to the position of office manager? (direct object)

The artist *whom* I believe he sponsored moved to New York. (Omit extra clause *I believe*.) (direct object)

You are a person *whom* I know Ms. Ferraro would be pleased to hire. (Omit extra clause *I know*.) (object of infinitive)

I'm sure the president will approve *whomever* you choose for the position. (direct object)

possessive case—"whose"

Whose book is lying here?

We do not know *whose* department will prove to be the most efficient under our new cost-saving plan.

i. Pronouns must agree in gender and number with any nouns or other pronouns they represent.

Everyone please open *his* or *her* book to page 73.

Both *Ms. Greer* and *Mr. Baty* received *their* orders yesterday.

The *puppy* caught *its* tail in the door.

Verbs

8–4. Regular Verbs

Verbs take various forms to designate periods of time. The principal parts of a verb include the present form, the past form, and the past participle.

Regular verbs are all formed in the same way: (1) the present part has the infinitive form without the accompanying *to,* (2) the past tense adds *ed* to the present form, and (3) the past participle uses the past form with at least one verb helper.

infinitive	present	past	past participle
to ask	ask	asked	(have, was) asked
to change	change	changed	(were, had been) changed
to collect	collect	collected	(has, have been) collected

8–5. Irregular Verbs*

Many verbs do not form their parts in the usual manner. These irregular verbs take a variety of forms. A list of parts for commonly used irregular verbs follows:

am	was	been	know	knew	known
arise	arose	arisen	lay	laid	laid
become	became	become	lead	led	led
begin	began	begun	leave	left	left
bite	bit	bitten	lend	lent	lent
blow	blew	blown	lie	lay	lain
break	broke	broken	lose	lost	lost
bring	brought	brought	make	made	made
burst	burst	burst	pay	paid	paid
buy	bought	bought	ride	rode	ridden
catch	caught	caught	ring	rang	rung
choose	chose	chosen	rise	rose	risen
come	came	come	run	ran	run
dig	dug	dug	see	saw	seen
do	did	done	set	set	set
draw	drew	drawn	shake	shook	shaken
drink	drank	drunk	shrink	shrank	shrunk
drive	drove	driven	sing	sang	sung
eat	ate	eaten	sink	sank	sunk
fall	fell	fallen	sit	sat	sat
fight	fought	fought	speak	spoke	spoken
fly	flew	flown	spring	sprang	sprung
forget	forgot	forgotten	steal	stole	stolen
forgive	forgave	forgiven	strike	struck	struck
freeze	froze	frozen	swear	swore	sworn
get	got	got	swim	swam	swum
give	gave	given	take	took	taken
go	went	gone	tear	tore	torn
grow	grew	grown	throw	threw	thrown
hang	hung	hung	wear	wore	worn
hide	hid	hidden	write	wrote	written

8

8–6. Use of *Lay* and *Lie*

a. The principal parts of *lay* and *lie* follow:

lay	laid	laid
lie	lay	lain

---

*Irregular verb forms are shown in the dictionary. They are listed after the present form of the verb.

b. Use a form of *lie* when the verb called for is intransitive (does not have a direct object) and a form of *lay* when the verb is transitive (has a direct object). The form is always transitive when the past participle is used with a *being* verb helper.

intransitive

The new shopping center *lies* at the foot of the Flintridge Foothills.

He *lay* in bed for three days with the flu.

transitive

Please *lay* the papers on my desk.

She *laid* the file folders in the "in" tray.

always transitive

These sandbags have *been laid* here because of impending flood damage.

The carpeting for our new building *was laid* yesterday.

8-7. Subject-Verb Agreement

a. The verb of a sentence must agree in person and number with the subject. To identify a subject, omit any prepositional phrase that separates the subject and the verb.

The *legs* of the table *were damaged* in transit.

b. A pronoun that represents the subject must agree in number and gender with the subject.

Mr. Charles was asked to prepare *his* report by the end of this week.

Would *every student* please be sure to submit *his* or *her* class schedule by February 5.

Ellen and Margaret were asked to resubmit *their* applications for employment.

The *company* filed bankruptcy because it was unable to meet *its* obligations.

c. Compound subjects joined by *and* generally require the use of a plural verb. When compound subjects are joined by *or* or *nor,* the form of the verb is determined by the element closer to the verb. If one element is plural and the other is singular, place the plural element, where possible, closer to the verb.

compound joined by "and"

My *son and daughter-in-law receive* monthly issues of <u>Business Weekly</u>.

Outgoing *letters and packages leave* our office on a regularly scheduled basis.

Mr. Lopez and his two assistants were requested to attend the board meeting.

compound joined by "or" or "nor"

Neither Sharon nor *John was* available for comment to the press.

Either you or *I am* responsible for writing this section of the report.

Ms. Binder or her *assistants are* reviewing the manuscript.

Candy or *flowers are* typically given on this occasion. (Not: Flowers or *candy is* typically given on this occasion.)

d. Subjects joined by *and* take singular verbs in only two cases: (1) when the parts separated by *and* constitute a single person or thing and (2) when the compound is preceded by *each, every,* or *many a (an).*

single person or thing

Our *accountant and tax attorney has* prepared all the reports for the Internal Revenue Service.

Her *nurse and companion works* six days a week.

Bacon and eggs is served in our coffee shop until 11 a.m. each day.

Luckily the *horse and carriage was* stolen after the cameraman shot the scene.

compound preceded by "each," "every," or "many a"

Each apartment and condominium was inspected by our general manager before being released for rental.

Every man, woman, and child is responsible for carrying his or her belongings during the tour.

Many a student and instructor has requested additional tickets to our Drama Department's production of "Picnic."

e. Indefinite pronouns such as *each, every, anyone, everyone, somebody, anybody, either,* and *neither* take singular verbs.

Each of the books *was* stamped with the company name.

Please give a copy of this report to *anyone* who *asks* for one.

Everyone was pleased with the hotel accommodations.

f. When *there* precedes the verb, select the singular or plural verb form on the basis of the number of the noun that follows. The same rule applies to those words such as *some, all, none, most, a majority, one fourth,* and *part* that indicate portions.

"there" preceding a verb form

There *are* three *people* on the reserve list.

There *appears* to be only one *reason* why we did not receive the contract.

portion preceding a verb form

Some of the *building has* been infested by mice.

Part of your *order has* been shipped.

All the *materials were* shipped to you yesterday.

Only *one half* of the *packages have* been inspected.

g. "A number" used as a subject requires a plural verb. "The number" used as a subject requires a singular verb.

"a number" subject

A number of our students *have* registered late this semester.

Under the circumstances, *a number* of our customers *are* requesting a full refund.

"the number" subject

The number of responses *was* greater than we had expected.

We believe that *the number* of employees selecting the DSE insurance option *has* increased.

h. To express the subjunctive mood, use *were* instead of *was* after *if, as if, as though,* or *wish* if the situation expressed is untrue or highly unlikely. The verb *was* is used only if the situation after *if, as if,* or *as though* could be true.

8

use of "were" instead of "was"

If I *were* you, I would submit another application before the deadline date.

Mr. Greeley took charge *as though* he *were* the owner of the store.

I *wish* I *were* able to answer that question for you.

use of "was"

If Mary *was* here, she did not return the overdue library books.

The customer acted *as though* he *was* irritated with our credit policies.

i. Avoid splitting an infinitive, that is, placing any words between *to* and the verb form.

Unfortunately, I was unable *to follow logically* the speaker's train of thought. (not *to logically follow*)

Were you able *to understand fully* the ramifications of this policy change? (not *to fully understand*)

j. Collective nouns such as *committee, jury, audience, group,* and *council* may take either singular or plural verbs, depending upon the situation in which the verb is used. If the elements of the noun are operating as a unit, use a singular verb; if the elements of the noun are acting separately, use a plural verb.

elements of noun acting as a unit

It is rewarding when an *audience gives* a speaker a standing ovation.

Has the *committee* finished its report?

elements of noun acting separately

The *jury were* arguing violently.

Unfortunately, the *council do* not agree on the purpose of this committee.

k. A relative pronoun clause must agree in gender and number with the noun or pronoun it modifies.

Ms. Cohen is a *person* who *is* concerned about maintaining *her* good health.

Our manager is the kind of *man* who *is* always considerate of *his* subordinates.

All the *children* who *attend* this school must maintain *their* grade averages at the "C" level.

Have you read all the *papers* that *were* placed on your desk?

Our committee *meeting,* which *was* scheduled for next Monday, has been canceled.

l. Those relative pronoun clauses preceded by such phrases as "one of those doctors," "one of those executives," "one of those books," or "one of those secretaries" agree with the plural noun and, therefore, must take a plural verb.

Mary is one of those business *executives* who *travel* considerably in *their* jobs.

He is one of those *salespersons* who regularly *visit* all *their* customers.

Joshua's Travels is one of those *books* that *have* an unhappy ending.

Adjectives

8–8. Adjectives Modify Nouns

Adjectives modify nouns. They answer such questions as what kind? how many? which one?

what kind?

damaged merchandise

green lawns

stylish dresses

how many?

three insurance salespersons

several years

two dozen pencils

which one?

that chair

those flight attendants

this idea

8–9. Use of the Articles *A* and *An*

Use the article *a* before a word that begins with a consonant sound, a long *u* sound, or an *h* that is pronounced. Use *an* before words that begin with a pronounced vowel sound (except long *u*) or before words that begin with a silent *h*.

use of "a"

a newspaper	a restaurant
a uniform	a union
a history class	a hillside development

use of "an"

an answer
an honest person
an unusual request
an hour

8–10. Adjective Comparison

a. Adjectives may be used to compare two or more nouns or pronouns. Use the comparative form for comparing two persons or things and the superlative form for comparing three or more.

b. Regular one-syllable adjectives ending in *e* add *r* for the comparative and *st* for the superlative. Regular one-syllable adjectives ending in consonants add *er* for the comparative and *est* for the superlative.

one-syllable adjectives ending in "e"

He has a *fine* set of golf clubs.

He has a *finer* set of golf clubs than I.

He has the *finest* set of golf clubs I have ever seen.

one-syllable adjectives ending in a consonant

This is a *short* letter.

The first letter is the *shorter* one.

This is the *shortest* letter I have typed today.

c. Most two-syllable adjectives and all adjectives containing three or more syllables use *more* or *less* and *most* or *least* to form the comparative and superlative. Forms for those two-syllable adjectives that do not follow this pattern are shown in the dictionary. These include *costly, friendly, happy, healthy, merry, lovely, pretty*—all ending in *y*.

two- and three-syllable adjectives with "more," "most," "less," or "least"

We purchased a *handsome* wallet yestereday.

This wallet is *more handsome* than the one we purchased yesterday.

This is the *most handsome* wallet in the store.

We purchased an *expensive* wallet yesterday.

This wallet is *less expensive* than the one we purchased yesterday.

This is the *least expensive* wallet in the store.

8

two-syllable adjectives using "er" or "est"

We initiated a *costly* program.

The state's highway program is *costlier* than its conservation program.

Our welfare program is the *costliest* one in the nation.

d. Irregular forms for adjective comparison appear in the dictionary. They are listed after the simple forms. A list of commonly used irregular adjectives follows:

simple	*comparative*	*superlative*
good, well	better	best
bad, ill	worse	worst
little	littler, less	littlest, least
many, much	more	most
far	farther, further	farthest, furthest

e. Use *other* or *else* when comparing one person or object with the other members of the group to which it belongs.

Our Dallas office earns more revenue than any of our *other* branch offices. (Not: "any of our branch offices.")

John is more intelligent than anyone *else* in the class. (Not: "anyone in the class.")

f. Some adjectives cannot be compared in the regular sense because they are absolute. A partial list of such adjectives follows:

finished   perfect   complete
round   dead   straight
unique   full   alive

Absolute adjectives may show comparison by use of the forms "more nearly" or "most nearly."

This water cooler is *full.*

The water cooler in your office is *more nearly full* (not *fuller*) than the one in ours.

The water cooler in the Personnel Office is the *most nearly full* (not *fullest*) one on this floor.

This victim is *dead.*

This victim is *more nearly dead* (not *deader*) than the other one.

This victim is the *most nearly dead* (not *deadest*) one in the emergency room.

8-11. Independent Adjectives

When two or more adjectives appearing before a noun independently modify the noun, separate these adjectives with commas.

His *direct, practical* approach to problems created high respect among his staff.

We returned that *boring, poorly written* manuscript to its author.

She handled the problem in a *sure, calm, decisive* manner.

8-12. Adjectives with Linking Verbs

Use adjectives, not adverbs, after linking verbs. Common linking verbs include *feel, look, smell, sound,* and *taste.*

I *feel bad* that you were not elected. (not *badly*)

This cake *tastes delicious. (not deliciously)*

After the fire the adjoining rooms *smelled terrible.* (not *terribly*)

8-13. Compound Adjectives*

When two or more words appearing before a noun function as a single adjective, place hyphens between the words.

---

*See Section 2-2 for detailed rules regarding the formation of compound adjectives.

Your *up-to-date* files have been very helpful in compiling this data.

Upon reading your *well-written* report, the committee members agreed to establish a new community center.

Do not exceed the *55-mile-an-hour* speed limit.

Adverbs

8–14. Function and Form of Adverbs

Adverbs modify verbs, adjectives, or other adverbs. They answer such questions as when? where? why? how? to what degree?

a. Most adverbs end in *ly*.

accidentally	daily	finally
carefully	definitely	steadily
cautiously	diligently	usually

b. Some adverbs (mostly ones containing one syllable) may either end in *ly* or take the adjective form of the word.*

Please drive *slowly* (or *slow*) on this icy road.

Your order will be processed as *quickly* (or *quick*) as possible.

You may call *directly* (or *direct*) to Chicago on this line.

c. Other adverbs do not take an *ly* form. Such adverbs include the following:

again	late	not	there
almost	never	now	very
here	no	soon	well

8–15. Adverb Comparison

a. One-syllable adverbs and some two-syllable adverbs are compared by adding *er* or *est*. For comparisons between two items, use *er;* for comparisons among more than two items, use *est.***

comparisons of two

You live *closer* to the library than I.

My assistant left *earlier* than I.

---

*Both forms are shown in the dictionary for those adverbs that may end in *ly* or take the adjective form.

**Two-syllable adverbs that show comparison by adding *er* or *est* are considered irregular. Therefore, they are shown in the dictionary following the simple form.

8

comparisons of more than two

Of all the students in the study group, you live *closest* to the library.

Who left the *earliest*—Bill, Paul, or Bob?

b. Most adverbs containing two syllables and all adverbs containing more than two syllables form the comparison by adding *more* or *most* to the positive form. Use *more* in comparing two items and *most* in comparing more than two items.

comparisons of two

This brand of soap is *more widely* used on the East Coast than in the South.

This conveyor belt travels *more slowly* than the one next to it.

Please pack these items *more carefully* than you have done in the past.

comparisons of more than two

This brand of soap is the *most widely* used one in the country.

Denver has been mentioned *most often* as the likely site for our next convention.

This conference is the *most unusually* conducted one I have ever attended.

8–16. Adverbs vs. Adjectives

8

Use an adverb after a verb that shows action; use an adjective, however, after a nonaction (or linking) verb.

action verb

You *did well* on your six-month evaluation.

The pedestrian *crossed* the street *cautiously*.

Most of the committee *opposed bitterly* the controversial measure.

Our bowling team *was beaten badly*.

nonaction or linking verb

This room *smells terrible*.

His coffee *tastes bitter*.

I *feel bad* about Mr. Johnson's predicament.

The Sunday evening banquet *was delicious*.

8–17. Double Negatives

Use only one negative word or limiting adverb to express a single idea.

Do *not* release this information to *anybody*. (not *nobody*)

I did *not* receive *anything* from our insurance agent. (not *nothing*)

I *can* (not *can't* or *cannot*) *scarcely* believe that our president would make such a foolish statement.

We *were* (not *weren't* or *were not*) *hardly* in the office when Ms. Murch gave us the disappointing news.

He *had* (not *hadn't* or *had not*) *barely* finished the report in time for the board meeting.

Prepositions

8–18. In, Between, or Among?

When a preposition has a single object, use *in*. For two separate objects, use *between;* for three or more objects, use *among.*

"in"

There are several discrepancies *in* the auditor's report.

The prosecution noted several discrepancies *in* the witness's testimony.

"between"

Between you and me, I believe our company stock will split within the next several months.

There were several discrepancies *between* the two witnesses' reports.

"among"

Please distribute these supplies *among* the various branch offices.

Among themselves the Board of Directors consented previously to withdraw that motion.

8–19. Prepositions Used With Certain Words

Certain words require certain prepositions depending upon the meaning to be conveyed. Other words often acquire prepositions incorrectly. A list of commonly used combinations follows:

Agree *on* or *upon* (reach an understanding)
Agree *to* (undertake an action)
Agree *with* (a person or his or her idea)

All *of* (use *of* when followed by a pronoun; omit *of* when followed by a noun)

Angry *about* (a situation or condition)
Angry *at* (things)
Angry *with* (a person or a group of persons)

Both *of* (use *of* when followed by a pronoun; omit *of* when followed by a noun)

Buy *from* (not *off*)

Comply or compliance *with* (not *to*)

Conform *to* (to act in accordance with prevailing standards)
Conform *with* (to be similar or in agreement)

Convenient *to* (a location)
Convenient *for* (a person)

Correspond *with* (by writing)
Correspond *to* (a thing)

Discrepancy *in* (one thing)
Discrepancy *between* (two things)
Discrepancy *among* (three or more things)

Different *from* (not *than*)

From (*from* a person)

Help (not help *from*)

Identical *with* (not *to*)

Inside (not inside *of*)

Off (not *off of; off* a thing)

Opposite (not opposite *to* or *of*)

Outside (not outside *of*)

Plan *to* (not *on*)

Retroactive *to* (not *from*)

Take *off* (a thing)
Take *from* (a person)

8–20. Prepositional Phrases

In determining subject-verb agreement, generally omit any prepositional phrases that separate the subject and the verb.

One of your brothers *is* waiting in your office.

A large *quantity* of goods *has* been ordered for the sale.

Last Monday our *supply* of paper goods and kitchen utensils *was* destroyed.

Conjunctions

8–21. Conjunctions Used in Pairs

a. Use *either . . . or* for positive statements; use *neither . . . nor* for negative statements.

positive statements, "either . . . or"

Either Ms. Saunders *or* Mr. Ramirez will inspect the property.

You may specify *either* black *or* brown on your order.

negative statements, "neither . . . nor"

Neither a Toyota *nor* a Datsun is available for rental this week.

I could not believe that *neither* Larry *nor* Debbie would accept the assignment.

b.   Use the same grammatical construction after each part of the conjunctive pair *not only . . . but also.*

Our company manufactures *not only* furniture *but also* major appliances. (Not: Our company *not only* manufactures furniture *but also* major appliances.)

Our company *not only* manufactures and services major appliances *but also* services small appliances.

c.   In comparisons use *as . . . as* for positive ideas and *so . . . as* for negative ideas.

positive ideas, "as . . . as"

Our Model 874 radio has become *as* popular *as* our Model 923.

I believe that her understudy is *as* talented *as* Ms. Saito.

negative ideas, "so . . . as"

Our Model 874 radio is not *so* popular *as* our Model 923.

Avocados are not *so* expensive *as* they were last year.

8–22.   As vs. Like

As is a conjunction and is used when the following construction is a clause (contains a subject and a verb). *Like* is a preposition and is used when the following construction is a prepositional object (a phrase ending with a noun or pronoun).

"as" with a clause

They did not package the order *as* (not *like) he expected they would.*

As (not *like) you indicated in your letter,* we cannot expect to make a profit during our first year of operations.

"like" with a prepositional phrase

We need more qualified agents *like you.*

Please order another typewriter *like the one* you have in your office.

Address Format and Forms of Address

9

Address Format and Forms of Address Solution Finder

Forms of Address

Ambassador, American   9–9
Ambassador, Foreign   9–9
Cabinet Members   9–9
Catholic Clergy   9–10
Chaplain   9–10
Chief Justice   9–9
Clergy   9–10
Company   9–8
Consul, American   9–9
Dean   9–8
Governor   9–9
Governor, Lieutenant   9–9
Head, Government Offices and
  Agencies   9–9
Jewish Clergy   9–10
Judge   9–9
Justice, Associate   9–9
Lawyer   9–8
Man   9–8
Man and Woman   9–8
Married Couple   9–8
Married Couple, Professional
  9–8
Mayor   9–9
Men, Two or More   9–8
Physician   9–8
President, Assistant to   9–9
President, Board of
  Commissioners   9–9
President, College or
  University   9–8
President, Former   9–9
President, United States   9–9
President, Wife of   9–9
Professor   9–8
Protestant Clergy   9–10

Representative, State   9–9
Representative, United States
  9–9
Secretaries, Deputy or Under
  9–9
Senator, State   9–9
Senator, United States   9–9
Service Personnel   9–8
Vice President, United States
  9–9
Widow   9–8
Woman and Man   9–8
Woman, Marital Status
  Unknown   9–8
Woman, Married   9–8
Woman, Single   9–8
Women, Two or More   9–8

General Address Format   9–1

Names and Titles

Company names   9–4
Courtesy titles   9–2
Professional titles   9–3
Signature lines   9–3b

Places

Buildings and units   9–5
City names   9–7a
State names   9–7b
Street addresses   9–6
Zip codes   9–7c

9

General Format

9–1. General Address Format

a. Use combinations of the following to address general business correspondence: full name with appropriate title, company name, street address, city, state, and zip code. Use the same format for both the inside address and the envelope, unless the company uses the envelope format recommended by the U.S. Postal Service described in Section 10–26.

addressed to individual

Ms. Elizabeth Bennett
2879 Balboa Boulevard, Apt. 2
San Clemente, California 92672

Dear Ms. Bennett:

addressed to individual within company

Mr. Jay V. Berger, Manager
Policy Issue Department
General Insurance Company of America
341 Prospect Avenue
Hartford, Connecticut 06105

Dear Mr. Berger:

addressed to company

F. M. Tarbell Company
2740 Troy Avenue, S.W.
Indianapolis, Indiana 46241

Attention: Mr. William F. Schlossinger, Manager, Personnel Department

Gentlemen:

b. An address may have a maximum of six lines and a minimum of two lines.

minimum two-line address

Phillips Foods, Inc.
Morristown, NJ 07960

maximum six-line address

Miss Stephanie R. Whitaker
Chief Operations Manager
Quality Control Department
Neware Aluminum Accessories
3618 Chelwood Boulevard, N.E.
Albuquerque, NM 87111

9

Names and Titles

9–2. Courtesy Titles

a. Abbreviate the courtesy titles *Mr.*, *Ms.*, and *Mrs.* when they are used with the names of individuals. Spell out, however, the title *Miss*.

Mr. Stanley Hutchinson

Ms. Nina Lopez

Mrs. Charlene Carnachan

Miss Frances Cates

b. When the name of an individual does not signify whether the person is a man or a woman, omit the courtesy title or use *Mr.* When addressing a woman, use the courtesy title *Ms.* unless *Miss* or *Mrs.* is specified by the addressee.

Chris Kenworth

Mr. Lynn V. Stauber

Ms. Elizabeth Rankin

c. The title *Master* is used for addressing young boys (boys too young to be called *Mister*).

Master William J. Clark

d. The abbreviated courtesy title *Esq.* is sometimes used after the surname. In such cases no courtesy title precedes the name.

Murray T. Silverstein, *Esq.*

9–3. Professional Titles

a. Except for *Dr.* and long professional titles consisting of more than one word, write out and capitalize all professional titles when they precede the names of individuals. *Professor, Dean, The Reverend, Governor, Senator, Colonel, Lieutenant,* and *The Honorable* are examples of titles that are capitalized and written in full.

"Doctor" abbreviated
Dr. Allen Kupsh

professional title written out
Professor Marly Bergerud

long professional title abbreviated
Lt. Col. Ret. Maurice P. Wiener

b. In addressing business correspondence or completing signature lines, capitalize and write out professional titles that follow an individual's name.

single-line address format
Mr. Ray Johnson, *Dean*

two-line address format
Ms. Jane S. Kenyon
Plant Superintendent

single-line signature format
Ruth Johnson, *Dean*

two-line signature format
John S. Minasian
Plant Superintendent

c. Capitalize professional titles not appearing in address format or signature lines only when they precede an individual's name. Do not capitalize titles following an individual's name, except in the case of high-ranking government officials (President of the United States, Vice President of the United States, Cabinet members, members of Congress, and governors).

title preceding name
President Robert I. Place will deliver the main address.

title following name
Robert I. Place, *president* of A & I Enterprises, will deliver the main address.

title of high-ranking government official
The Honorable John Linn, *Senator* from Pennsylvania, has agreed to deliver the main address.

d. Only one professional courtesy title with the same meaning should appear with a single name. Use *Dr.* or *M.D.* but not both titles with the same name.

titles with the same meaning
Dr. James V. Glaser
James V. Glaser, *M.D.*

titles with different meanings
Dr. Barbara Simi, *Professor*

e. Do not capitalize professional titles that substitute for individuals' names except in the case of high-ranking government officials.

187

title substituted for name

The *general* scheduled a staff meeting for Thursday afternoon.

title of high-ranking government official

Did the *Governor* appear for the press conference?

9–4. Company Names

Spell out company names in full unless the company itself uses abbreviations in its official name. *Inc.* and *Ltd.* usually appear in abbreviated form.

company name written in full

Pacific Mutual Life Insurance Company

Richter and Sons

Watson Corporation

company name containing abbreviation

Consolidated Factors, *Ltd.*

McKnight, Fisher & Donovan

International Computer Corp.

9 Places

9–5. Buildings and Units

Capitalize the names of buildings and units therein.

Capitol Building, Office 243F

Medical Arts Center, Suite 680–681

Greenwich Apartments, Unit 3

9–6. Street Addresses

a. Use figures to express house numbers. Only the house number *one* is written in word form.

house number "one"

One Lakeview Terrace

house number in figures

8 Burbank Lane

b. Spell out compass directions that appear within a street address. Compass points following the street address are preceded by a comma and abbreviated.

compass point within street address

1864 *East* 37 Street

compass point following street address

180 Central Avenue, *S.W.*

c. All numbered street names *ten* and below are written in words (using ordinal numbers—*first, second, third,* etc.). Numbered street names above *ten,* however, are written in figures. Use cardinal numbers (*11, 12, 13,* etc.) when a compass point appears between the house and street numbers; use ordinal numbers (*11th, 12th, 13th,* etc.) when no such compass point is present.

numbered street name "ten" or below

1183 *Fifth* Avenue   983 West *First* Street

numbered street name above "ten"—with compass point

980 North *81* Street

numbered street name above "ten"—without compass point

2036 *48th* Street

d. Spell out street designations such as *Boulevard, Avenue, Street, Place, Drive,* and *Lane.* Only the street designation *Boulevard* (Blvd.) may be abbreviated with exceptionally long street names.

street designation spelled out

18394 Lankershim *Boulevard*

street designation abbreviated

19263 North Coldwater Canyon *Blvd.*

9

e. Spell out where possible mailing designations such as *Rural Route* or *Post Office Box* that are used in the place of street addresses. Abbreviate the mailing designation only with long addresses.

postal designation spelled out

Post Office Box 107

postal designation abbreviated

P.O. Box 269, Terminal Annex

f. Apartment, building, and unit numbers are expressed in figures and are typed on the same line as the street address. The terms *Apartment* and *Building* may be abbreviated when they are included with a street address.

unit number

6176 Arroyo Road, *Unit 2*

apartment number

3964 West 81 Street, *Apt. 3*

no specific designation

16932 Wilshire Boulevard, *C-110*

9–7. City, State, and Zip Code

a. Spell out in full the names of cities.

   Saint Louis   New York   Fort Worth   Los Angeles

b. Use the two-letter post office designation for state names or spell out in full the state name. Select either mode based upon (1) the degree of formality of the correspondence or (2) the one that provides better balance for setting up the entire address. Should both be equally suitable, use the two-letter postal designation. Use the same form for both the inside address and the envelope unless the company chooses to use the U.S. Postal Service recommendations for addressing envelopes described in Section 10–26.

   state two-letter zip code designation

   Ms. Jessica Moore
   108 Academy Avenue
   Boston, MA 02188

   state name written in full

   Mr. William R. Stephenson
   257 American Legion Highway
   Boston, Massachusetts 02131

c. Zip codes are typed a single space after the state.

   Atlanta, Georgia 30331   Atlanta, GA 30331

Forms of Address

9–8. Personal and General Professional Titles

The following table lists the proper forms of address, salutation, and complimentary close for correspondence addressed to a general individual, two or more individuals, certain professionals, and a company.

Addressee	Address on Letter and Envelope	Salutation and Complimentary Close
Man	Mr. (full name) (local address) 00000	Dear Mr. (surname): Sincerely,
Married Woman	Mrs. (husband's first name, last name) (local address) 00000	Dear Mrs. (surname): Sincerely,
	or	
	*Mrs. or Ms. (wife's first name, last name) (local address) 00000	Dear Mrs. or Ms. (surname): Sincerely,
Single Woman	Miss or Ms. (full name) (local address) 00000	Dear Miss or Ms. (surname): Sincerely,
Woman, Marital Status Unknown	Ms. (full name) (local address) 00000	Dear Ms. (surname): Sincerely,
Widow	Mrs. (husband's first name, last name) (local address) 00000	Dear Mrs. (surname): Sincerely,
	or	
	Mrs. or Ms. (wife's first name, last name) (local address) 00000	Dear Mrs. or Ms. (surname): Sincerely,
Two or More Men	Mr. (full name) and Mr. (full name) (local address) 00000	Dear Mr. (surname) and Mr. (surname): Dear Messrs. (surname) and (surname): Gentlemen: Sincerely,
Two or More Women	Mrs. (full name) and Mrs. (full name) (local address) 00000	Dear Mrs. (surname) and Mrs. (surname): Dear Mesdames (surname) and (surname): Mesdames: Sincerely,
	or	
	Miss (full name) and Mrs. (full name) (local address) 00000	Dear Miss (surname) and Mrs. (surname): Sincerely,
	or	
	Ms. (full name) and Ms. (full name) (local address) 00000	Dear Ms. (surname) and Ms. (surname): Dear Mses. (surname) and (surname): Sincerely,
One Woman and One Man	Ms. (full name) and Mr. (full name) (local address) 00000	Dear Ms. (surname) and Mr. (surname): Sincerely,
Married Couple	Mr. and Mrs. (husband's full name) (local address) 00000	Dear Mr. and Mrs. (surname): Sincerely,

*This form is also used for a woman who is separated or divorced from her husband.

Address Format and Forms of Address

Addressee	Address on Letter and Envelope	Salutation and Complimentary Close
Professional Married Couple	(title) (full name of husband) (title) (full name of wife) (local address) 00000	Dear (title) and (title) (surname): Dear (plural of title and surname if both husband and wife have same title): Sincerely,
President of a College or University (Doctor)	Dr. (full name), President, (name of institution) (local address) 00000	Dear Dr. (surname): Sincerely,
Dean of a School or College	Dean (full name) School of (name) (name of institution) (local address) 00000	Dear Dean (surname): Sincerely,
	or	
	†Dr. or Mr. (full name) Dean of (title) (name of institution) (local address) 00000	Dear Dr. or Mr. (surname): Sincerely,
Professor	Professor (full name) (name of department) (name of institution) (local address) 00000	Dear Professor (surname): Sincerely,
	or	
	Dr. (full name), Professor (name of department) (name of institution) (local address) 00000	Dear Dr. (surname): Sincerely,
	or	
	†Dr. or Mr. (full name) Assistant Professor (name of department) (name of institution) (local address) 00000	Dear Dr. or Mr. (surname): Sincerely,
Physician	(full name), M.D. (local address) 00000	Dear Dr. (surname): Sincerely,
Lawyer	†Mr. (full name) Attorney at Law (local address) 00000	Dear Mr. (surname): Sincerely,
Service Personnel	(full rank, full name, and abbreviation of service designation) (Retired is added if applicable.) (title and organization) (local address) 00000	Dear (rank) (surname): Sincerely,
Company or Corporation, Men	(full name of organization) (local address) 00000	Gentlemen: Sincerely,

†When the addressee is a woman, substitute *Miss, Mrs.,* or *Ms.* for *Mr.*

Addressee	Address on Letter and Envelope	Salutation and Complimentary Close
Company or Corporation, Men and Women	(full name of organization) (local address) 00000	Gentlemen: or Ladies and Gentlemen: Sincerely,
Company or Corporation, Women	(full name of organization) (local address) 00000	Ladies: Sincerely,

9-9. Government Officials

The following table shows the proper forms of address, salutation, and complimentary close for specific government officials. When the addressee is a woman, substitute one of the following for the salutation shown:

Madam for *Mr.* before formal terms such as *President, Vice President, Chairman, Secretary, Ambassador,* and *Minister.*

Ms., Miss, or *Mrs.* for *Mr.* before the name of a member of the House of Representatives, a senator-elect, a representative-elect, or a lesser government official.

Addressee	Address on Letter and Envelope	Salutation and Complimentary Close
The President	The President The White House Washington, DC 20500	Dear Mr. President: Respectfully,
*Former President	Honorable (full name) Former President of the United States (local address) 00000	Dear Mr. (surname): Sincerely,
Wife of the President	Mrs. (full name) The White House Washington, DC 20500	Dear Mrs. (surname): Sincerely,
Assistant to the President	Honorable (full name) Assistant to the President The White House Washington, DC 20500	Dear Mr. (surname): Sincerely,
The Vice President	The Vice President United States Senate Washington, DC 20510 or The Honorable (full name) Vice President of the United States Washington, DC 20501	Dear Mr. Vice President: Sincerely,

*This form of address may be adapted to address other former high-ranking government officials.

Address Format and Forms of Address

Addressee	Address on Letter and Envelope	Salutation and Complimentary Close
The Chief Justice	The Chief Justice of the United States The Supreme Court of the United States Washington, DC 20543	Dear Mr. Chief Justice: Sincerely,
Associate Justice	Mr. Justice (surname) The Supreme Court of the United States Washington, DC 20543	Dear Mr. Justice: Sincerely,
United States Senator	Honorable (full name) United States Senate Washington, DC 20510 *or* Honorable (full name) United States Senator (local address) 00000	Dear Senator (surname): Sincerely,
United States Representative	Honorable (full name) House of Representatives Washington, DC 20515 *or* Honorable (full name) Member, United States House of Representatives (local address) 00000	Dear Mr. (surname): Sincerely,
Cabinet Members	Honorable (full name) Secretary of (name of department) Washington, DC 00000	Dear Mr. Secretary: Sincerely,
	or Honorable (full name) Postmaster General Washington, DC 20260	Dear Mr. Postmaster General: Sincerely,
	or Honorable (full name) Attorney General Washington, DC 20530	Dear Mr. Attorney General: Sincerely,
Deputy Secretaries, Assistants, or Under Secretaries	Honorable (full name) Deputy Secretary of (name of department) Washington, DC 00000 *or* Honorable (full name) Assistant Secretary of (name of department) Washington, DC 00000 *or* Honorable (full name) Under Secretary of (name of department) Washington, DC 00000	Dear Mr. (surname): Sincerely,

9

Addressee	Address on Letter and Envelope	Salutation and Complimentary Close
Head of Independent Offices and Agencies	Honorable (full name) Comptroller General of the United States General Accounting Office Washington, DC 20548	Dear Mr. (surname): Sincerely,
	or	
	Honorable (full name) Chairman, (name of commission) Washington, DC 00000	Dear Mr. Chairman: Sincerely,
	or	
	Honorable (full name) Director, Bureau of the Budget Washington, DC 20503	Dear Mr. (surname): Sincerely,
American Ambassador	Honorable (full name) American Ambassador (City), (Country)	Sir: (formal) Dear Mr. Ambassador: (informal) Very truly yours, (formal) Sincerely, (informal)
American Consul General or American Consul	Mr. (full name) American Consul General (or American Consul) (City), (Country)	Dear Mr. (surname): Sincerely,
Foreign Ambassador in the United States	His Excellency (full name) Ambassador of (country) (local address) 00000	Excellency: (formal) Dear Mr. Ambassador: (informal) Very truly yours, (formal) Sincerely, (informal)
Governor of State	Honorable (full name) Governor of (name of state) (City), (State) 00000	Dear Governor (surname): Sincerely,
Lieutenant Governor	Honorable (full name) Lieutenant Governor of (name of state) (City), (State) 00000	Dear Mr. (surname): Sincerely,
State Senator	Honorable (full name) (name of state) State Senate (City), (State) 00000	Dear Senator (surname): Sincerely,
State Representative, Assemblyman, or Delegate	Honorable (full name) (name of state) House of Representatives (or State Assembly or House of Delegates) (City), (State) 00000	Dear Mr. (surname): Sincerely,
Mayor	Honorable (full name) Mayor of (name of city) (City), (State) 00000	Dear Mayor (surname): Sincerely,

9

Addressee	Address on Letter and Envelope	Salutation and Complimentary Close
President of a Board of Commissioners	Honorable (full name) President, Board of Commissioners of (name of city) (City), (State) 00000	Dear Mr. (surname): Sincerely,
Judge	Honorable (full name) (name of court) (local address) 00000	Dear Judge (surname): Sincerely,

9–10. Religious Dignitaries

The following table shows the proper forms of address, salutation, and complimentary close for specific religious dignitaries.

Addressee	Address on Letter and Envelope	Salutation and Complimentary Close
Catholic Clergy	His Eminence (given name) Cardinal (surname) Archbishop of (diocese) (local address) 00000	Your Eminence: (formal) Dear Cardinal (surname): (informal) Sincerely,
	or	
	The Most Reverend (full name) Archbishop of (diocese) (local address) 00000	Your Excellency: (formal) Dear Archbishop (surname): (informal) Sincerely,
	or	
	The Most Reverend (full name) Bishop of (city) (local address) 00000	Your Excellency: (formal) Dear Bishop (surname): (informal) Sincerely,
	or	
	The Right Reverend Monsignor (full name) (local address) 00000	Right Reverend Monsignor: (formal) Dear Monsignor (surname): (informal) Sincerely,
	or	
	The Very Reverend Monsignor (full name) (local address) 00000	Very Reverend Monsignor: (formal) Dear Monsignor (surname): (informal) Sincerely,
	or	

9

Addressee	Address on Letter and Envelope	Salutation and Complimentary Close
	The Reverend (full name) (add initials of order, if any) (local address) 00000	Reverend Sir: (formal) Dear Father (surname): (informal) Sincerely,
	or	
	Mother (full name) (initials of order, if used) Superior (name of convent) (local address) 00000	Dear Mother (full name): Sincerely,
	or	
	Sister (full name) (initials of order, if used) (name of convent) (local address) 00000	Dear Sister (full name): Sincerely,
Jewish Clergy	Rabbi (full name) (local address) 00000	Dear Rabbi (surname): Sincerely,
Protestant Clergy	The Right Reverend (full name) Bishop of (name) (local address) 00000	Right Reverend Sir: (formal) Dear Bishop (surname): (informal) Sincerely,
	or	
	The Very Reverend (full name) Dean of (name of church) (local address) 00000	Very Reverend Sir: (formal) Dear Dean (surname): (informal) Sincerely,
	or	
	The Reverend (full name) Bishop of (name) (local address) 00000	Reverend Sir: (formal) Dear Bishop (surname): (informal) Sincerely,
	or	
	The Reverend (full name) (title), (name of church) (local address) 00000	Dear Reverend (surname): Dear Mr. (surname): Sincerely,
Chaplains	Chaplain (full name) (full rank, service designation) (post office address of organization and station) (local address) 00000	Dear Chaplain (surname): Sincerely,

9

Business Letters and Memorandums

10

Business Letters and Memorandums Solution Finder

Addressing Envelopes

Addressee notations   *10–24*
Mailing address   *10–23*
 Format   *10–23a*
 Manila envelopes, letter-
  sized   *10–23e*
 No. 5⅛ envelopes   *10–23d*
 No. 6¾ envelopes   *10–23c*
 No. 7 envelopes   *10–23d*
 No. 10 envelopes   *10–23b*
Mailing notations   *10–25*
Nine-digit zip code   *10–27*
Return address   *10–22*
 Printed   *10–22a*
 Typewritten   *10–22b*
U.S. Postal Service
 recommendations   *10–26*
Zip + 4   *10–27*

Folding and Inserting Correspondence

No. 6¾ envelopes   *10–29*
No. 7 envelopes   *10–28*
No. 10 envelopes   *10–28*
Window envelopes   *10–30*

Letter Styles

Full block   *10–1*
Modified block   *10–2*
 Blocked paragraphs   *10–2a*
 Indented paragraphs   *10–2b*
Simplified   *10–4*
Social business   *10–3*

Memorandums

Preparation   *10–32*
Second-page heading   *10–32*
Usage   *10–31*

Placement of Major Letter Parts

Addressee notations   *10–7a, c*
Attention line   *10–9*
Blind carbon copies   *10–17d*
Body of the letter   *10–12*
Carbon copy notation   *10–17*
Complimentary close   *10–13*
Date   *10–6*
Enclosure or attachment
 notation   *10–16*
Formating guide   *10–8c*
Inside address   *10–8*
Mailing notations   *10–7b, c*
Margins   *10–8c*
Postscripts   *10–18*
Reference initials   *10–15*
Return address   *10–5*
 Printed   *10–5a*
 Typewritten   *10–5b, c*
Salutation   *10–10*
Second-page headings   *10–19*
Signature lines   *10–14*
Subject line   *10–11*

Punctuation Style

Mixed punctuation   *10–20*
Open punctuation   *10–21*

10

Letter Styles*

10–1. Full Block

The full block letter style is the most efficient letter style because all parts and all lines begin at the left margin.

full block letter

```
1
2
3        Gibraltar Insurance Company of America
4
5
6                        916 New Britain Avenue
7                        Hartford, Connecticut 06106
8                        Telephone: (203) 743-1200
9
10
11
12
13          June 16, 1985




                 Lynch & Marten Insurance Agency
                 16320 San Fernando Mission Boulevard
                 Sepulveda, California 91343
1 blank line ➞
                 Gentlemen
1 blank line ➞
                 SUBJECT:  CLAIM NO. AT 6509, INSURED THOMAS A. GLASCO
1 blank line ➞
                 The claim of your client, Mr. Thomas A. Glasco, for $450 to
                 replace the golf clubs that were stolen from him in Las Vegas
                 is covered under his homeowner's policy, No. 19362084.

                 To process Mr. Glasco's claim, we must have a copy of the
                 police report filed at the time of the theft.  Please contact
                 the police agency handling the theft report and have them
                 forward us a copy addressed to my attention.

                 As soon as we receive the necessary information, Mr. Glasco's
                 check will be sent to your office.

                 Sincerely yours
1 blank line ➞
                 GIBRALTAR INSURANCE COMPANY OF AMERICA


3 blank lines ➞

                 Mariam R. Marsh, Claims Adjuster
1 blank line ➞
                 fd
1 blank line ➞
                 cc:  Mr. Thomas A. Glasco
```

IO

---

*All letters appearing in this chapter have been designed by the authors for illustrative purposes. They are not reproductions of actual letters.

10–2. Modified Block

a. The modified block letter style with blocked paragraphs is the most popular letter style used in business. All lines except the return address (if used), the date, and the closing lines begin at the left margin.

modified block letter with blocked paragraphs

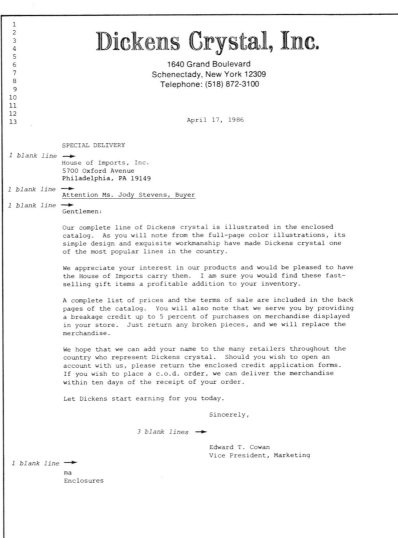

b. The modified block letter style with indented paragraphs is also used frequently. All lines except the first line of each paragraph, the return address (if used), the date, and the closing lines begin at the left margin.

modified block letter with indented paragraphs

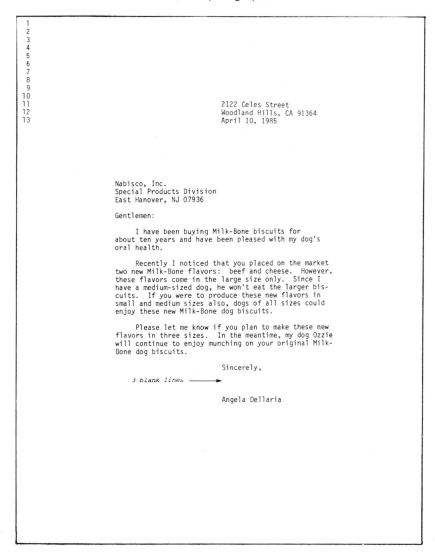

```
1
2
3
4
5
6
7
8
9
10
11                              2122 Celes Street
12                              Woodland Hills, CA 91364
13                              April 10, 1985




        Nabisco, Inc.
        Special Products Division
        East Hanover, NJ 07936

        Gentlemen:

            I have been buying Milk-Bone biscuits for
        about ten years and have been pleased with my dog's
        oral health.

            Recently I noticed that you placed on the market
        two new Milk-Bone flavors:  beef and cheese.  However,
        these flavors come in the large size only.  Since I
        have a medium-sized dog, he won't eat the larger bis-
        cuits.  If you were to produce these new flavors in
        small and medium sizes also, dogs of all sizes could
        enjoy these new Milk-Bone dog biscuits.

            Please let me know if you plan to make these new
        flavors in three sizes.  In the meantime, my dog Ozzie
        will continue to enjoy munching on your original Milk-
        Bone dog biscuits.

                            Sincerely,

        3 blank lines ────────►

                            Angela Dellaria
```

IO

10–3. Social Business

The social business letter style is used for social business correspondence. The inside address is placed after the closing lines in this informal format. The salutation may be followed by a comma instead of a colon. Paragraphs are either indented or blocked. The typed signature line is optional. Reference initials, enclosure notations, and carbon copy notations are usually omitted on the original, but these parts may be typed below the inside address on the file copy or on the copies for distribution. Leave a double space after the inside address and single-space the information to be included.

social business letter

United Bank of Iowa

Park Fair Shopping Center
Des Moines, Iowa 50313
Telephone: (515) 273-9600

January 23, 1985

Dear Jim,

Congratulations on your appointment as president of Bayview Savings and Loan Association and executive vice president of the parent holding company, Consolidated Financial Corporation.

You are certainly deserving of this promotion because you have contributed immeasurably to the rapid growth and development of Bayview and Consolidated. I know, too, that under your leadership both organizations will continue to move forward in the savings and loan industry.

Sincerely,

← *3 blank lines*

John S. Moore

← *2 blank lines*

Mr. James T. Montague, President
Bayview Savings and Loan Association
5800 West Camelback Road
Phoenix, Arizona 85033

1
2
3
4
5
6
7
8
9
10
11
12
13

10

10–4. Simplified

The simplified letter style was introduced by the Administrative Management Society. All parts of the letter begin at the left margin. In this style a subject line typed in all capital letters replaces the salutation. Two blank lines are left before and after the subject line. No complimentary close is used in the simplified letter style. Instead, the signature line is typed on the fifth line below the last line of the message. Use all capital letters and a single line for the signature line.

simplified letter

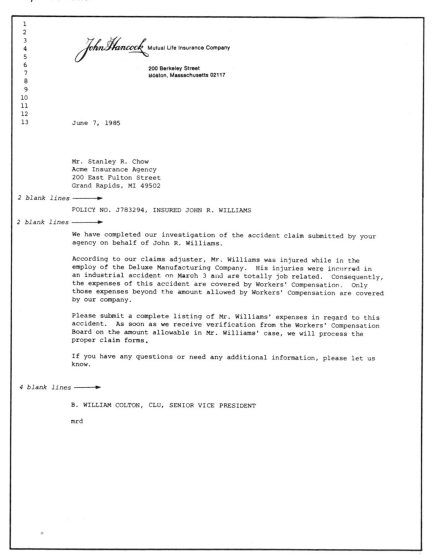

Placement of Major Letter Parts

10–5. Return Address

a. No return address is needed for business letters typed on paper containing a complete company letterhead. When plain bond paper or letterhead paper without a mailing address is used, a return address must be included. The return address in the modified block letter style is illustrated in Section 10–2b.

b. On plain paper begin the return address so that the last line is 2 inches from the top of the paper. The following table may be used to determine return address placement.

Return Address Placement

Number of Lines in Address	Typing Line for First Line of Address
2	11
3	10
4	9
5	8

In the full block and simplified letter styles, all lines begin at the left margin. In the modified block or social business styles, the return address may (1) begin at the center of the page, (2) begin five spaces to the left of the page center, (3) have the longest line back-spaced from the right margin to determine the placement, or (4) have each line centered.

return address in full block or simplified letter style without letterhead

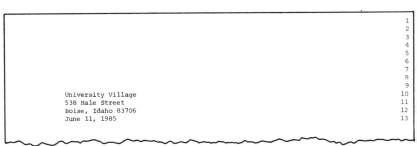

```
                                                            1
                                                            2
                                                            3
                                                            4
                                                            5
                                                            6
                                                            7
                                                            8
                                                            9
        University Village                                 10
        538 Hale Street                                    11
        Boise, Idaho 83706                                 12
        June 11, 1985                                      13
```

return address in modified block or social business letter style without letterhead

```
                                                    1
                                                    2
                                                    3
                                                    4
                                                    5
                                                    6
                                                    7
                                                    8
                                                    9
                                                   10
                       2034 Mason Street           11
                       Macon, Georgia 31204         12
                       May 3, 1986                  13
```

c. On letterhead paper without a mailing address, begin the return address a double space below the last line in the letterhead or end it 2 inches below the top edge of the paper. Select the procedure that places the return address in the lower position.

return address begun a double space below letterhead—full block or simplified letter

```
                                                              1
                                                              2
        Committee for the Reelection of the Governor          3
                 A Nonprofit Organization                     4
     Endorsed by:                                             5
                                                              6
        _____    _____    _____    _____          7
        _____    _____    _____    _____          8
                                                              9
        _____    _____    _____    _____         10
        _____    _____    _____    _____         11
                                                             12
        _____    _____    _____    _____         13
     9978 Access Road                                        14
     Minneapolis, MN  55431                                  15
     September 27, 1985                                      16
```

return address ending 2 inches from top edge of paper—modified block or social business letter

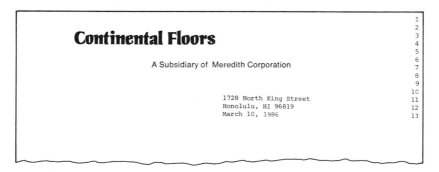

```
                                                         1
                                                         2
   Continental Floors                                    3
                                                         4
                                                         5
         A Subsidiary of Meredith Corporation            6
                                                         7
                                                         8
                                                         9
                                                        10
                 1728 North King Street                 11
                 Honolulu, HI 96819                      12
                 March 10, 1986                          13
```

10–6. Date

a. On letterhead paper with a mailing address, type the date a double space below the last line in the letterhead or with a 2-inch margin from the top edge of the paper (line 13). Select the procedure that places the date in the lower position.

In full block or simplified letters, type the date at the left margin. In modified block and social business letters, the date may be centered, begun at the center of the paper, or back-spaced from the right margin.

date typed a double space below letterhead—full block letter

date typed 2 inches below top edge of paper—modified block or social business letter

b. In letters requiring return addresses, type the date on the line directly below the last line of the return address. A date used with the return address in a complete letter is illustrated in Section 10–2b.

date with return address

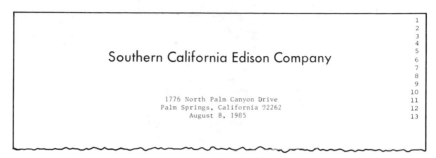

10–7. Addressee and Mailing Notations

a. Addressee notations such as *Personal* and *Confidential* are typed in all capital letters either (1) a double space below and even with the date or (2) a double space above the inside address.

even with date

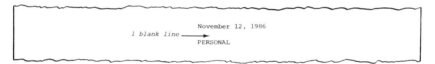

double space above inside address

b. Mailing notations such as *Special Delivery, Registered Mail,* and *Certified Mail* are typed in all capital letters (1) a double space below and even with the date, (2) a double space above the inside address, or (3) a single or double space below the reference initials or enclosure notation, whichever appears last. A mailing notation is illustrated in a complete letter in Section 10–2a.

even with date

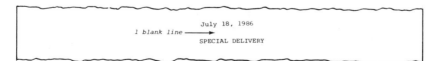

double space above inside address

```
CERTIFIED MAIL--RETURN RECEIPT REQUESTED
        ◄────1 blank line
Dr. Edward L. Adams
933 Westminster Street
Providence, RI 02904
```

after reference initials or enclosure notation

```
dls
Enclosures 3
REGISTERED MAIL
cc:  Mr. Roland B. Sink
```

c. If an addressee notation and a mailing notation appear in the same letter, place the addressee notation a triple space above the inside address and the mailing notation on the line directly below. Both notations are typed in all capital letters. Leave *at least* two blank lines between the date and addressee notation.

addressee and mailing notation in same letter

```
February 11, 1986
            ◄────at least 2 blank lines
CONFIDENTIAL
SPECIAL DELIVERY
            ◄────1 blank line
Mr. Frank D. Parsons
Vice President, Sales
Western Foundry, Inc.
3210 West Polk Street
Chicago, IL 60612
```

10

10–8. Inside Address

a. The inside address contains some or all of the following: courtesy title, name, professional title, company name, street or mailing address, city, state, and zip code. Single-space and begin at the left margin those parts necessary to direct the letter to the addressee.

arrangement of an inside address

Ms. Phyllis I. Prescott
Manager, Accounting Department
Eastern Savings and Loan Association
6750 East Independence Boulevard
Charlotte, North Carolina 28212

b. Abbreviate only the courtesy titles *Mr., Mrs., Ms.,* and *Dr.* Spell out all street designations such as *Street, Avenue,* and *Boulevard. Boulevard* may be abbreviated, however, with exceptionally long street names. Spell out the state name or use the two-letter post office designation, whichever achieves balance with the remaining lines. Each inside address should contain a minimum of two lines and a maximum of six lines.

two-line inside address

Holiday Inn
Cedar Rapids, IA 52406

six-line inside address

Mr. M. J. Fujimoto
Airline Training Specialist
Division of Personnel Instruction
Trans Continental Airlines
12700 East Funston Street
Wichita, Kansas 67207

c.   In the modified block, full block, and simplified letter styles, the inside address usually follows the date. The number of blank lines between the date and the inside address is determined by the length of the letter. Generally, the following table may be used for 8½- by 11-inch paper to determine (1) the number of lines between the date and the inside address and (2) the margins to be used for typing the letter.

Letter Formatting Guide

Approximate Number of Words in Body of Letter	Spaces in Line Length		Blank Lines Between Date and Inside Address	
	Elite	Pica	Elite	Pica
Under 150	50	40	6–10	5–7
150–250	60	50	4–8	3–5
250–350	70	60	2–4	2–3
Over 350 (two pages)	70	60	2–3	2–3

inside address in modified block letter

d. In the social business letter, the inside address is placed after the closing lines. If the typed signature line is omitted, leave five or six blank lines after the complimentary close before beginning the inside address. If a typed signature line is included, leave two blank lines after the typed signature before beginning the inside address.

social business letter without typed signature

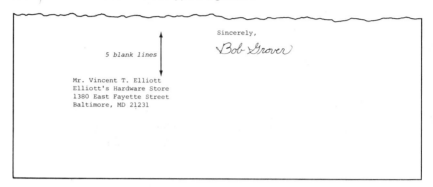

social business letter with typed signature

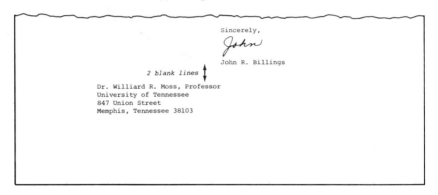

10–9. Attention Line

a. The attention line is used for directing correspondence to an individual or department within a company while still officially addressing the letter to the organization. In the modified block style, the attention line is placed at the left margin, centered, or indented to align with the paragraphs in the letter. Place the attention line a double space below the last line of the inside address. Use all capital letters or a combination of capital and lowercase letters underlined. The word *attention* may be typed with or without a colon following it. An attention line is illustrated in a complete letter in Section 10–2a.

attention line at left margin

```
                    Prescott Industries, Inc.
                    5450 North 37 Street
                    Tampa, Florida 33610

                    ATTENTION:  DR. JAMES MANOS
```

attention line centered

```
                    Phillips Bootery
                    3182 Jackson Street
                    San Francisco, CA 94115

                        Attention Ms. Sydney Corveau, Manager
```

attention line aligned with paragraph indentions

```
                    Freestone Rubber Company
                    1200 North Clybourn Avenue
                    Chicago, Illinois 60610

                        Attention Personnel Director

                    Gentlemen:

                        As accounts supervisor for a major industrial firm
                    in the Detroit area, I have had the opportunity to handle
                    transactions involving wholesalers throughout the country.
```

b. In the full block letter style, the attention line is placed at the left margin a double space below the last line of the inside address. Use all capital letters or a combination of capital and lowercase letters underlined. The word *attention* may or may not be followed by a colon.

10

```
                    SST Products, Inc.
                    840 30th Street
                    Boulder, CO 80303

                    ATTENTION ADJUSTMENT DEPARTMENT
```

c. In the simplified letter style, the attention line is included in the inside address and is typed directly below the organization name. Treat the attention line as you would any other line in the inside address. The word *attention* may or may not be followed by a colon. Some companies who use the modified or full block letter styles also prefer to treat the attention line in this manner and use the same format for the envelope address.

attention line included in inside address

```
Valley Manufacturing Company
Attention:  Ms. Karen Long, Manager
18692 Sierra Bonita Boulevard
San Bernardino, California 91783
```

10–10. Salutation

a. Type the salutation a double space below the last line of the inside address or the attention line, if used. Omit the salutation in the simplified letter style. Begin the salutation at the left margin for all other letter styles. In letters addressed to individuals, use one of the following salutations, depending upon the degree of formality desired. Use a colon after the salutation if mixed punctuation is used; use no punctuation mark if open punctuation is used.

informal salutation

Dear Fred: Dear Elsie:

standard business letter salutation to a single addressee

Dear Mr. Hampton: Dear Miss Baker:

Dear Ms. Harris: Dear Mrs. Chin:

standard business letter salutation to two men

Dear Mr. Hampton and Mr. Cranston:
    or
Dear Messrs. Hampton and Cranston:
    or
Gentlemen:

standard business letter salutation to two women

Dear Ms. Reed and Ms. Johnson:
    or
Dear Mses. Reed and Johnson:

standard business letter salutation to two single women

Dear Miss Frazier and Miss Goodlad:
    or
Dear Misses Frazier and Goodlad:

standard business letter salutation to two married women

Dear Mrs. Koonce and Mrs. O'Donnell:
    or
Dear Mesdames Koonce and O'Donnell:
    or
Mesdames:

10

standard business letter salutation to two persons with different courtesy titles

Dear Ms. Knott and Mr. Wade:

standard salutations to persons with professional titles

Dear Dr. Parsons:

Dear Professor Bredow:

Dear Colonel Jones:

formal salutations for certain government officials and religious dignitaries

Sir:

Excellency:

Reverend Sir:

Your Eminence:

b. If it is not known whether the addressee is a man or a woman, use the courtesy title *Mr.* or the full name of the person without a courtesy title. Use the courtesy title *Ms.* for a woman unless another title is specified by the addressee.

courtesy title "Mr."

Mr. Orolyn Ruenz (Dear Mr. Ruenz:)

Mr. Chris Meister (Dear Mr. Meister:)

Mr. J. T. Weyenberg (Dear Mr. Weyenberg:)

full name without courtesy title

Orolyn Ruenz (Dear Orolyn Ruenz:)

Chris Meister (Dear Chris Meister:)

J. T. Weyenberg (Dear J. T. Weyenberg:)

courtesy title for a woman

Ms. Sharon Reember (Dear Ms. Reember:)

Ms. Laura Nguyen (Dear Ms. Nguyen:)

c. In correspondence addressed to companies, associations, or other groups, use one of the following salutations:

*salutations for groups composed of men and women**

Gentlemen: (most common)

Ladies and Gentlemen:

Gentlemen and Ladies:

---

*While advocated by some persons, the terms *Gentlepersons* and *Gentlepeople* have not yet achieved widespread acceptance in business.

salutation for groups composed entirely of men

Gentlemen:

salutations for groups composed entirely of women

Mesdames:

Ladies:

d. Letters addressed to a firm but directed to the attention of an individual within the company receive the salutation used to open a letter to a group: *Gentlemen, Ladies and Gentlemen, Gentlemen and Ladies, Mesdames,* or *Ladies.* *

```
Grand Avenue Merchants Association
2834 Central Avenue, N.W.
Albuquerque, New Mexico 87105

ATTENTION MR. CORDAY WESTPHAL, PRESIDENT

Ladies and Gentlemen:
```

10–11. Subject Line

a. In the modified block style, begin the subject line at the left margin, center it, or align it with the paragraph indentions. Place it a double space below the salutation. The word *subject* may or may not precede the line. If it is used, it is followed by a colon. Type the subject line in all capital letters or capital and lowercase letters underlined. If an attention line appears in the same letter, select the same typewritten form for both lines.

subject line at left margin

```
Gentlemen:

SUBJECT: HOURLY RATE INCREASE FOR EMPLOYEES
```

two-line subject with book title

```
Gentlemen:

SUBJECT:   ALTERNATE DISTRIBUTION CHANNELS FOR THE SIXTH EDITION
           OF OUR STATISTICS TEXTBOOK, STATISTICAL ANALYSIS
```

---

*See Sections 9–8, 9, and 10 for proper use of formal titles, salutations, and complimentary closings.

subject line centered

```
    Dear Mr. Fanu:

                 ANTICIPATED COST REDUCTIONS
```

subject line aligned with paragraph indention

```
        Dear Mr. Haley:

            Subject:  New Membership Applications

                Several perspective members have indicated an interest
            in joining the women's assistance guild.  These women are
            interested in volunteer work. . . .
```

attention and subject lines in the same letter

```
        Attention Personnel Manager

        Gentlemen:

        Subject:  Insurance Benefits for Regular Employees
```

b. In the full block style, begin the subject line at the left margin a double space below the salutation. The word *Subject:* may or may not precede the line. Type the subject line in all capital letters or capital and lowercase letters underlined. If an attention line appears in the same letter, select the same typewritten form for both lines. The subject line is illustrated in a full block letter in Section 10–1.

```
        ATTENTION ORDER DEPARTMENT

        Gentlemen

        PURCHASE ORDER 14978 DATED JUNE 28, 1985
```

10

217

c. The subject line replaces the salutation in the simplified style. Begin the subject line at the left margin a triple space below the inside address. Type it in all capital letters without the term *subject:*. Triple-space between the subject line and the first line of the body of the letter.

```
Mr. Jack Rochester, Editor
Wadsworth Publishing Company
10 Davis Drive
Belmont, California 94002


PURCHASE OF WORD PROCESSING EQUIPMENT


We appreciate receiving your letter inquiring about our new word processing
equipment.  Our salesman, Bill Retkoe, will be in the area soon, and he
```

d. Insurance and financial institutions, attorneys, and government offices often use the reference *Re:* or *In re:* in place of the word *Subject:*.

IN RE: TOLBERT VS. FEINBERG

Re: Policy 489–6342, Insured Michael T. Block

e. When initiating or replying to correspondence that has a special policy number, order number, or other such reference, include this information in a subject line (as illustrated in Section 10–11a–d) or in a specific reference below and aligned with the date. If references are not printed on the letterhead, use designations such as *When replying, refer to:, File No.:, In reply to:, Re:, Your reference:, Refer to:,* etc. These notations are typed a double space below the date or a double space below an addressee or a mailing notation appearing below the date.

below date

```
                    (Letterhead)



                    June 8, 1985
                                    ◄——————— one blank line
                    In re:   Policy 893621P
```

below addressee or mailing notation

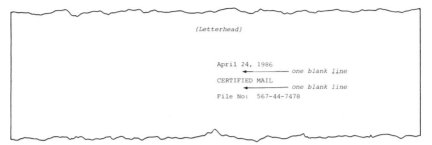

10–12. Body of the Letter

a. For the majority of business letters, single-space paragraphs within the body of the letter and double-space between each paragraph. For the modified block style with blocked paragraphs, the full block style, and the simplified style, begin each paragraph at the left margin. For the modified block style with indented paragraphs, indent the first line of each paragraph from five to ten typewritten spaces. Paragraphs may be either indented or blocked in the social business letter style.

body of letter with blocked paragraphs

```
        Dear Mr. Bedrosian:

        Your Zippo portable radio arrived yesterday, along with
        your explanation of the needed repairs.

        As you suggested, the station tuning mechanism has been
        replaced under the terms of the warranty.  In examining
        your radio, however, our serviceman noticed that the
        speaker had been damaged from an apparent jarring or
        dropping.  The cost and installation of a new speaker
        would be $15.98.
```

10

body of letter with indented paragraphs

```
        Dear Mrs. Russell:

            We enjoyed the presentation on color coordination
        that you gave to Dr. Halpern's secretarial workshop
        last Saturday.  Thank you for sharing your valuable
        ideas with us.

            The class especially appreciated the material you
        gave us on the Wilson color wheel.  Everyone agreed
        that this information will certainly be helpful in
        making wardrobe selections for the office.
```

b. The body of letters consisting of one or two short paragraphs may be double-spaced using the modified block style with indented paragraphs or the social business style with indented paragraphs.

short, one-paragraph letter

Connecticut Life Insurance Company

916 New Britain Avenue   Hartford, Connecticut 06106
Telephone: (203) 761-8211

July 7, 1985

Aaron, Aaron, & Cohen
Attorneys at Law
9324 Wilshire Boulevard
Beverly Hills, CA 90212

Gentlemen:

Our copy of the Bixby contract arrived today.

Thank you for forwarding it so promptly.

Sincerely yours,

Frances T. Archer
General Counsel

rn

10

short, two-paragraph letter

The Ironworks

2520 Eastern Avenue
Las Vegas, NE 89109

September 12, 1986

Mr. Perry Sneed, Manager
Green Thumb Nursery
3619 Kyrene Road
Tempe, Arizona 85282

Dear Mr. Sneed:

Your order for 3 dozen wrought iron pot racks was shipped today.

We appreciate receiving Green Thumb Nursery as a new account. Thank you for your initial order, and we look forward to a pleasant business relationship.

Sincerely,

Lorraine Holloway
Sales Manager

fb

IO

10–13. Complimentary Close

a. The complimentary close selected to end a business letter must comply with the formality of the salutation. Sample salutations as well as suitable complimentary closes are listed here.

Salutation	Complimentary Close
formal correspondence	
Dear Mr. President	Respectfully
His Excellency	Very truly yours
Dear Senator Monroe	Sincerely yours
general business correspondence	
Dear Mr. Siebert	Sincerely yours
Dear Ms. Mendoza	Sincerely
Gentlemen	
informal business correspondence	
Dear Bill	Sincerely yours
Dear Karen	Sincerely
	Cordially yours
	Cordially

10

b. In the modified block styles and the social business style, the complimentary close is typed a double space below the last line of the body. Begin the closing (1) at the page center, (2) five spaces to the left of the page center, or (3) aligned with the longest closing line that has been back-spaced from the right margin.

complimentary close begun at page center

```
As soon as we receive your reply, we will either
repair the radio speaker or return it to you in
the condition it was received.
                              Sincerely,

                      center
```

complimentary close begun five spaces to the left of page center

```
          We would appreciate receiving your check within
          the next week so that we can mark your account
          "paid."
                              Sincerely yours,

                              center
```

complimentary close aligned with longest closing line back-spaced from right margin

```
              Don't delay; act now to receive a copy of Your
              Banking Future--while the supply lasts.

                          Sincerely yours,

                          BARCLAY TRAINING INSTITUTE



                          Morgan Barclay, Director
```

c. In the full block letter style, the complimentary close is typed at the left margin a double space below the last line of the body.

```
              May I please have an opportunity to review my
              qualifications with you?  Just call me at
              349-8211, and I will be pleased to come to
              your office for an interview.

              Sincerely yours,
```

10

d. No complimentary close is used in the simplified letter style.

10–14. Signature Lines

a. Some business firms include the name of the company in the signature lines. In such cases the name of the company is typed in all capital letters a double space below the complimentary close. The first letter of the company name is aligned with the first letter of the complimentary close. Company signature lines are not used in the social and simplified letter styles. Use of the company name in the signature lines is illustrated in a full block letter in Section 10–1.

modified block letter

```
                                    Sincerely yours,

                                    GREENBAY TRAVEL AGENCY
```

full block letter

```
                        Sincerely yours,

                        REDVIEW TILE COMPANY
```

b. In the modified and full block letter styles, begin typing the name and title of the person writing the letter on the fourth blank line below the last line, which will be either the complimentary close or the company name. Align the first letter of the individual's name with the first letter of the company name or the complimentary close.

full block letter

```
                Sincerely,

                        3 blank lines

                Lewis A. List
                Vice President
```

modified block letter

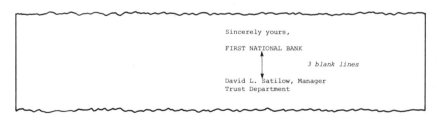

```
                        Sincerely yours,

                        FIRST NATIONAL BANK

                                        3 blank lines

                        David L. Satilow, Manager
                        Trust Department
```

c. Type combinations of names and titles so that balance is achieved in the signature lines. The name and title may appear on the same line or on separate lines, depending upon the length of each item.

single-line typed signature

Philip Ashton, President

two-lined typed signatures

Wilma T. Washington
Manager, Accounting Department

John S. Ross, Manager
Data Processing Department

Horace F. Tavelman
Accounts and Sales Representative

three-line typed signature

Roberta Casselman
Senior Film Editor
Division of Secondary Education

d. Signature lines containing the names of men are not preceded by the courtesy title *Mr.* Signature lines containing the names of women are not preceded by a courtesy title unless the writer prefers to make the distinction of *Ms., Mrs.,* or *Miss.* The title may or may not be placed in parentheses.

signature lines containing name of man

George R. Bezowski
Regional Manager

signature lines containing name of woman

Mary R. Stevens
Regional Manager
or

| Ms. Mary R. Stevens | (Ms.) Mary R. Stevens |
| Regional Manager | Regional Manager |

or

| Miss Mary R. Stevens | (Miss) Mary R. Stevens |
| Regional Manager | Regional Manager |

or

| Mrs. Mary R. Stevens | (Mrs.) Mary R. Stevens |
| Regional Manager | Regional Manager |

10

e. Correspondence that is signed by a person other than the one whose name appears in the typed signature line usually shows the initials of the person signing the letter.

Sincerely yours,

Wallace C. Murietta (lc)
Wallace C. Murietta

f. In the simplified letter style, the entire signature line is typed in all capital letters on a single line. It begins at the left margin on the fifth line below the last line of the message.

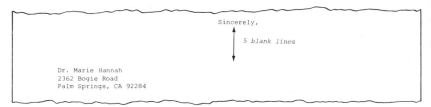

```
      appreciate receiving your reply within the next week.


      JOANN STEVENS, ASSISTANT TO THE VICE PRESIDENT
```

g. In the social business style, the typed signature line may be omitted. If it is included, only the individual's name, not title, is written.

typed signature line omitted

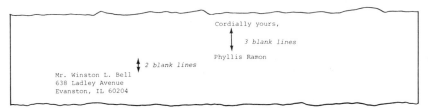

```
                                    Sincerely,

                                        ↑
                                        | 5 blank lines
                                        ↓

      Dr. Marie Hannah
      2362 Bogie Road
      Palm Springs, CA 92284
```

typed signature line included

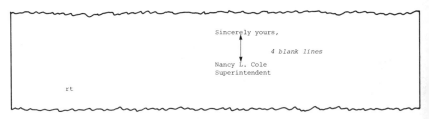

```
                                    Cordially yours,

                                        ↑ 3 blank lines
                                        ↓
                                    Phyllis Ramon
                        ↕ 2 blank lines
      Mr. Winston L. Bell
      638 Ladley Avenue
      Evanston, IL 60204
```

10–15. Reference Initials

a. Except in the social business style, reference initials are used to show who typed the letter. The typist's initials are typed in lowercase letters at the left margin a double space (or single space in longer letters) below the last line in the signature block.

```
                                    Sincerely yours,
                                        ↑
                                        | 4 blank lines
                                        ↓
                                    Nancy L. Cole
                                    Superintendent

      rt
```

10

b. Both the initials of the dictator and the typist may be included in the reference notation. When the person who has signed the letter is the one who dictated it, his or her initials appear in capital letters before the typist's initials. The initials are separated by a colon or a diagonal line.

```
                              Sincerely yours,

                              JAMESTOWN PLUMBING SUPPLY


                              Owen F. Toburg, Manager
          OFT:md
```

c. When correspondence is written by a person other than the one whose signature appears in the typed signature line, the dictator's initials in capital letters or his name precedes the initials of the typist. Separate the initials or name of the dictator from the typist's initials by a colon or a diagonal line.

```
                              Sincerely yours,



                              Stephen T. Pendleton
                              President
          KWashburn/rt
```

10–16. Enclosure or Attachment Notations

a. If any enclosures are included with the letter, an enclosure notation is typed a double space (or single space in longer letters) below the reference initials. Place the enclosure notation at the left margin. Following are some examples of enclosure notations:

Enclosures: Check for $20   2 Enclosures
           Copy of Invoice 1362

Enc.   Enclosure   Enclosures 3   Enc. 2

b. When an enclosure is attached to the letter, the word *Attachment* or its abbreviation may be used in place of the enclosure notation.

Attachments: Application for admission   Attachment
            Student information form

Att.   Att. 2   Attachments 2

10–17. Carbon Copy Notations

a. When carbon copies of correspondence are directed to other individuals, note the distribution at the bottom of the letter. The carbon copy notation is typed a double space (or single space in longer letters) below the enclosure notation, if used; otherwise, a single or double space below the reference initials. However, if a mailing notation follows the reference initials or enclosure notation, the carbon copy notation is typed below it.

Carbon copy notations may include a combination of the courtesy title, name, position, company, and complete address of an individual. Following are some examples of appropriate carbon copy notations:

cc: Mr. John R. Robinson

CC: Francis P. Olsen, President, Wilson Corporation

cc Alice Morley, Credit Clerk

CC Gene Rupe

carbon copy notation following reference initials

carbon copy notation with additional notations

b. In many cases copies are made on a copying machine rather than with carbon paper. Some companies prefer to note these copies in the following ways:

copy: Ms. Janice Welch   c: Sales Department Staff

copies: Bill Acevedo   C: Mrs. Phuong Nguyen
       Donna Mellert

copy to Mr. Bill Hughes, Manager, Hillsdale Paper Corporation

pc: Vernon R. Milliken, M.D.

c. If copies are directed to more than one individual, list the individuals according to rank. If the individuals are equal in rank or ranking is unimportant, alphabetize the list. The list may be typed either vertically or horizontally.

ranked list

cc: R. F. Gillham, President
    T. L. McMillan, Vice President
    F. S. Simpkins, General Manager

alphabetized list

cc Marcus L. Brendero, Adam S. Langville, David M. Silverman

  d. If it is unnecessary or inappropriate for an addressee to know that a copy or copies of the letter are being sent to other individuals, use a blind carbon copy notation.

To do this, position the carriage where you wish to begin typing. Then, disengage the paper release lever and carefully remove the original without disturbing the carbon pack. Return the paper release lever to the lock position and type the blind carbon copy notation so that the first copy and all others will contain the notation.

The blind carbon copy notation may be typed (1) on the seventh line from the top of the page at the left margin or (2) where the regular copy notation normally appears.

bcc: Bruce R. Caldwell

bcc Ms. Miriam Minkoff

10–18. Postscripts

A postscript may be used to add an idea that was inadvertently omitted from the body of the letter or an idea that requires emphasis. The postscript appears in last position; it may be typed or handwritten with or without the abbreviation *P.S.* If typewritten, leave a blank line between the previous letter part and the postscript. If the postscript runs longer than one line, indent subsequent lines under the first word of the message.

10

with abbreviation "P.S."

```
              cr
       Enclosure

       P.S.  Don't miss the opportunity to order Living World Today.
             Remember that this offer ends October 31!
```

```
           cr
       Enc. 2
       P.S.  Don't miss the opportunity to
             order Living World Today.
             Remember that this offer ends
             October 31!
```

without abbreviation "P.S."

```
JNT/rpn
cc:  Ellen Anderson, Kathleene Basil, Sylvia Cohen

Don't miss the opportunity to order Living World Today.  Remember that
this offer ends October 31!
```

```
JNT/rpn

CC Joyce Mason, Leo Sirakides, Agner Streebing
```

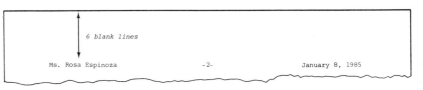

10–19. Second-Page Headings

a. Type headings for second and succeeding pages on plain paper. Begin typing on the seventh line, using the same margins that appear on the first page. These page headings include the name of the addressee, the page number, and the date. Either a horizontal or vertical format may be used.

horizontal format

```
            ↑
            │  6 blank lines
            │
            ↓
Ms. Rosa Espinoza              -2-                January 8, 1985
```

vertical format

```
            ↑
            │  6 blank lines
            │
            ↓
Ms. Rosa Espinoza
Page 2
January 8, 1985
```

b. Before resuming the message, space down three lines from the last line of the heading.

c.   Do not divide the last word on the previous page, and include at least two lines of a new paragraph at the bottom. Likewise, at least two lines from a paragraph need to be carried forward to any additional page. Leave from six to nine blank lines at the bottom of each page, except, of course, for the last one.

d.   The closing lines of a business letter should not be isolated on a continuation page. At least two lines of the message must precede the complimentary close or signature line (when no complimentary close is used).

IO

Punctuation Style

10–20. Mixed Punctuation

The most popular punctuation style for business letters is mixed punctuation. In this format a colon is placed after the salutation and a comma appears after the complimentary close. No other closing punctuation marks are used except those concluding an abbreviation or ones appearing within the body of the letter.

Dickens Crystal, Inc.

1640 Grand Boulevard
Schenectady, New York 12309
Telephone: (518) 872-3100

April 17, 1986

House of Imports, Inc.
5700 Oxford Avenue
Philadelphia, PA 19149

Attention Ms. Jody Stevens, Buyer

Gentlemen:

Our complete line of Dickens crystal is illustrated in the enclosed catalog. As you will note from the full-page color illustrations, its simple design and exquisite workmanship have made Dickens crystal one of the most popular lines in the country.

We appreciate your interest in our products and would be pleased to have the House of Imports carry them. I am sure you would find these fast-selling gift items a profitable addition to your inventory.

A complete list of prices and the terms of sale are included in the back pages of the catalog. You will also note that we serve you by providing a breakage credit up to 5 percent of purchases on merchandise displayed in your store. Just return any broken pieces, and we will replace the merchandise.

We hope that we can add your name to the many retailers throughout the country who represent Dickens crystal. Should you wish to open an account with us, please return the enclosed credit application forms. If you wish to place a c.o.d. order, we can deliver the merchandise within ten days of the receipt of your order.

Let Dickens start earning for you today.

Sincerely,

Edward T. Cowan
Vice President, Marketing

ma
Enclosures

10–21. Open Punctuation

Writers of business letters sometimes use open punctuation. No other closing punctuation marks except those concluding an abbreviation appear after the letter parts. The only other ending punctuation marks are those used within the body of the letter.

Gibraltar Insurance Company of America

916 New Britain Avenue
Hartford, Connecticut 06106
Telephone: (203) 743-1200

June 16, 1985

Lynch & Marten Insurance Agency
16320 San Fernando Mission Boulevard
Sepulveda, California 91343

Gentlemen

SUBJECT: CLAIM NO. AT 6509, INSURED THOMAS A. GLASCO

The claim of your client, Mr. Thomas A. Glasco, for $450 to
replace the golf clubs that were stolen from him in Las Vegas
is covered under his homeowner's policy, No. 19362084.

To process Mr. Glasco's claim, we must have a copy of the
police report filed at the time of the theft. Please contact
the police agency handling the theft report and have them
forward us a copy addressed to my attention.

As soon as we receive the necessary information, Mr. Glasco's
check will be sent to your office.

Sincerely yours

GIBRALTAR INSURANCE COMPANY OF AMERICA

Mariam R. Marsh, Claims Adjuster

fd

cc: Mr. Thomas A. Glasco

10

Addressing Envelopes

10–22. Return Address

a. The return address is usually printed in the upper left corner of the envelope. In large companies the initiator's initials or name and location are typed above the company name and return address. This practice facilitates routing the letter to the sender in case of nondelivery by the post office.

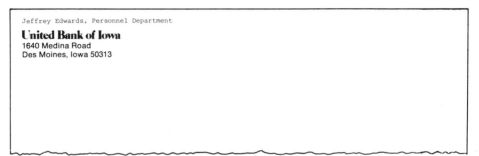

b. On an envelope without a printed return address, type the return address in the upper left corner. Single-space the typewritten lines and include (1) the name of the individual or the individual and the company; (2) the mailing address; and (3) the city, state, and zip code. Begin typing on the third line from the top of the envelope and on the fourth space from the left edge.

10–23. Mailing Address

a. Single-space the mailing address, using at least two lines. The last line of the address should contain the city, state, and zip code. If the envelope is used to mail correspondence, type the address exactly as it appears in the inside address.

b. On legal-sized envelopes, No. 10 envelopes (4½ by 9½ inches), space down to line 12 or 13. Begin typing the address 4 to 4½ inches from the left edge, depending upon the line length of the mailing address.

No. 10 envelope

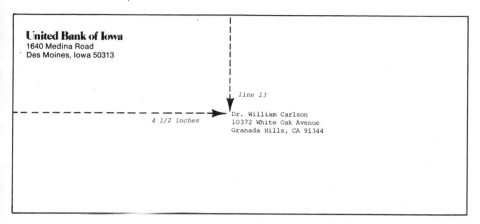

c.   On letter-sized envelopes, No. 6¾ envelopes (3⅝ by 6½ inches), space down to line 11 or 12. Begin typing the mailing address 2 to 2½ inches from the left edge, depending upon the line length of the mailing address.

No. 6¾ envelope

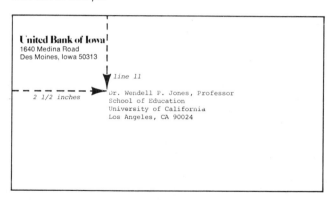

d.   No. 7 (3⅞ by 7½ inches) and No. 5⅛ (4⅝ by 5¹⁵⁄₁₆ inches) envelopes are used less frequently than the standard No. 10 and No. 6¾ envelopes. On No. 7 envelopes space down to line 12; on No. 5⅛ envelopes space down to line 14. Begin typing the mailing address ½ to 1 inch left of the envelope center, depending upon the length of the address lines.

10

No. 7 envelope

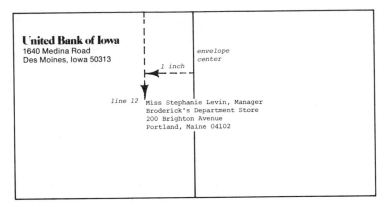

No. 5⅛ envelope

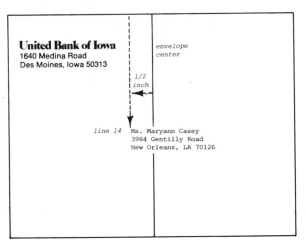

e. Letter-sized manila envelopes (9 by 12 inches or 10 by 12 inches) may have the address typed directly on the envelope or have a label with the address affixed to the envelope. In either case, the first line of the mailing address is placed 6 inches from the top edge of the envelope. Locate the address from 1 to 1½ inches left of the envelope center, depending upon the length of the address lines.

letter-sized manila envelope

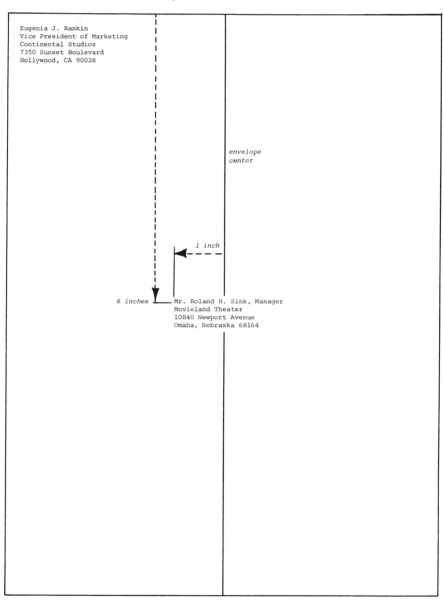

Eugenia J. Rankin
Vice President of Marketing
Continental Studios
7350 Sunset Boulevard
Hollywood, CA 90028

envelope center

1 inch

6 inches

Mr. Roland H. Sink, Manager
Movieland Theater
10840 Newport Avenue
Omaha, Nebraska 68164

10

10–24. Addressee Notations

   a.   Type an attention line or a special notation such as *Personal, Confidential,* or *Please Forward* a double space below the last line of the return address or 1½ inches (line 9 for standard typewriters) from the top edge of the envelope, whichever position is lower. Use capital and lowercase letters and underline the notation. Begin typing ½ inch from the left edge of the envelope.

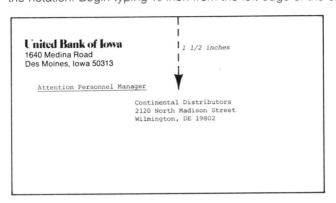

   b.   If an attention line is included with the mailing address instead of typed on a separate line, place it directly below the organizational name.

10–25. Mailing Notations

a. Type mailing notations such as *Airmal* (for foreign destinations), *Express Mail, Special Delivery, Certified Mail,* or *Registered Mail* in all capital letters below the stamp, 1½ inches (line 9 for standard typewriters) from the top edge of the envelope. End the notation ½ inch from the right edge of the envelope.

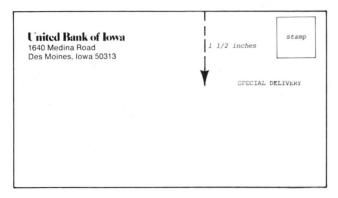

b. If an addressee and a mailing notation appear on the same envelope, type both in all capital letters. The addressee notation appears a double space below the last line of the return address or 1½ inches (line 9 for standard typewriters) from the top edge of the envelope, whichever position is lower. Mailing notations are placed below the stamp, 1½ inches (line 9 for standard typewriters) from the top edge of the envelope.

10–26. Addressing Envelopes for Optical Character Recognition (OCR)

In 1972 the U.S. Postal Service introduced a format for faster handling of mail addressed by plates or computerized equipment (Customer Services Publication 59). This publication was updated in 1975. In a 1974 publication (Customer Services Notice 23-B) and again in a 1977 publication (Customer Services Publication 62), the U.S. Postal Service recommended that a similar addressing format be used for all other mail.

For general business correspondence most companies still prefer the formality of using the same form of address for both the inside address and the envelope. This format is described in Sections 10–23 through 10–25. If a company follows the U.S. Postal Service recommendations, however, use the following guidelines for addressing all mail. These guidelines are based on the information given in Notice 23-B (January 1982) and Notice 221 (September 1983) issued by the U.S. Postal Service.

a. Addresses should be placed at least 1 inch from the left and right edges of the envelope. The bottom of the last line must be at least ⅝ of an inch from the bottom edge of the envelope, and it may be no more than 2¼ inches from the bottom edge. Keep the lower right half of the envelope free of extraneous printing or symbols, and be careful not to type the address at a slant.

b. Use block-style type or print (no italic, script, artistic, foreign-type, or certain dot matrix [in which dots do not touch] styles). The address area on all mail materials should be blocked, with all lines having uniform margins. Typed addresses in all capital letters without punctuation are preferred, but they are required only when the vertical line spacing contains eight lines per inch. Consequently, combinations of capital and lowercase letters may be used for mail addressed on standard typewriters.

c. The bottom line of the address should include the city, state, and zip code in that sequence. Use the two-letter state abbreviation separated from the zip code by one or two spaces. When addressing foreign mail, use the country name as the last line of the address block, placing it a double space below the city line.

bottom line of domestic addresses

DALLAS TX 75201

CY OF INDUSTRY CA 90014

concluding lines of foreign address

WIESBADEN

GERMANY

d. The delivery point for the mail, whether it is a street address or a box number, must be shown on the second line from the bottom, directly above the city, state, and zip code. When apartment numbers, suite numbers, room numbers, etc., are used, they should be placed immediately after the street address on the same line.

When mail is addressed to a box number, place the box number first and then the station name, both on the same line.

street address

8325 W HALBY ST APT 27
DENVER CO 80202

10

box number with station name

PO BOX 3302 JEFFERSON STN
DETROIT MI 48214

e. Attention lines or other information may be shown on any line of the address block above the second line from the bottom. The attention line is usually typed directly following the organization name.

attention line

GENERAL MANUFACTURING COMPANY
ATTEN MR EDWARD R KING
PO BOX 3302 JEFFERSON STN
DETROIT MI 48214

other information

MR H JENKINS MGR
ACCOUNTING DEPT
ABC CORP RM 809
3515 E INDUSTRIAL PKY
CLEVELAND OH 44135

f. Account numbers, subscription numbers, presort codes, etc., may be located within the address block. Such numbers are typed immediately above the addressee's name.

973-81269346
MS ROBERTA W FRANK
8325 W HALBY ST APT 27
DENVER CO 80202

g. The following common address abbreviations may be used for addressing correspondence in conjunction with the U.S. Postal Service recommendations.

10

Apartment	APT	Post Office	PO
Attention	ATTEN	Ridge	RDG
Avenue	AVE	River	RV
Boulevard	BLVD	Road	RD
East	E	Room	RM
Expressway	EXPY	Route	RT
Heights	HTS	Rural	R
Hospital	HOSP	Rural Route	RR
Institute	INST	Shore	SH
Junction	JCT	South	S
Lake	LK	Square	SQ
Lakes	LKS	Station	STA
Lane	LN	Street	ST
Meadows	MDWS	Terrace	TER
North	N	Turnpike	TPKE
Palms	PLMS	Union	UN
Park	PK	View	VW
Parkway	PKY	Village	VLG
Plaza	PLZ	West	W

envelope prepared according to postal service recommendations

M D RIVERTON

PiERᶜE COᒪᒪEGE

6201 Winnetka Avenue, Woodland Hills, California 91371

CONFIDENTIAL

CERTIFIED MAIL
RETURN RECEIPT REQUESTED

DR ALICE T MILLS
SUPVR BUS ED DEPT
CALIF STATE DEPT OF EDUC
51 CAPITOL MALL RM 2142
SACRAMENTO CA 95814

acceptable envelope address format for OCR

M. D. Riverton

PiERᶜE COᒪᒪEGE

6201 Winnetka Avenue, Woodland Hills, California 91371

CONFIDENTIAL

CERTIFIED MAIL
RETURN RECEIPT REQUESTED

Dr. Alice T. Mills, Supervisor
Business Education Department
California State Department of Education
51 Capitol Mall, Room 2142
Sacramento, California 95814

10

10–27. Zip + 4

a. For the faster and more economical processing of mail, the U.S. Postal Service has assigned four additional digits to the present zip code of mailing addresses. This series of four digits is separated from the original zip code with a hyphen.

Northridge, CA 91325-*6213*   Boise, Idaho 83702-*4819*

Jackson, MS 39203-*1073*   Reno, Nevada 89503-*2103*

b. The use of Zip + 4 is optional. Its use on individual mail pieces does not ensure that the item will reach its destination in a shorter time period, but the U.S. Postal Service hopes to reduce its operating costs by encouraging the public to use the nine-digit code. Reduced rates, however, for the use of Zip + 4 can be obtained by bulk mailers.

c. While zip codes may be located through a directory published by the U.S. Postal Service, the additional four digits result in producing too many codes to be published in volumes for public distribution. Zip + 4 National State Directory Computer Tapes are available for computerized mailers. Zip + 4 codes will be provided free of charge by the U.S. Postal Service to those institutions and businesses that do not have access to large-scale computers. Lists from these institutions and businesses will be updated once for each customer, but the U.S. Postal Service may grant exceptions.

Folding and Inserting Correspondence

10–28. No. 10 and No. 7 Envelopes

a. Fold up one third of the page

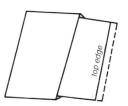

b. Fold down the upper third of the page so that the top edge is approximately ½ inch above the first fold.

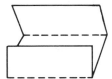 

c. Insert the page so that the top edge is near the top edge of the envelope.

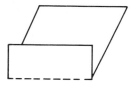

IO

10–29.   No. 6¾ Envelopes

a.   Fold up one half of the page so that the bottom edge is approximately ½ inch below the top edge.

b.   From the right side fold over one third of the page.

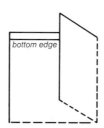

c.   Fold over the second third of the page so that the left edge is approximately ½ inch from the right fold.

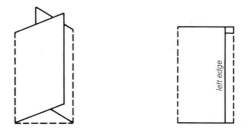

d.   Insert the page so that the left edge is near the top edge of the envelope.

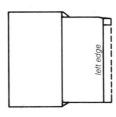

10

10–30. Window Envelopes

a. Fold up one third of the letter.

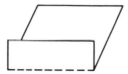

b. Turn the folded letter face down.

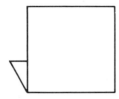

c. Fold down the upper third of the letter so that the top edge meets the first fold.

d. Insert the letter so that the address appears in the window of the envelope.

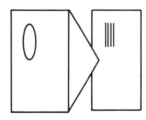

10

Memorandums

0–31. Usage

Letters generally involve the transmission of written messages sent outside an organization. Written messages sent within the organization, however, more often take the form of a memorandum. Memorandums comprise the major medium for internal written communication.

10–32. Preparation

a. Procedures for preparing memorandums vary widely from office to office, but there are a few general guidelines. Most organizations have prepared forms for typing memorandums. These forms contain printed headings for directing the message to the addressee, designating the source of the message, indicating the date written, and identifying the subject content. While the arrangement and design may vary, these basic ingredients are found in most printed memorandum forms.

printed memorandum form

Northridge Manufacturing Company

To:

From:

Date:

Subject:

b. Some companies do not have standardized forms for typing memorandums. In these cases use the following procedures for typing the memorandum on plain paper or paper containing the company letterhead.

(1) A memorandum is usually typed on 8½- by 11-inch paper. For short memorandums, however, a half sheet (8½ by 5½ inches) may be used.

(2) Type the date 2 inches (line 13) from the top of the paper. The date may be typed at the left margin, centered, begun at the center of the page, or back-spaced from the right margin. Double- or triple-space after the date.

(3) Type in all capital letters and double-space the headings *TO:, FROM:,* and *SUBJECT:* at the left margin.

(4) Align the information following the headings two spaces after the *SUBJECT:* heading.

(5) Triple-space after *SUBJECT:* and begin typing the body of the memorandum. Single-space the message, but double-space between paragraphs. For short, one-paragraph memorandums, the body may be double-spaced.

typewritten memorandum

Northridge Manufacturing Company

6201 Winnetka Avenue   Woodland Hills, California 91364
Telephone: (213) 347-0551

April 24, 1986

TO: All Employees

FROM: Donna Anderson, President

SUBJECT: GROUP HEALTH INSURANCE

As you know, Stanley Hutchinson, your employee representative, proposed
to the Board of Directors last January that we consider adopting an
employee group health insurance plan. He pointed out the many medical
expenses incurred by our employees throughout the year and the benefits
a group health insurance policy would have in helping meet some of the
medical expenses resulting from sickness and injuries.

After careful study of several group health insurance policies, the
board concluded that the group policy proposed by the Edgewater
Insurance Company would give the most comprehensive medical coverage
for its cost. As a result, the board voted unanimously to adopt this
policy at no cost to the employees, effective June 1.

Attached is a brochure that explains in detail the health-care services
covered by the Edgewater policy. If you have any questions, please
call Don Curry at Ext. 7351. He will be glad to assist you.

rm

IO

c. When a memorandum contains more than one page, the heading for the second and succeeding pages should have a 1-inch margin from the top edge of the page. Show the name of the person to whom the memorandum is addressed, the page number, and the date. This information may be arranged vertically at the left margin or be placed on a single line with the name beginning at the left margin, the page number centered, and the date back-spaced from the right margin. Triple-space after the heading before continuing the body of the memorandum.

second-page headings

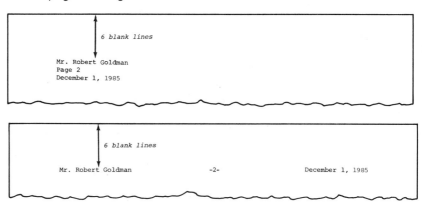

Reports, Manuscripts, and Minutes

Reports, Manuscripts, and, Minutes Solution Finder

Body of the Report or Manuscript

Headings   11–6
    First-degree   11–6
    Fourth-degree   11–6
    Second-degree   11–6
    Third-degree   11–6
Illustration of report pages   11–5
Illustrations   11–9
    Bar charts   11–9c
    Figures   11–9b, c, d
    Line charts   11–9d
    Pie charts   11–9b
    Tables   11–9a
Listings   11–7
    Horizontal   11–7
    Vertical   11–7
Referencing notations   11–8
    Bibliographical notes   11–8b
    Endnotes   11–8c
    Footnotes   11–8a
    New MLA referencing style
        11–8d

End Sections of the Report or Manuscript

Appendix   11–11
Bibliography   11–10

Meeting Minutes   11–12, 13

Preliminary Pages of the Report or Manuscript

Letter of Transmittal   11–2
List of Illustrations   11–4
List of Tables   11–4
Table of Contents   11–3
Title Page 11–1

Typing the Report or Manuscript   11–5

Manuscript typing guide   11–5d
Margins   11–5a, d
Pagination   11–5c
Spacing   11–5b

Reports and Manuscripts

11–1. Title Page

    a.   The title page will generally contain (1) the name or title of the report or manuscript; (2) the name or name and title of the person, group, or organization for whom it was written; (3) the name or name and title of the person or group who wrote it; and (4) the date it was submitted. The contents of a title page are not restricted to these items.

    b.   All lines appearing in the title page should be centered. The title of the report or manuscript should be single-spaced in all capital letters and begun 2 inches (line 13) from the top of the paper. Space equally all other items below the title, allowing a 2-inch bottom margin. An illustration of a title page is on page 252.

11–2. Letter of Transmittal

    a.   The letter of transmittal is used to introduce the reader to the report or manuscript. Although the content of the transmittal letter will depend upon the complexity and scope of the report or manuscript, it should basically tell the reader (1) what the topic is, (2) why the report was written, (3) how the report was compiled (method of research), (4) who worked on it or helped with its development, and (5) what major findings or conclusions resulted (if a synopsis or summary page is not included).

    b.   The letter of transmittal should be friendly and concise, usually concluding with the writer showing appreciation for the opportunity to do the report or manuscript. It appears directly after the title page and may be typed in any acceptable business letter format. An illustration of a letter of transmittal is on page 253.

11–3. Table of Contents

The content and format of a table of contents depend upon the length and complexity of the report or manuscript but are usually prepared in the following way:

    (1)   Type the heading *TABLE OF CONTENTS* or *CONTENTS* in all capital letters centered 2 inches (line 13) from the top edge of the paper.

    (2)   Type *Page* a triple space below the table of contents heading, backspaced from the right margin (set 1¼ inches from the right edge of the paper).

    (3)   Type in all capital letters and double-space the preliminary sections of the report (i.e., letter of transmittal, list of tables, list of interviews). Begin a double space below *Page* and 1¼ inches from the left edge of the paper (the left margin). Although it is paginated, the table of contents is not included in this listing.

(4) Begin the major division heading of the report (i.e., *Chapter, Section, Unit, or Topic*) at the left margin. The major division heading may either appear on the same line as *Page* or be typed a double space below the preliminary parts.

(5) Beginning at the left margin, type the major sections of the report in all capital letters. Those sections of lesser degree should be indented,

title page

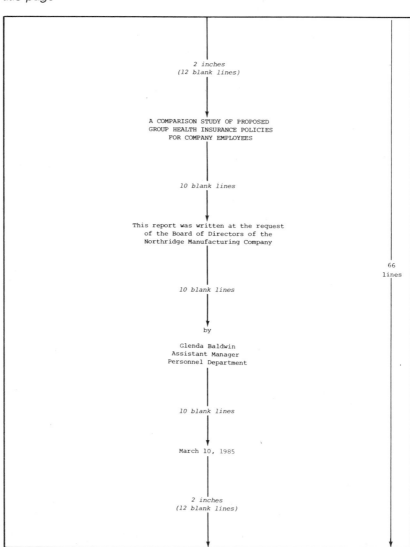

typed in capital and lowercase letters, and placed in the same sequence as they appear in the report.

(6) Major sections of a report may be numbered by using uppercase Roman numerals. Type the longest numeral at the left margin and indent the shorter numerals so the periods following the numerals are aligned.

letter of transmittal

Northridge Manufacturing Company

6201 Winnetka Avenue   Woodland Hills, California 91364
Telephone: (213) 347-0551

March 10, 1985

Mr. Don Washington, President
Northridge Manufacturing Company
402 West Main Street
Northridge, Illinois 60162

Dear Mr. Washington:

As requested by our Board of Directors, here is the report comparing the employee group health insurance policies that were submitted by eight companies.

The policies were compared in the following ways:

1. Company cost per employee
2. Cost to employees
3. Kinds of illnesses and/or injuries covered
4. Hospital, out-patient, and home-visit coverage
5. Total annual health benefits allowed
6. Miscellaneous coverages such as medicines, X rays, physical therapy, private nursing, etc.
7. Family members covered

As shown by the summary table on page 19, the Edgewater policy is superior in all categories except one--company cost per employee. I recommend we select the Edgewater proposal. The additional $3.16 annual cost per employee is relatively small considering the substantial benefits over any one of the other less expensive policies.

Thank you for the opportunity to conduct this study. I appreciate the help and cooperation I received from the employees' representative and from the representatives of the insurance companies.

If you have any questions or if I can be of further help, please let me know.

Sincerely,

Glenda Baldwin, Assistant Manager
Personnel Department

ba

ii

---

(7) Use leaders (a line of alternating periods and spaces) to assist the reader in locating the page number of a particular section, and align vertically the leaders for each section or subsection of the report. While all major headings must have corresponding page numbers, the assignment of page numbers to subheadings appearing in the table of contents is optional. An example of a table of contents appears below.

table of contents

TABLE OF CONTENTS

                                                                        Page

LETTER OF TRANSMITTAL ii

LIST OF TABLES iv

Section

   I.   INTRODUCTION.   1

        Purpose of the Report   1
        Scope of the Report   1
        Organization of the Report.   1

  II.   A COMPARISON OF THE EIGHT HEALTH INSURANCE POLICIES   4

        Company Cost Per Employee   4
        Cost to Employee.   5
        Family Members Covered.   7
        Kinds of Illnesses and/or Injuries Covered.   8
        Hospital, Out-Patient, and Home-Visit Coverage. 11
        Miscellaneous Coverage. 14
        Total Annual Health Benefits Allowed. 15

 III.   SUMMARY, CONCLUSIONS, AND RECOMMENDATIONS 17

        Summary 17
        Conclusions 18
        Recommendations 20

BIBLIOGRAPHY. 23

APPENDIXES. 24

        Appendix A: Copy of the initial letter from the
                     employees' representative requesting
                     health insurance coverage. 25

        Appendix B: Copies of the eight health insurance
                     policies submitted 26

                                  iii

11–4. List of Tables or List of Illustrations

a. When a report or manuscript contains several tables, it is often helpful as a reference to the reader to include a list of tables after the table of contents. The format for the list of tables follows:

(1) Type the heading *LIST OF TABLES* in all capital letters centered 2 inches (line 13) from the top edge of the paper.

(2) Triple-space after the list of tables heading, and type *Table* at the left margin and *Page* back-spaced from the right margin.

(3) Indent three spaces from the left margin and type the number of each table followed by its title in all capital letters. Single-space each title; double-space between titles.

(4) Use leaders (a line of alternating periods and spaces) to assist the reader in locating the page number of a particular table.

list of tables

LIST OF TABLES

Table		Page
1	A COMPARISON OF THE ANNUAL COST PER EMPLOYEE OF HEALTH INSURANCE POLICIES SUBMITTED BY EIGHT COMPANIES	8
2	EMPLOYEE CLAIMS SUBMITTED OVER A TEN-YEAR PERIOD BY THREE COMPANIES OF EQUAL SIZE	14
3	ESTIMATED COST OF HEALTH EXPENSES PER EMPLOYEE OVER A TEN-YEAR PERIOD WITHOUT HEALTH INSURANCE	17
4	A COMPARISON OF THE COST OF GROUP INSURANCE VS. INDIVIDUAL HEALTH POLICIES	25

b. A list of illustrations may be used for a report that contains figures or a combination of tables and figures. For one that contains only figures, use the same format described in the previous section for a list of tables. Change only the title to *LIST OF ILLUSTRATIONS* and the subtitle *Table* to *Figure*. Use the following procedures to format a list of illustrations that contains both tables and figures.

(1) Type the heading *LIST OF ILLUSTRATIONS* in all capital letters centered 2 inches (line 13) from the top edge of the paper.

(2) Triple-space after the list of illustrations heading, and center in capital and lowercase letters underlined the subheading *A. Tables.* Double-space after the subheading, and type *Table* at the left margin and *Page* back-spaced from the right margin.

(3)   Indent three spaces from the left margin, and type the number of each table followed by its title in all capital letters. Use leaders (a line of alternating periods and spaces) to assist the reader in locating the page number. Single-space each title; double-space between titles; and triple-space after the last title.

(4)   Center and underline the subheading *B. Figures* in capital and lowercase letters. Double-space after the subheading, and type *Figure* at the left margin and *Page* back-spaced from the right margin.

(5)   Indent three spaces from the left margin, and type the number of each figure followed by its title in all capital letters. Use leaders to assist the reader in locating the page number. Single-space each title; double-space between titles.

list of illustrations

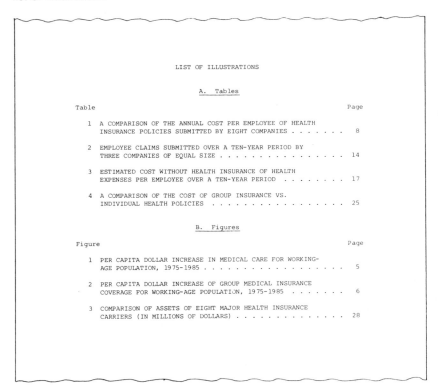

11–5.   Typing the Report or Manuscript

a.   Use the following margins for typing reports and manuscripts:

(1)   A 1¼-inch left and right margin. When the report or manuscript will be bound, allow 1½ inches for the left margin.

(2)　A 1-inch top margin for all pages except those with first-degree headings. Pages with first-degree headings have 2-inch top margins.

(3)　A 1- to 1½-inch bottom margin. Allow at least two lines of a paragraph to appear at the bottom and top of each page, adjusting the bottom margin, if necessary, to accommodate the ending and beginning lines. Avoid single lines that carry over to end a paragraph or section at the top of a new page.

b.　Double-space the body of the report or manuscript. Each paragraph should be indented five to six spaces to offset it clearly from the previous one. Example pages appear on pages 258–259.

c.　Number each page as follows:

(1)　For pages with first-degree headings, either omit the page number or center it on the third line from the bottom of the page.

(2)　For pages without first-degree headings, type the page number on the third line from the page top, ½ inch from the right edge of the paper.

(3)　Number preliminary pages consecutively in lowercase Roman numerals ½ inch from the bottom of the page; horizontally center each number. Count the title as page i even though no number is shown on that page.

d.　Use a manuscript typing guide for setting up reports and manuscripts. Commercially prepared guides made of manila tag that indicate the remaining number of lines on a page are available. Usually these guides are larger than the standard-sized paper so that the remaining number of lines is readily visible.

When commercially prepared typing guides are not available, use an 8½- by 11-inch sheet of paper to design your own. Draw heavy black lines to represent the left and right margins as well as the top and bottom margins. Allow 1-inch top and bottom margins and 1¼-inch left and right margins, unless the manuscript or report is to be bound at the left; then allow a 1½-inch left margin. Draw a heavy black horizontal line 2 inches from the top edge (to signify the location of major headings) and a vertical line directly between the left and right margins (to aid in centering). At the right edge of the paper, number the lines of the last 4 inches of paper. Separate each inch with a 1-inch horizontal line as illustrated in the example on page 260 (to assist in gauging the end of the paper and in setting up footnotes). Finally, type ¼-inch lines where both the top and bottom page numbers are to be located.

body of report

SECTION I

INTRODUCTION

The following report is a comparison of the employees' health insurance policies submitted by eight major insurance companies.

Purpose of the Report

In January Mr. Norman Rittgers, the employees' representative for our company, requested that health insurance be considered by the Board of Directors as a supplement to our wage schedule. Consequently, the board directed the Personnel Department to (1) contact insurance companies to determine what health insurance policies were available and (2) compare the coverages to determine which policy would best meet our employees' health needs for the least cost.

Scope of the Report

The scope of this investigation was limited to the written policies submitted by participating insurance companies. Of the 28 insurance companies contacted, most gave verbal explanations as to what the estimated coverage and cost of a group health insurance policy for our company employees would be. Only eight of these companies, however, submitted written policies for our consideration. These eight policies were then compared in several ways:

body of report, continued

Company Cost Per Employee

Each health insurance package was analyzed to determine the cost per employee to the company. This analysis took into consideration such variables as discount for insuring over a certain number of people and added interest for making payments on a quarterly rather than an annual basis.

Cost to Employees

None of the health insurance packages shown in this report included any cost to employees. Some of the policies did, however, include options whereby individual employees could increase the amount of coverage at their own expense.

Kinds of Illnesses and/or Injuries Covered

Although all the health insurance packages shown in this report covered most of the common types of illnesses and injuries, there were differences in specific coverages. The most common differences appeared in coverage for illnesses resulting in operations, and these differences were analyzed in reaching the final recommendation.

Hospital, Out-Patient, and Home-Visit Coverages

Each health insurance package was analyzed to determine (1) hospital, out-patient, and home-visit coverages and (2) length of time for which the patient was covered under these categories.

Dollar Amounts of Coverage

Information regarding the basic dollar amount of coverage, the deductible amount (if any) for each family member, and the availability of extended coverage was obtained and analyzed for each of the eight

typing guide

1/4-inch line for
top page number location ___

1-inch
margin

major heading line

1 1/4-inch
margin

1 1/4-inch
margin

center line

24
23
22
21
20
19
18
17
16
15
14
13
12
11
10
9
8
7
6
5
4
3
2
1

1-inch
margin

___ 1/4-inch line for bottom
page number location

11–6. Headings

Headings of different degrees are used to signal content in a report or manuscript. An explanation of how each degree heading should be typed follows.

first-degree heading

                    FIRST-DEGREE HEADINGS

      Place a first-degree heading 2 inches from the top edge of the page.

Center the heading and type it in all capital letters. Triple-space

after a first-degree heading.

second-degree heading

              Second-Degree Headings

    A second-degree heading is centered and typed in capital and

lowercase letters with a continuous underline. Triple-space before

a second-degree heading and double-space after it.

third-degree heading

    Third-Degree Headings

      Begin a third-degree heading at the left margin. Use capital and

lowercase letters with a continuous underline. Triple-space before a

third-degree heading and double-space after it.

fourth-degree heading

> Fourth-degree headings. The fourth-degree heading is part of the
> paragraph that follows. Only the first word in the heading is capital-
> ized. The entire heading is underlined and followed by a period.
> Double-space before a fourth-degree heading and begin typing the
> paragraph on the same line as the heading.

11-7. Listings

Both vertical and horizontal lists are often used in letters, memos, reports, and manuscripts. A description and illustration of each type follow.

vertical lists

> Use the following format for listing items vertically:
>
> 1. Introduce a vertical listing with a complete thought.
>
> 2. Double-space before the first item, between items, and after the last item in the list.
>
> 3. Indent the listed items three to five spaces from both the left and the right margins.
>
> 4. Single-space items that are more than one line.
>
> 5. Begin the second and succeeding lines of an item directly under the first word, not under the number.
>
> 6. Capitalize the first word in each listed item.
>
> 7. Use a period after each item only in listings of complete sentences.

horizontal lists

> Use the following format for listing items horizontally: (a) use a colon
> before the list when it is preceded by a complete thought; (b) capitalize
> the first word of each item only when it is a proper noun; and (c) identify
> the listed items by enclosing either letters of numbers in parentheses.

11–8. Methods of Citing Sources

When either direct quotations or other information needs to be cited in a report or manuscript, any one of four methods may be used. These include footnotes, bibliographical notes, endnotes, and the new MLA (Modern Language Association) style of notation.

a. *Footnotes*
Indicate the presence of a footnote by typing a superior (slightly raised) figure after the reference material to be documented. Type the footnote itself at the bottom of the page where the reference notation appears.

(1) Set the footnotes off from the rest of the page by typing a 1½-inch line at the left margin, single-spaced after the last line on the page. Use the underline key, and double-space after typing this line.

(2) Indent five spaces and number each footnote consecutively by typing a superior figure at the beginning of the footnote.

(3) Single-space each footnote, but double-space between footnotes.

(4) Type the name of the author, if any, in a first-name, last-name sequence.

(5) Indicate the complete title of the cited reference. Place the titles of magazine articles, sections of books, and newspaper columns in quotation marks. Underline the titles of books, pamphlets, magazines, and newspapers.

(6) Follow the complete title with the geographical location of the publisher, the name of the publisher, and the date of publication—all enclosed in parentheses. Eliminate the state name from the geographical location when the city is commonly known; otherwise, use the standard state abbreviation with the city name.

(7) Follow the complete title of magazines and newspapers with the date of publication.

(8) Conclude footnotes with reference to the page location of the cited material.

book, one author

```
        ¹Richard R. McCready, Solving Business Problems With Computers,
2nd ed., (Boston:  Kent Publishing Company, 1981), p. 86.
```

book, two authors

```
        ²E. Bryant Phillips and Sylvia Lane, Personal Finance, 3rd ed.,
(New York:  John Wiley & Sons, Inc., 1984), p. 109.
```

paperback book

> [3]Harold J. Leavitt, <u>Managerial Psychology</u>, 3rd ed., (Chicago: University of Chicago Press, 1980), pp. 26-27.

magazine article with author

> [4]John Hoerr, "Why Recovery Isn't Gutting Cooperation in the Workplace," <u>Business Week</u>, 20 February 1984, p. 32.

magazine article without author

> [5]"Electronic Calculators," <u>Changing Times</u>, July 1985, pp. 40-42.

newspaper article with author

> [6]Richard A. Donnelly, "Commodities Corner," <u>Los Angeles Times</u>, 12 December 1985, Sec. 3, p. 8, cols. 3-4.

government publication

> [7]<u>Statistical Abstract of the United States</u>, U.S. Bureau of the Census, (Washington, D.C.: U.S. Government Printing Office, 1980), p. 56.

signed encyclopedia article

> [8]William Austin, "Cromwell, Oliver," <u>Encyclopedia Americana</u>, 9th ed.

unsigned encyclopedia article

> [9]"Pope, Alexander," Encyclopaedia Britannica, 15th ed.

Once a reference has been cited, a shortened form may be used when the same reference is shown again.

> [6]Ibid. (Used when the reference is identical to the one in the preceding footnote. Ibid. means "in the same place.")
>
> [7]Ibid., pp 14-15 (Used when the reference is identical to the one in the preceding footnote except for the page numbers cited.)
>
> [8]Donnelly, loc. cit. (Used when the reference has been cited previously, the same page numbers are being referenced, but intervening footnotes have occurred.)
>
> [9]Leavitt, op. cit., p. 74. (Used when the reference has been cited previously, different page numbers are being referenced, and intervening footnotes have occurred.)

b. *Bibliographical notes*
    References to the bibliography may be used as alternatives to formal footnotes. The reference to the bibliography is shown in parentheses at the end of the cited material by referring first to the number of the reference in the bibliography followed by a colon and the page number(s) of the source. The complete source appears in the bibliography following the body of the paper (see Section 11–10).

bibliographical notes

> . . . Income has risen 16 percent during the last fiscal period. To offset this increased income, however, expenses have risen 21 percent over the same period. (6:10-11)

c. *Endnotes*
    Another alternative to footnotes is endnotes. Endnotes are placed on a separate page at the end of the report or at the end of each chapter in a long report. Use the following format for showing endnotes:

(1) Type the heading *NOTES* in all capital letters centered 2 inches (line 13) from the top edge of the page.

(2) Triple-space after the heading. Single-space each note, but double-space between notes.

(3) Indent the first line of each note five spaces. Number the notes consecutively using arabic numerals followed by a period and two spaces.

(4) Use the same format for endnotes as shown for footnotes in Section 11–8a.

endnotes page

NOTES

1. Michael A. Hitt, R. Dennis Middlemist, and Robert L. Mathis, Effective Management, (St. Paul, Minn.: West Publishing Company, 1983), pp. 42-44.

2. Richard M. Steers and Lyman W. Porter, Motivation and Work Behavior, 2nd ed., (New York: McGraw-Hill Book Company, 1980), p.88.

3. Ibid., p. 109.

4. Jack Halloran, Applied Human Relations, 2nd ed., (Englewood Cliffs, N.J.: Prentice-Hall, Inc., 1982), pp. 9-11.

5. Hitt, op. cit., p. 60.

d. *New MLA referencing style*
Another method for citing sources is the new MLA style. In this style a short description of the source and the pertinent page number(s) appear in parentheses after the information to be cited. Common practice for citing the first reference to a source would include the primary author's last name, a short title, the date for a magazine or newspaper, and page or page numbers, for example (Greenburg, *Human Relations in Business,* 281–85). Ensuing references to the same source may be shortened by including only the source title and appropriate page number(s). A full description of the cited source is given in the bibliography (see Section 11–10).

new MLA referencing style

> According to recent surveys, investment in personal computers
> now ranks as the fifth largest investment item for United States
> corporations. "Between now and 1990," forecasts David Dell, director
> of research at the Diebold Group, New York, "corporations will spend
> between $12 billion and $20 billion on personal computers." (Datamation,
> 15 April 1984, 85). As you can see, the use of personal computers in
> industry does not appear to be a temporary phase.

11–9. Illustrations

Visuals in the form of tables, pie charts, bar charts, or line charts may be used to illustrate data in a report. Where possible, a table or chart should appear on the same page as the narrative describing it. If there is insufficient space on the same page for the table or chart and its explanation, then the illustration should be placed on the following page. A statement such as "As shown by Table 3 on page 9, ..." must be used in the narrative to direct the reader to the illustration. The type of illustration used will vary according to the kind of data presented; suggestions for preparing each type of illustration are presented here.

a. *Tables*
As shown in the illustration on page 269, tables are used to clarify data in an orderly fashion by using a system of headings and columns to present information. Although the length, number of columns, and style of tables will vary according to the type of data presented, use the following general procedures to set up tables.

(1) Leave three blank lines before and after a table if it does not appear on a separate page.

(2) If more than one table appears in the report, number each table consecutively using arabic numerals. Center *Table* and its corresponding number over the proposed position of the table.

(3) Double-space and then center under the table number the title of the table; use all capital letters. If a secondary title is needed, center and use capital and lowercase letters for this subtitle, beginning a double-space below the main title. Triple-space after the final line of either the main title or subtitle.

(4) If columnar headings are used, allow a sufficient number of lines to center these headings attractively and to allow a double space between the last line of the heading and the first line of the data. After

the columns have been typed, center the carriage over the longest line in each column and then back-space once for every two spaces in the column heading. Type each heading in capital and lowercase letters and underline the last line of the heading.

(5) Center tabular columns horizontally using either the back-space or arithmetic method of horizontal centering.

Use these procedures for the back-space method of horizontal centering:

(a) Center the carriage halfway between the left and right margins of the report.

(b) Determine the number of spaces to be left between columns. Leave from 4 to 12 spaces between columns, depending upon the number and length of the columns.

(c) Back-space once for every two spaces between columns and once for every two characters and spaces in the longest line of each column (including the heading). Set the left margin of the typewriter at this point.

(d) Set tabulator stops at the beginning of each column by spacing forward one space for each character and space in the longest line of each column and once for each space to be left between the columns.

Use these procedures for the arithmetic method of horizontal centering:

(a) Count the number of characters and spaces in the longest line of each column (including the heading) plus the total number of spaces to be left between the columns.

(b) Divide the total of step (a) by two. Subtract this number from the center point of the typewriter (51 for elite and 43 for pica). Set the left margin of the typewriter at this point.

(c) Set tabulator stops at the beginning of each column by spacing forward one space for each character and space in the longest line in each column and once for each space to be left between the columns.

(6) A table appearing on a separate page should be centered vertically as well as horizontally.

(a) Count the number of lines and the spaces between the lines to be used in the table.

(b) Subtract the total number of lines and spaces from 66 (the number of lines on standard, 11-inch typing paper).

(c) Divide the difference obtained in step (b) by two. The result is the number of *blank* lines between the top edge of the paper and the table number.

a table

```
                              Table 1

          A COMPARISON OF THE ANNUAL COST PER EMPLOYEE
                OF HEALTH INSURANCE POLICIES
                SUBMITTED BY EIGHT COMPANIES

                        March 1, 1985


    Company            Plan A¹        Plan B²        Plan C³

Chicago General        $375.00        $492.50        $545.00
Concord                 325.00         450.00         510.00
D & P Life              385.50         485.50         585.50
Edgewater               312.50         443.50         513.50
Lincoln                 415.00         500.00         655.00
Morgan                  309.34         440.25         524.15
New Jersey              350.00         475.00         530.00
Western                 405.60         595.00         620.30


    ¹$100,000 maximum coverage
    ²$200,000 maximum coverage
    ³$300,000 maximum coverage
```

b. *Pie charts*

Pie charts are used to illustrate the part of a whole when that whole represents 100 percent of something. To achieve maximum clarity in this visual, do not exceed seven or eight segments in the illustration. Notice how the example pie chart in Figure 1 shown on page 270 follows the guidelines outlined below.

(1) Begin by drawing a circle approximately three blank spaces below the last line of type.

(2) Starting at the 12 o'clock position of the circle and moving clockwise, slice the pie in appropriate wedges, showing the largest wedge first. The remaining wedges may or may not be in descending order of size, but the size of each wedge should be proportional to the percentage of the whole it represents.

(3) If possible, within each wedge identify what it represents and its corresponding percentage. Place this information outside the circle, however, and draw a line to the appropriate wedge if the wedges are too small.

(4) Numbers and titles of pie charts are usually centered in upper- and lowercase letters a triple space below the bottom of the chart. Leave three blank lines before resuming the typewritten narrative.

a pie chart

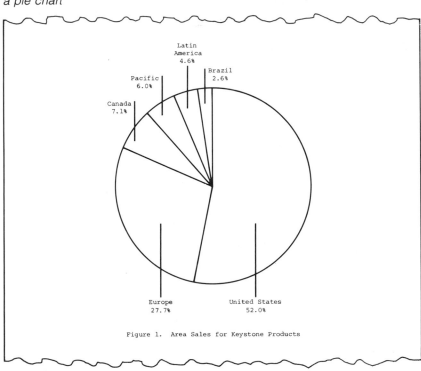

Figure 1. Area Sales for Keystone Products

c. *Bar charts*
Bar charts are used to compare quantities within a class or over a time period. They may be illustrated either horizontally or vertically, as shown in Figures 2 and 3 on pages 271 and 272. Use the following procedures for constructing bar graphs.

(1) Leave three blank lines before and after a bar chart when it interrupts the narrative.

(2) Bar charts require both a vertical axis and a horizontal axis. One axis represents the quantity and the other represents the varying items in the class or the time period over which the quantities are measured.

a horizontal bar chart

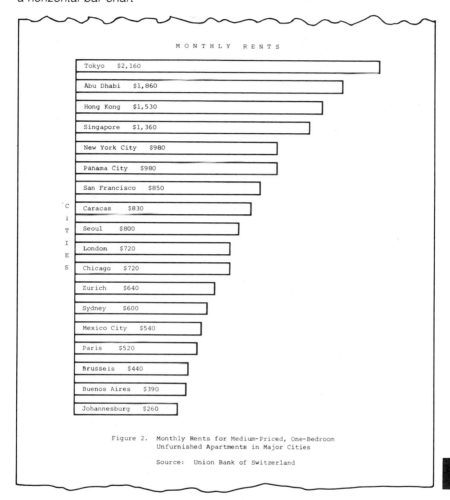

M O N T H L Y   R E N T S

Tokyo	$2,160
Abu Dhabi	$1,860
Hong Kong	$1,530
Singapore	$1,360
New York City	$980
Panama City	$980
San Francisco	$850
Caracas	$830
Seoul	$800
London	$720
Chicago	$720
Zurich	$640
Sydney	$600
Mexico City	$540
Paris	$520
Brussels	$440
Buenos Aires	$390
Johannesburg	$260

C I T I E S

Figure 2. Monthly Rents for Medium-Priced, One-Bedroom
Unfurnished Apartments in Major Cities

Source: Union Bank of Switzerland

a vertical bar chart

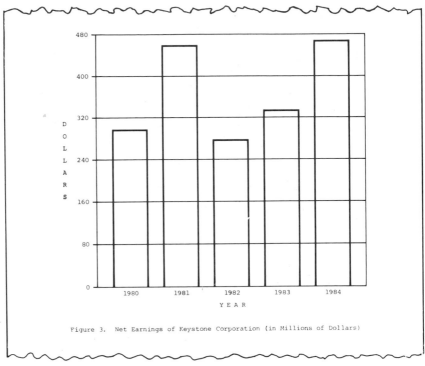

Figure 3.   Net Earnings of Keystone Corporation (in Millions of Dollars)

(3)   In constructing horizontal bar charts, the horizontal axis is used to represent the different quantities for each variable or time period; the vertical axis represents the variable or time period. Each axis must be labeled clearly.

(4)   For vertical bar charts use the vertical axis to represent the different amounts for each variable or time period; use the horizontal axis to represent the variables or time periods. Be sure to label both axes clearly.

(5)   In constructing bar charts, make sure that each bar is of the same width. If the bars are not touching, they should be placed equidistant in the chart.

(6)   Numbers and titles of bar charts are centered a triple space below the last line of the chart. Capitalize the main words in the title.

d.   *Line charts*
Line charts are used to illustrate movement or trends over a time period. They may also be used to compare two or more sets of data over a time period. Study Figure 4 on page 273 to see how the following guidelines were used to construct this line chart.

(1) Leave three blank lines before and after a line chart that interrupts text.

(2) At the left of the line chart, draw a straight vertical line to represent the quantity scale. The bottom of the scale represent the lowest quantity and the top of the scale should represent the largest quantity in question. At the bottom of the vertical line, draw at right angle a horizontal line that extends to the right side of the line chart. This horizontal line represents the time periods encompassed by the chart. Each quantity and time period should be placed equidistant on its respective scale.

a line chart

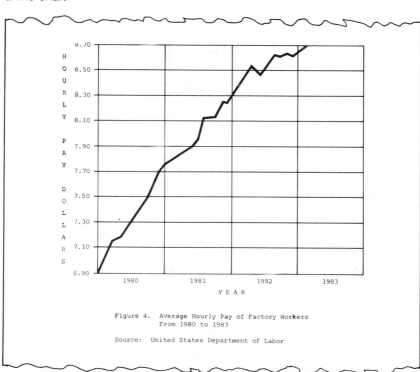

Figure 4.   Average Hourly Pay of Factory Workers
From 1980 to 1983

Source: United States Department of Labor

(3) Quantities should be plotted above the time period indicated and these time periods should be connected. When one or more factors are plotted on the same graph, various colors or line demarcations may be used for each set of data

(4) Numbers and titles of line charts are centered a triple space below the last line contained in the chart, and all main words in the title are capitalized.

11–10. Bibliography

a. The bibliography follows immediately after the body of the report or manuscript and contains all sources cited in the text. Any source material that is not cited but that has contributed directly to the development of a report or manuscript should also be included.

b. List the items in the bibliography alphabetically by authors' last names. Consecutively number each item in the bibliography if the bibliographical form of footnoting is used (Section 11–8b).

(1) Center the heading *BIBLIOGRAPHY* in all capital letters 2 inches (line 13) from the top edge of the page.

(2) Triple-space between the heading and the first reference.

(3) Single-space each reference and double-space between references. If a reference requires more than one line, indent the second and succeeding lines five spaces.

(4) If an author has more than one reference listed, type a five-space underline in place of his or her name, starting with the second reference.

(5) When the author is unknown, alphabetize the reference by title.

(6) End the references for magazines, journals, or other multisource articles with page references.

unsigned encyclopedia article

BIBLIOGRAPHY

"Adams, John." Encyclopedia Britannica. 17th ed. Vol. I. 241-243.

signed encyclopedia article

Austin, William. "Cromwell, Oliver." Encylcopedia Americana.
Vol. III. 1984. 239-240.

newspaper column with author

Donnelly, Richard A. "Commodities Corner." Los Angeles Times,
13 August 1984, Sec. 2, p. 4, cols. 1-2.

magazine article with author

Drew, Sanford. "Multinational Corporations in a Tough New World."
Business Week, 15 August 1984, 52-56.

magazine article without author

"Electronic Games Capture the Market." American News Monthly,
March 1985, 43-53, 97.

article in professional journal with volume number

Humphrey, Susan R. and Gerald F. Donaldson. "Make Your Technical
Report 'People Oriented.'" American Business Communication
Association Bulletin 35 (December 1983): 26-32.

paperback book

Leavitt, Harold J. Managerial Psychology. 3rd ed. Chicago:
University of Chicago Press, 1983.

book, one author

McKittrick, Richard D. Solving Business Problems With Computers.
2nd ed. Boston: Kent Publishing Company, 1986.

book, same author

_____. Personal Computer Applications. Boston: Kent Publishing
Company, 1985.

book, two authors

Phillips, E. Bryant and Sylvia Lane. Personal Finance. 5th ed.
New York: John Wiley & Sons, Inc., 1986.

book, three or more authors

Ruston, Alice R., Justin C. Rosen, and C. R. Terimoto. Principles
of Data Processing. 6th ed. Springfield, Ill.: The Fordney
Press, 1986.

government publication

> Statistical Abstract of the United States. U.S. Bureau of the
> Census. Washington, D.C.: U.S. Government Printing Office,
> 1980.

11–11. Appendix

a. The appendix follows the bibliography and contains material of a supportive nature. This material may include such items as letters, copies of question-naires, maps, contracts, lists, tables, and other documents not shown elsewhere.

b. The appendix may be preceded by a page entitled *APPENDIX* or *APPENDIXES* (typed in all capital letters and centered both horizontally and vertically). This introductory page may also include a list of the items contained in the appendix. In this case both the title and the listing are centered vertically or the title may be typed 2 inches from the top edge of the page with the listing beginning a tripe space thereafter. The material may be numbered with alphabetic letters if more than one item appears in the appendix.

introductory appendix page

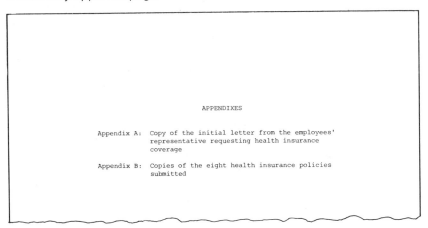

Meeting Minutes

11–12. Purpose and Contents

Minutes are compiled to provide a written record of announcements, reports, significant discussions, and decisions that have taken place during a meeting. While the degree of formality and extent of coverage may vary, the specific information contained in meeting minutes usually includes the following:

(1) Name of group and meeting

(2) Date, place, time meeting called to order, and time of adjournment

(3) Names of persons present (if applicable, names of persons absent)

(4) Disposition of any previous minutes

(5) Announcements

(6) Summary of reports

(7) Motions presented and action taken on motions

(8) Summary of significant discussions

(9) Name and signature of person compiling minutes

11–13. Organization and Format

a. Use 8½- by 11-inch white bond paper, and set the typewriter margins for a 6-inch line. Begin typing and center the name of the group and/or meeting in all capital letters on line 10, leaving a 1½-inch top margin. Double-space down; then center in capital and lowercase letters the date and scheduled time of the meeting. The place where the meeting was held appears another double space below the time and date. This information, too, is centered in capital and lowercase letters. See page 279 for an illustration of the heading format for meeting minutes.

b. A listing of those persons present at the meeting follows the preliminary information. This listing is typed a triple space below the meeting place. Begin the listing with a phrase such as *Members Present:, Managers Present:,* or *Persons Present:.* Then list horizontally or vertically the names of the individuals present at the meeting in the order of their importance or in alphabetical order.

In addition to showing the members or persons in attendance, those regular members absent from a meeting may be noted. In this case a separate listing appears a double space below the listing of members present. It is usually preceded by *Members Absent:, Persons Absent:,* or another such designation. Examples of vertical attendance listings appear on page 279.

c. The initial paragraph of the meeting minutes appears a triple space below the attendance listing or listings. It generally begins with a statement giving the exact time the meeting was called to order and by whom. This statement is usually followed by a discussion of the dispensation of any previous minutes.

d. If there were any announcements, these are listed after the opening paragraph. Use a third-degree heading to introduce the announcements, allowing two blank lines above the heading and one blank line below it. Then number and list each announcement made. If only one announcement occurred, show it in paragraph form without a number.

e. Most meeting agendas are organized according to old business and new business. These two categories may be used for topic headings (use third-degree headings) in presenting the motions and discussions that have taken place during short meetings. However, for lengthy meetings it is easier to locate information in minutes if the topic headings describe concretely the information discussed, reported, or voted upon.

f. Reports presented at a meeting should be noted and in some cases summarized. The amount of information provided in the minutes will depend upon their purpose, formality, and use. Include with the reference to the report contents the name of the person giving the report as well as its disposition.

g. The exact wording of motions must be given in the meeting minutes. Persons making and seconding the motions may be named in the motion statement. Include a brief summary of the discussion for each motion. Finally, indicate whether the motion was passed, defeated, or tabled. The number of yeses, noes, and abstentions for each motion should be recorded.

h. If the meeting is not concluded with a motion for adjournment, the secretary preparing the minutes should indicate the time the meeting was adjourned and by whom. This information is placed in the concluding paragraph of the meeting minutes.

i. The typed signature of the person preparing the minutes usually appears on the fourth line below the concluding paragraph. It may be typed at the left margin or begun at the page center. The preparer's signature is placed directly above the typed signature line.

In formal minutes the complimentary closing *Respectfully submitted* may precede the signature line. In this case the entire signature block simulates the signature block of a business letter. Place *Respectfully submitted* a double space below the concluding paragraph and leave three blank lines for the written signature before typing the preparer's name. This style signature block may also begin at the left margin or page center.

The major components of meeting minutes are illustrated in the following example on pages 279–282.

II

meeting minutes

STATE MUTUAL LIFE INSURANCE COMPANY
MINUTES, MONTHLY MEETING OF HOME OFFICE DEPARTMENT MANAGERS

April 12, 1985, 2 p.m.

Room 625, State Mutual Building

Officers Present: Louise Brannon, Agency Accounting
Robert Childress, Legal
Anthony Coletta, Claims
Phillip Horowitz, Personnel
Vern Knudsen, Vice President, Operations
Gaylord Martin, Policy Issue
Robert Miles, Actuarial
Wayne Nugent, Data Processing
Doris Penrose, Investments
George Ross, Treasurer
Dwayne Schramm, Central Records
Fred Wyatt, Finance

Officers Absent: Neil Tsutsui, Group Insurance
Diane Zimmerman, Public Relations

The meeting was called to order at 2:05 p.m. by Vern Knudsen. Minutes from the previous meeting held on March 15, 1985, were read and approved.

Announcements

1. Effective June 1 Anthony Coletta will assume the position of administrative assistant to the vice president of operations. This new position has been created because of the increased workload within the last three years in the home office. John Davis, the present assistant manager of the Claims Department, will assume the role of manager on June 1.

2. Two new State Mutual agencies will be opened on July 1. The Chadwick Agency (located in Fort Worth, Texas) will become Agency No. 137, and Graff & Phelps (located in Salem, Oregon) will become Agency No. 138. Marian Rosetti in Agency Accounting will coordinate the opening of these agencies.

3. The employee cafeteria will be closed from May 17 to May 26 for renovation. It will be enlarged to accommodate 100 more people. This new renovation should help to ease the overcrowded conditions we are now experiencing. Barring any unforeseen circumstances, the cafeteria will reopen on May 27. All department managers were requested to inform their staffs of this temporary shutdown.

meeting minutes, continued

2

Financial Report for Period Ending March 31, 1985

George Ross distributed copies of the financial report for the first
quarter of 1985. He pointed out that overall life insurance sales
had increased 8 percent over the same period for last year. The
greatest increase in sales had taken place in the Southwest, mainly
in New Mexico, Nevada, and Arizona. Sharp declines, however, were
noticeable in the Eastern Seaboard area; namely in states such as
Connecticut, Rhode Island, and Massachusetts. These regional differences
have not been so apparent in previous years.

Claims for the period from January 1 to March 31, 1985, increased
6 percent over the same period for last year. This rise is within the
statistical projection based on sales and volume presently carried by
the company.

Income from other sources has risen 4 percent over the last comparable
period. Operational expenses during the first quarter have increased
12 percent, mainly because of rising prices due to inflationary factors.
Net operations income, consequently, for this period has decreased .5
percent over the same period for last year.

Progress Report, Central Records Microfilm Conversion

Dwayne Schramm reported that a committee had been formed of representatives
from those departments that use or store records in the Central Filing
Department. These representatives met to discuss which records could be
placed on microfilm and which should be retained in their present form.
Those records referred to frequently and those that are current (within
the last year) will be retained in their original form. The committee
also decided that records dated prior to May 31, 1984, needed to be
analyzed individually to determine which ones should be microfilmed.

Each department was given a list of records presently maintained by the
Central Filing Department. Departmental representatives were asked to
survey their respective departments to determine which of the listed
records were used. The representative is to note those records used, the
purpose and frequency of their use, and by whom they are used. On the
basis of this information, individual decisions will be made by subcom-
mittees to determine the precise time line for microfilming each kind of
stored data.

Microfilm readers must be purchased, and the cost of these readers is $738
each. Viewers may be placed in individual departments or centralized in
the Central Filing Department. Capital investment in equipment would be
reduced considerably by centralizing the viewers in the Central Filing
Department; however, additional time would be lost by persons using the
equipment if the viewers were isolated here.

Louise Brannon moved that a microfilm viewer be placed in those departments
that frequently use microfilm records and have the space in which to
place the viewer. Viewers should also be placed in the Central Filing
Department for those departments that do not need direct access to them.
The motion was seconded by Robert Miles.

meeting minutes, continued

3

In the discussion that followed, most of the department managers agreed that too much time would be lost in traveling to and from the Central Filing Department if viewers were placed exclusively in that area. It was pointed out, however, by other managers that the additional cost associated with purchasing viewers for individual departments would be an excessive capital outlay. Also, the premium space required for each viewer is not always available. The motion was passed 8-2-0.

Revision of Employee Dress Code

Phillip Horowitz reported that a number of employees are concerned about our present dress code. They believe the present code reflects last decade's styles and has not been updated to incorporate new fashion trends. Basically, these employees feel that smartly styled, well-pressed jeans should be permissible attire for women employees.

At present the only pants allowed for women employees are pantsuits with matching jackets. These employees maintain that pantsuits are no longer stylish and are sold in few stores. Jeans with coordinating tops have replaced the traditional pantsuit they argue, and therefore the present dress policy should be revised.

The department managers expressed concern over revising the dress standards to include jeans. Many indicated that jeans are not appropriate in an office situation because they are too casual. Also, it would be difficult to control their condition, i.e., fadedness and wrinkled appearance.

Gaylord Martin moved that the present dress policy be retained and that jeans not be allowed as acceptable attire for women employees. Doris Penrose seconded the motion. The motion was passed 10-0-0.

Employment Freeze on Office Personnel

Phillip Horowitz reported that in February the company established a Word Processing Group to assist all departments with their written communications. Eight clerical employees plus a supervisor were hired to staff this group, which was placed under the direction of the Data Processing Department.

At the time the group was established, it was decided that the new positions created would be offset by the natural attrition of clerical persons within the company. In the cases where this natural attrition has occurred, the departments losing the positions have indicated that their function is being impaired. Phillip Horowitz recommended that this body appoint a committee to study the problem and determine if and where clerical positions may be eliminated or consolidated.

Wayne Nugent moved that a five-person committee be formed to study the work flow generated to the Word Processing Group and the effect of this delegation on the workloads in all affected departments. The committee is to be charged with making recommendations regarding the staff size

II

meeting minutes, continued

4

of the Word Processing Group and the staff size of clerical employees in other departments. The motion was seconded by Fred Wyatt. It was passed 7-2-1.

Vern Knudsen appointed the following persons to the committee: Louise Brannon, Phillip Horowitz, Gaylord Martin, Neil Tsutsui, and Fred Wyatt.

The meeting was adjourned at 4:15 p.m. by Vern Knudsen. The next meeting of the department managers is scheduled for May 10 at 2 p.m. in Conference Room 621-A.

Respectfully submitted,

Chris Weiser, Secretary

kc

Mail, Telegrams, and Cablegrams

12

12

Mail, Telegrams, and Cablegrams Solution Finder

Cablegrams

Charges for cablegrams 12–15
Classes of cablegrams 12–14
   Full rate 12–14a
   Letter rate 12–14b

Mail

Domestic mail classes
  First class 12–2
    Business-reply mail 12–2b
    Mailgram service 12–2c,
     12–12c
    Priority mail 12–2a
  Fourth class (parcel post)
   12–5
    Bound printed matter
     rate 12–5d
    Bulk rate 12–5a
    Library rate 12–5c
    Special rate 12–5b
  Mixed classes 12–6
  Parcel post 12–5
  Second class 12–3
  Third class 12–4
Express mail 12–1
  Next-day service 12–1a
  Same-day airport service
   12–1b

Insured mail 12–9
  C.o.d. 12–9c
  Fourth class 12–9b
  Postal money orders 12–9d
  Registered 12–9a
  Third class 12–9b
Proof of mailing and delivery
  12–10
  Certificate of mailing 12–10b
  Certified mail 12–10a
  Return receipts 12–10a
Special delivery 12–7
Special handling 12–8
United Parcel Service (UPS)
  12–11

Telegrams

Classes of telegrams 12–12
  Full rate 12–12a
  Mailgram 12–2c, 12–12c
  Overnight 12–12b
Sending telegrams 12–13
  Charges 12–13b
  Wording 12–13a

12

Domestic Mail Classes and Services

There are a number of mail classes and services. Each varies in (1) the type, weight, and size of the matter that may be sent; (2) the cost of mailing; and (3) the priority in which the mail will be delivered.

12–1. Express-Mail Service

Express mail receives the highest priority handling in terms of destination arrival time. It is a high-speed intercity delivery system geared to the special needs of business and industry for the fast transfer of letters, documents, or merchandise. All domestic shipments sent by express mail are insured up to $500 (negotiable items are limited to $15) against loss or damage at no extra charge. For an extra charge return receipts are available.

a. *Express-mail next-day service* is available in major cities throughout the United States, and each city has its list of other cities to which it guarantees this service. Express mail may be sent post office to post office or post office to addressee. This means that mail brought in by the local cut off time or deposited in an express-mail collection box by the posted time will be delivered to its destination city by the next day. The mailing will be delivered to the addressee by 3 p.m. the next day (weekends and holidays included), or it can be picked up at its destination post office by 10 a.m. of the next business day the office is open for regular business.

b. *Express-mail same-day airport service* provides service between major airports within the United States. Items are sent on the first available flight to the destination airport, to be picked up by the addressee upon arrival.

12–2. First-Class Mail

The following examples are always considered first-class mail if the weight is 12 ounces or less:

(1) Handwritten and typewritten messages, including identical copies, but excluding computer material

(2) Bills and statements of account

(3) Notebooks or account books containing handwritten or typewritten entries

(4) Postcards and postal cards

(5) Canceled and uncanceled checks

(6) Printed forms filled out in writing

(7) Printed price lists with written or typed changes

(8) Greeting cards, sealed and not marked "Third Class"

(9) Business-reply mail

(10) Any other type of mail weighing 12 ounces or less sent as first class at the option of the mailer

12

First-class mail pieces that are ¼ inch or less in thickness are nonmailable unless they are (1) rectangularly shaped, (2) at least 3½ inches high, (3) at least 5 inches long, and (4) at least .007 inch thick. Items such as keys and identification devices are not subject to the minimums except the .007-inch thickness minimum.

A surcharge is assessed on each piece of first-class mail weighing one ounce or less if it exceeds any one of the following criteria: (1) A height of 6⅛ inches, (2) a length of 11½ inches, (3) a thickness of ¼ inch. In addition, the surcharge is assessed if the length is less than 1.3 times or more than 2.5 times the height.

For oversized materials (larger than legal-sized envelopes), use the white envelopes with a green diamond border. This border automatically indicates that these materials are to be sent first class. These envelopes are available for purchase at the post office.

a. *Priority mail* is first-class mail weighing over 12 ounces. The rate schedule is determined by weight and zone, but the delivery time is faster than for fourth-class mail. The maximum weight for priority mail is 70 pounds, and its dimensions are limited to 108 inches in length and girth combined, a maximum standard set for all mailings handled by the U.S. Postal Service.

b. *Business-reply mail* is a first-class mail service supplied to mailers who want to encourage responses by paying the postage. The mailer guarantees that he will pay the postage plus a fee for all replies returned to him.

c. *Mailgram service* provides next-business-day delivery for messages to addresses in the United States and Canada. By taking directly or telephoning a message to a Western Union office, the sender can ensure delivery with the next business day's mail. The message is transmitted electronically to a post office near its destination from where it is placed in a special envelope and delivered with regular mail. (See also Section 12–12c.)

12–3. Second-Class Mail

12

Second-class mail is used primarily by newspaper and magazine publishers to mail publications at a special bulk rate. A publisher mails at the second-class rate on the basis of a permit obtained from the post office.

Publications must be issued at least four times annually to qualify for the special bulk rate. The regular second-class postage rate varies depending upon the frequency of publication, the advertising portion of the publication's content, and whether or not the publication is mailed to addresses within the county of publication.

A mailer other than a publisher can mail individual, complete copies of a publication by paying what is called a "transient rate." This mail should be marked "Second Class."

12–4. Third-Class Mail

Third-class mail consists of circulars, booklets, catalogs, and other printed materials such as newsletters or proof sheets. It also includes merchandise, farm and factory products, photographs, keys, and printed drawings.

Each piece of third-class mail is limited in weight to fewer than 16 ounces. The same material weighing 16 ounces or more is classified as fourth-class, or parcel post, mail.

Third-class mail may be sent at a single-piece rate or at a bulk rate. Additionally, certain nonprofit organizations qualify for a special third-class bulk postage rate. Keys and identification devices may be mailed for still another rate.

12–5. Fourth-Class Mail (Parcel Post)

Fourth-class mail is generally called "parcel post." The minimum weight for fourth-class mail is 16 ounces per item; mail under this weight is sent at third-class rates. Maximum weight and size restrictions are 70 pounds and 108 inches combined length and girth. Postage rates for this class are determined by the weight of the parcel and the distance from its point of origin to its destination.

a. A *bulk-rate fourth-class mail* is available for sending 300 or more pieces that are identical in weight.

b. A *special fourth-class rate* may be used for mailing books, certain kinds of films, printed music, printed test materials, sound recordings, play scripts, manuscripts, educational reference charts, and medical information. Books containing advertising for merchandise, telephone directories, corporation reports, house organs, and periodicals do not qualify for this special rate.

All items mailed with the *special fourth-class rate* should be marked as such. In addition, note a description of the item, such as "Books," "Sound Recordings," "Films," etc.

c. *Library rate* is used for certain kinds of materials that are loaned, exchanged between, or mailed by or to schools, colleges, libraries, museums, or certain nonprofit organizations. Materials include books, printed music, academic theses, sound recordings, etc. All items must be marked "Library Rate."

d. Securely bound advertising, promotional, directory, or educational material may be sent at a special *bound printed matter rate*. Material may not have the nature of personal correspondence and cannot be a book.

12

12–6. Mixed Classes

A first-class letter may be attached to or enclosed in a parcel sent by a lower class. If the letter is attached to the parcel, each item should have separate postage. If the letter is enclosed in the package, "First-Class Mail Enclosed" should be marked on the outside of the parcel, along with the correct postage affixed for both items.

12-7. Special Delivery

This special service is used to hasten the delivery of a mailed item. It provides for delivery, even on Sundays and holidays, during prescribed hours that extend beyond the hours for delivery of ordinary mail. The purchase of special delivery does not always mean the article will be delivered by messenger. Special delivery may be delivered by a regular carrier if it is available before the carrier departs for morning deliveries. While sending an item special delivery virtually ensures delivery on the day received at that post office, it does not necessarily speed up the transportation time to that point from its origin.

This service is available to all customers served by city carriers and to other customers within a one-mile delivery radius of the delivery post office. All classes of mail except bulk third class may be sent special delivery for an additional fee.

12-8. Special Handling

A special handling service is provided for preferential handling in the dispatch and transportation of third- and fourth-class mail. A special handling fee must be paid on parcels that take special care, such as baby chicks, baby alligators, etc.

12-9. Insured Mail

a. *Registered mail* may be used only for first-class mail, priority mail, or c.o.d. parcels with prepaid postage at the first-class mail rate. Except for c.o.d. parcels, each mailing may be insured for its full value up to $25,000; c.o.d. service is limited, however, to items valued at a maximum of $400. Registered mail may not be deposited in collection boxes since a receipt must be issued at the point of mailing.

This service is offered for the protection of valuable papers, jewelry, and other items of value. The registry fees, in addition to first-class mail or priority-mail postage, are scaled according to the declared value of the mail. For an additional fee a mailer can obtain a return receipt and/or restrict to whom the mail is delivered.

b. *Insured mail* consists of third- and fourth-class mail items insured for protection against loss or damage. This service is also available for merchandise that is mailed at the priority-mail or first-class mail rates.

Unnumbered or minimum-fee insured mail is delivered as ordinary parcel mail, and the limit of indemnity is $20. Numbered insured mail insures mail valued at over $20, with a maximum indemnity of $400. A receipt is given to the mailer

12

at the time of mailing, and a signature is required upon delivery. For insured mail of more than $20 declared value, a return receipt and/or restricted delivery can be requested.

c. *C.o.d.* (collect on delivery) may be used for first-, third-, and fourth-class mail. When the mail is delivered, the addressee pays the amount due for the contents. The addressee may also be required to pay the postage and the c.o.d. fee, depending upon the prior agreement between the sender and receiver.

The c.o.d. fee includes insurance against loss, damage, or failure to receive the amount collected from the addressee. The maximum amount that can be collected for one item is $400. The goods shipped must have been ordered by the addressee, and the sender agrees to pay any return postage unless specified differently on the mail.

Senders of c.o.d. mail may (1) request restricted delivery, (2) alter the charges or direct delivery to a different address, or (3) register first-class mail.

d. *Postal money orders* provide for sending money through the mail safely. If they are lost or stolen, they can be replaced. Domestic money orders up to $500 may be purchased and redeemed at any post office. Mailers may obtain copies of paid money orders for two years after the date they have been paid.

2–10. Proof of Mailing and Delivery

The U.S. Postal Service provides ways in which proof may be obtained that an item has been mailed or received. These optional services are available to any mailer.

a. *Certified mail* is used for first-class and priority-mail items that have no money value since there is no insurance feature with this service. Certified mail provides for a record of delivery to be maintained by the post office from which the item was delivered. The carrier delivering certified mail obtains a signature from the addressee on a receipt form that is kept for two years. In this way the sender can prove that items were received by the addressee. Proof of delivery may be obtained at a later time during the two-year period following delivery.

Return receipts showing to whom, when, and where the item was delivered may be obtained for an additional charge for mail that is registered, insured, certified, or sent c.o.d. During the two-year period after delivery, proof of delivery may be obtained from the post office from which the item was delivered.

12

Certified mail may be deposited in a collection box if the mailer has attached a "Certified" sticker and the appropriate postage and fees.

b. A *certificate of mailing* for any item may be obtained from the sender's post office. Unlike certified mail, however, the post office does not keep any record of the certificate issued or of the delivery of the item. It only provides proof that the item was mailed.

12–11. United Parcel Service

United Parcel Service (commonly called UPS) is a commercial company that is widely used throughout the United States to deliver small packages. Packages may be sent by truck or air, and customers may either take their packages to their local UPS office or have UPS pick up the packages at their home or place of business for a small extra charge. Packages sent by UPS may not weigh over 70 pounds or be over 108 inches in length and girth combined. All packages are automatically insured for up to $100.

Telegrams

12–12. Classes of Telegrams

a. *Full-rate telegrams* have first priority over other messages and are available for sending and phone delivery 24 hours a day, including Sundays and holidays. There is a base charge for up to 15 words, which does not include the recipient's address or telephone number and the sender's name and title. An additional charge is assessed for each word over the 15-word base.

The telegram provides two basic types of delivery—messenger and telephone. Messenger delivery is guaranteed within five hours, but this type of delivery is not available everywhere or at all times. Phone delivery is guaranteed within two hours, and a written copy of the message can be sent by mail.

A variety of special options are available at varying costs. If the sender wants a written record of the telegram as it was transmitted, a confirmation copy can be sent. If the sender wishes a report of delivery, whether by telephone or messenger, a telegram or mailgram giving the time and date the message was delivered can be sent to the originator. The sender may also avail himself or herself of personal delivery only or alternate delivery services. In addition, two other services offer financial protection in situations where a telegram has a monetary value of $500 or more.

b. *Overnight telegrams* are priced lower than the full-rate telegram. Messages can be sent at any time up until midnight and delivery is guaranteed by 2 p.m. the following day. There is a base charge for up to 50 words and an additional charge for each word over the 50-word base. The local Western Union office will telephone the message to the recipient unless the sender pays an extra charge to have a written message delivered.

c. *Mailgrams* are sent by Western Union to the local post office of the addressee for delivery with the next day's mail. A mailgram may be sent by telephone 24 hours a day, seven days a week. There is a base charge for up to 50 words and an additional charge for each 50 words or fewer over the base. Mailgram messages are eligible for the following services at an additional cost: (1) multiple-address messages, (2) business-reply messages, (3) confirmation copies of messages relayed, and (4) signed receipts acknowledging delivery.

12

12–13. Sending Telegrams

Although telegraph messages that are telephoned to a Western Union office will be accepted, the chance of the message being misunderstood can be lessened if the message is typed on either an official telegraph form or on regular paper and delivered to the telegraph office. Official telegraph forms can be readily obtained at any Western Union office. The following are some suggestions in preparing telegraph messages.

a. Use only those words that are necessary to make the message clear. Unnecessary words such as *I, you, the, a, and,* etc., should be omitted. For example, it is better to write, "Arriving United Flight 424 LAX 8 p.m., Jan 24. Please meet.," than "I will arrive on United Flight 424 at Los Angeles International Airport at 8 p.m. on Friday, January 24. I would appreciate your meeting me."

b. The wording of a telegram is charged as follows:

(1) Regular words used in a standard dictionary are counted as one word regardless of length. Other words are counted as one word for every five letters.

(2) Proper names are counted as they are written (New Mexico, 2 words; Van Der Meter, 3 words).

(3) Abbreviations, code words, and groups of figures are counted as one word for each five characters.

(4) Punctuation marks are not counted.

Cablegrams

Cablegrams are similar to telegrams, except they are sent outside the continental United States.

2–14. Classes of Cablegrams

a. *Full rate* is the fastest and, consequently, the most expensive type of cablegram. Either ordinary words, coded words, or a combination of the two may be used. There is a base charge for up to 7 words, but there is no charge for specifying that the cablegram is to be sent full rate (FR).

b. *Letter-rate* cablegrams are normally delivered the day after they are sent. There is a base charge for up to 22 words, including the letter-rate symbol (LR), which is counted as one word. Only ordinary words may be used at this rate.

2–15. Charges for Cablegrams

The wording of a cablegram is charged as follows:

(1) A word of 15 letters or more counts as two words.

12

(2) Each word in the address counts as one word except for the name of the country where the cablegram is to be sent.

(3) Each word in the signature counts as one word.

(4) Initials with spaces between are counted as separated words.

(5) Abbreviations, code words, and groups of figures are counted as one word for each five characters.

12

Appendix A
Terminology Used
in the Automated Office

A

Terminology Used in the Automated Office Solution Finder

All entries in this appendix are in alphabetical order.

Acoustic coupler
A special type of modem that allows a standard telephone headset to be attached to a computer terminal for the transmission of data from one computer to another or from one terminal to another.

Address
That portion of a computer instruction that references the location within the computer of the data to be processed.

American Standard Code for Information Interchange (ASCII)
A seven-bit code widely used in data communications.

Assembler language
A symbolic programming language that uses symbols and abbreviations to represent the function to be performed.

Asynchronous transmissions
The transmission of a single character at a time preceded by a start bit and followed by a stop bit.

Auxiliary storage
Storage by using usually either magnetic tapes or disks to supplement the working storage of the computer

Batch
A collection of data that can be processed during one operation.

BASIC
A programming language now commonly used on personal and small business computers.

Binary numbering system
A numbering system with a base 2 that uses either 0 or 1 to represent values.

Bit
A binary digit (either 0 or 1).

Boilerplate
A series of standardized paragraphs that can be arranged in a specific order as needed to produce a document.

Byte
A group of eight bits used as a measure of the storage capacity of computers, e.g., 32K = 32,000 bytes of data that can be stored in memory. One byte may be equated to a single letter or space.

Cathode ray tube (CRT) terminal
A computer terminal or word processor with a television-like screen for displaying data.

Central processing unit
Components of word processing and computer systems that cause processing to occur by controlling the input and output functions.

Character printer
A printer that prints like a typewriter one character at a time. [cf. line printer]

COBOL
A common business-oriented computer language.

Communicating computer or word processor
A computer or word processor that is connected through a modem to other computers and/or word processors so that data may be exchanged between or among the terminals.

Cursor
A mark on a display screen that shows where the next character will appear.

Daisy wheel
A circular print wheel used in high-speed printers.

Data base
A collection of interrelated data that may be accessed in a nonsequential manner.

Dedicated
A piece of computer equipment used for only one type of work, such as word processing.

Default
A setting in a computer that is automatically implemented if no other choice is designated.

Disk or diskette
A magnetic storage device on which information can be stored. Disks may be either "floppy" or "hard." "Hard" disks have much more storage capacity than do "floppy" disks.

Documentation
A set of instructions that enables an operator to run a computer or program.

Dot matrix
A type of high-speed printer that employs closely spaced dots to form a printed character. [cf. letter-quality printer]

Dual-density disk
A magnetic storage disk that has twice the storage capacity of a standard disk of the same size.

Dual pitch
Capacity to print two type sizes, usually 10 pitch and 12 pitch.

Electronic mail
The transmission of documents from one point to another through the use of telephone lines, satellite, microwaves, or direct cable.

Execute
A command on a computer to carry out an instruction, perform an operation, or run a program.

Facsimile
A device used to scan and transmit copies of documents electronically, specifically charts, graphs, photographs, and other graphic data.

Fiber optics
A new technology that uses hair-like glass fibers to enable telecommunications systems to transmit data at high rates of speed.

Field
A defined group or block of data.

File
A location within a computer's memory into which data can be placed.

Flowchart
A diagram that graphically illustrates the sequential steps involved in solving a problem.

FORTRAN
A computer language designed primarily for use by mathematicians, scientists, and engineers.

Global search
A computer search throughout a document for words, characters, or other data that might need to be changed.

Hard copy
A document printed on paper that has usually been transferred from the document displayed on a CRT screen.

Hardware
A term used to describe the actual equipment, in contrast to the programs, used in the computing process. [cf. software]

Information processing
The movement of words, symbols, or numbers from the origination of an idea to its destination.

Input
Data entered into a computer for processing.

Interface
The process that connects one part of the computer or word processor with another or one computer with another.

Keyboarding
Using a keyboard to enter data into a computer.

Laser printer
A high-speed, nonimpact printer that utilizes a narrow beam of electromagnetic light to enable it to print over 20,000 lines per minute.

Letter-quality printer
A printer that produces typewriter-quality print. [cf. dot matrix]

Line printer
A high-speed printer that prints one entire line at a time. [cf. character printer]

Loop
A sequence of instructions that is repeated continuously.

Mag
Shortened form of the word "magnetic." "Mag card" and "mag tape" are commonly used to refer to these magnetic devices.

Medium
The material on which information is recorded; e.g., magnetic tape, cards, or disks.

Memory
That part of a computer that stores information for future use.

Memory, programmable read only (PROM)

ROM chips whose memory can be programmed before they are set into the computer and become a fixed part of the system. Data in PROM memory is retained after the computer is turned off.

Memory, random access (RAM)

RAM is temporary memory within the computer and is used primarily for loading programs from disk or tape. Data in RAM memory is lost when the computer is turned off.

Memory, read only (ROM)

Permanent programs are stored in ROM, and these programs may not be altered. They are the ones that instruct the computer what to do when the power is turned on and how to do various jobs like loading from disk or tape. ROM will not lose its information when the power is turned off.

Menu

A list of possible actions an operator may take to perform tasks on a computer.

Merge

A word processing function that allows the data in two prefiled locations to be combined.

Modem

A device attached to computer or word processing terminals that allows the transmission of data between terminals over telephone wires by converting digital signals to analog signals at one end and reconverting the analog signals back to digital signals at the other end.

Network

A group of computers and/or word processors connected into a planned system to enable the transmission of data among the members of the system.

OCR (Optical character recognition)

Data read into a computer by scanning a document electronically.

Peripheral

Equipment such as typewriters and printers that work in conjunction with the computer but are not part of the computer itself.

Processing

Changes the input in a computer undergoes that result in the final product.

Program

A set of instructions designed to provide a computer solution to a problem by directing the computer to carry out a desired sequence of operations.

Programming

Writing instructions to direct a computer to perform a desired process.

Protocol
A set of conventions for the electronic transmission of data including modes, speed, character length, and code.

Reprographics
The duplication of hard copy usually by employing a computer peripheral such as a high-speed film or photocopier.

Scrolling
The process of moving text up or down on a CRT screen.

Software
Programs written to direct the operations of a computer or word processor. [cf. hardware]

Stand-alone system
A computer or word processing work station that is independent or can function by itself without being connected to a main frame computer.

Terminal
A device for entering and retrieving computer data. The most common computer terminal consists of a CRT screen and a keyboard.

User friendly
The degree to which the operations of a computer or word processor are made relatively easy to learn through the use of function keys, software, and documentation.

Turtle graphics
A method of drawing on a CRT screen by using a drawing cursor called a "turtle" to produce geometric shapes.

Word processing
The use of personnel and automated equipment to keyboard, edit, produce, and store business documents.

Appendix B
Secretarial Shortcuts

B

Secretarial Shortcuts Solution Finder

Secretarial Procedures

Color distinctions   B–10
   Filing systems   B–9d
   Forms   B–10d
   Memorandums   B–10c
   Reports   B–10b
   Shorthand notebooks   B–10a
Filing procedures   B–9
   Color, use of   B–9d
   Conserving file space   B–9c
   Out systems   B–9b
   Placement of materials   B–9a
   Special containers   B–9e
Follow-up files   B–8
   Card system   B–8b
   Folder system   B–8a
Time savers   B–11
   Alphabetical indexes   B–11f
   Collating device   B–11g
   Numbered desks   B–11a
   Postal cards   B–11e
   Sealing envelopes   B–11c
   Shorthand notebooks and
     pens   B–11b
   Stamping envelopes   B–11d
   Word processing
     equipment   B–11h

Simplified Typing Practices

Blind copies   B–7
Cards and labels   B–4
Corrections   B–3

Drawing lines   B–6
   Drawn lines   B–6b, c
   Typewritten lines   B–6a
Envelopes, chain feeding   B–5
   Back feeding   B–5b
   Front feeding   B–5a
Labels and cards   B–4
   Chain feeding   B–4b
   Continuous-feed labels   B–4a
   Pleat sheets   B–4a
Multiple copies   B–2
   Carbon packs   B–2b-d
   Photocopies   B–2a
Placement guides   B–1
   Letter placement guide   B–1a
   Manuscript placement
     guide   B–1b
   Placement rulers   B–1c
Typewritten corrections   B–3
   Bottom of page   B–3e
   Correction knives   B–3b
   Correction tape   B–3b
   Erasure corrections   B–3c, d
   Lift-off tapes and ribbons
     B–3a
   Opaquing fluid   B–3b
   Reinserting pages for
     corrections   B–3f
   Top-bound manuscripts, making
     corrections   B–3g

B

Simplified Typing Practices

B–1. Placement Guides

a. Use a letter placement guide for setting up correspondence. Place the guide directly behind the original but in front of any carbon copies. The lines on the guide will assist you in setting margins, placing the date, and calculating the letter length. Make your own guide on 8½- by 11-inch paper by following the specifications on the sample guide shown on page 304.

The heavy horizontal line at the top of the guide signifies the location of the date for standard-depth letterhead stationery. Should the letterhead drop farther, type the date a double space below the last line of the letterhead.

The outermost group of lines represents the parameters of a long letter (250 or more words); the middle group of lines represents the parameters of a medium-length letter (150 to 250 words); and the innermost group of lines represents the parameters of a short letter (fewer than 150 words). Estimate the length of your letter and set the left margin at the corresponding line. For the right side, set the margin five spaces to the right of the appropriate line to allow for the typewriter warning bell.

For a long letter the guide uses a 6-inch typing line, which corresponds closely to a 70-space line on an elite typewriter and exactly with a 60-space line on a pica typewriter. A 5-inch line length (60-space line on elite typewriters and 50-space line on pica typewriters) is used for a medium letter. The 4-inch line length shown for short letters approximates closely the 50-space line on elite typewriters and corresponds exactly with the 40-space line on pica typewriters.

The numbers at the bottom right edge of the placement guide indicate the number of standard typewritten lines remaining on the page. These numbers may be used to assist in determining whether the closing lines should be expanded or condensed so that a balanced placement can be achieved. The line indicators will also be useful for typing two-page letters by showing the remaining number of lines on the page.

The letter placement guide may be altered to accommodate other than standard-sized stationery and standard-spacing typewriters.

b. Use a manuscript typing guide for setting up reports and manuscripts. Commercially prepared guides made of manila tag that indicate the remaining number of lines on a page are available. Usually these guides are larger than the standard-sized paper so that the remaining number of lines is readily visible. An illustration appears on page 305.

When commercially prepared typing guides are not available, use an 8½- by 11-inch sheet of paper to design your own. Draw heavy black lines to represent the left and right margins as well as the top and bottom margins. Allow 1-inch top and bottom margins and 1¼-inch left and right margins, unless the manuscript or report is to be bound at the left; then allow a 1½-inch left margin. Draw a heavy black horizontal line 2 inches from the top edge (to signify the location of major headings) and a vertical line directly between the left and right margins (to aid in centering). At the right edge of the paper, number the

B

lines of the last 4 inches of paper. Separate each inch with a 1-inch horizontal line (to assist in gauging the end of the paper and in setting up footnotes). Finally, type ¼-inch lines where both the top and bottom page numbers are to be located. An illustration of this guide is shown on page 260 in Chapter 11.

letter placement guide

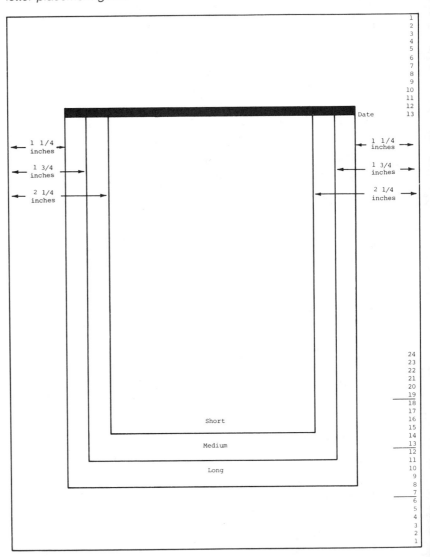

commercial typing guide

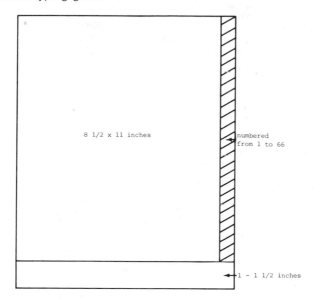

8 1/2 x 11 inches   numbered from 1 to 66   1 - 1 1/2 inches

c. When you type tabulations requiring spacing identical to that of a previously typed report, use a horizontal and vertical measurement ruler that measures spacing for both elite and pica typewriters. By placing the ruler on the previously typed report, you can determine where margins and tabulator stops were set and the number of blank lines between typewritten lines. These rulers are available commercially and may be purchased from South-Western Publishing Co., 5101 Madison Road, Cincinnati, Ohio 54227.

B–2. Multiple Copies

a. Use photocopying equipment when two or more copies are required. The time saved in preparing copy not requiring multiple corrections makes up for the cost of photocopies.

b. When photocopying equipment is not available for making multiple copies, use carbon packs. Place a backing sheet of manila tag behind the last sheet to prevent the carbon paper from wrinkling and printing "trees" on your copies. Should trees still result after using the backing sheet, have a typewriter service person check your platen.

c. To keep multiple carbons in alignment when inserting a carbon pack into the typewriter, place a folded half sheet of paper at the top of the pack.

B

Turn the carbon pack so that the top edge is at the bottom, with the last copy or backing sheet facing you.

Insert the carbon pack into the typewriter so that the folded page of the half sheet enters the typewriter first. Upon insertion, remove the half sheet of paper. Your carbon pack should have retained its alignment.

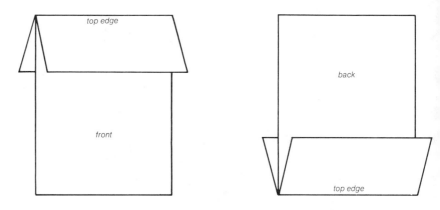

d.   Occasionally it is necessary to use extra large carbon packs that will not readily be accepted by the typewriter platen. In these cases use an old file folder to feed the carbon pack into the typewriter. Cut the folder according to the diagram.

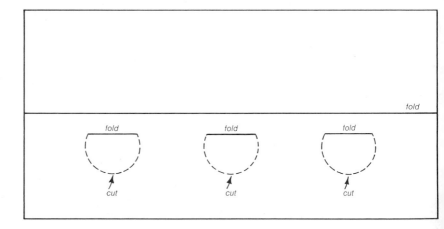

Place the top edge of the carbon pack in the center fold with the back of the carbon pack facing you.

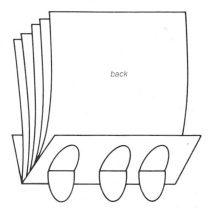

Insert the carbon pack into the typewriter by first allowing the platen to grip the cut-outs from the slots in the folded strip. Once the platen grasps the cut-outs, the carbon pack may be rolled in smoothly. Remove the folded strip after inserting the carbon pack.

B–3. Typewritten Corrections

a. Modern typewriters are equipped with special ribbons and lift-off tapes that enable the typists to remove errors by lifting them from the typewritten page. Older models of IBM typewriters (Selectric Is and Selectric IIs) may be equipped to make lift-off corrections. By purchasing special typewriter ribbons made especially for lift-off corrections, you may use lift-off tabs to remove typewritten errors. With the special ribbon the typist need only insert the lift-off tab, retype the error to have it disappear from the page, and then retype the correct letter. This technique of using lift-off tabs may be accomplished only by using the accompanying ribbons made for this purpose. These ribbons and lift-off tabs are available through various vendors and are manufactured in the various ribbon configurations for all models of IBM Selectric typewriters.

b. When possible, simplify corrections by using an opaquing fluid or correction tape to block out errors. Such a procedure is faster than erasing. For quality results be sure the color of the fluid or tape matches closely the color of the stationery you are using.

When using opaquing fluid or correction tape, make additional copies on a photocopy machine. If carbon copies are preferred, however, corrections may be made in the following manner. When using correction tape, insert an eraser guard between the original and the carbon. Retype the error on the original. Remove the eraser guard and type the correct letter. Use a fine surgical blade to remove the incorrect carbon deposits on the carbon copies.

An alternate procedure for correcting carbon-copy errors is to use a special copy correction tape simultaneously with the correction tape for originals. Sheets are inserted before each copy; the incorrect letter is typed; the sheets are removed; and the correct character is then imposed where the previous letter was blocked out.

B

When using opaquing fluid for correcting originals that require additional copies, type the correct letter over the opaqued area, allowing the letter to print on the carbon copies. Remove incorrect imprints from the copies with a fine surgical blade.

c. To erase smoothly, use a soft eraser, a hard eraser, and a small brush. On standard-carriage typewriters, move the carriage to the extreme right or left so that eraser or paper crumbs will not fall into the type basket. Begin erasing by removing the excess ink with the soft eraser. Remove the embedded ink with the hard eraser, and smooth out the surface with the soft eraser. Be sure to brush away all eraser crumbs before continuing to type. When carbon copies are involved, insert an eraser guard behind each copy as you erase so that the carbon copies will not become smudged by the erasing strokes.

Corrections on erased carbons are often fainter than the remainder of the type. To avoid this occurrence, place the ribbon position on stencil after making the correction. Type the correct letter once. Then return the ribbon to its regular position and type the letter again. In this way, the density of the carbon copy correction will be increased while not affecting the density of the correction on the original.

d. Keep your eraser clean by affixing a piece of fine sandpaper to the side of your typewriter with transparent tape. Then, when black marks appear on your eraser, you can remove them by rubbing your eraser against the sandpaper.

e. Make corrections at the bottom edge of the paper by releasing the ratchet and feeding back the paper until the error is free of the platen. Erase, return the page to the original position, and secure the ratchet. You are now ready to continue typing.

f. If a correction must be made after work has been removed from the typewriter, make corrections on each sheet individually. To align the work properly, use your paper release and align a straight letter (*i* or *l*) with one of the markings on the typewriter scale. Move your ribbon position to stencil and type the correct letter. A faint outline will allow you to determine whether or not you have achieved the proper placement. You may then return your ribbon to its typing position and strike the letter again.

If your typewriter does not have a carbon ribbon, be sure your correction key is clean by typing the character several times on a scrap piece of paper. Residual ink on the typewriter key may leave an imprint, even though the ribbon is in stencil position.

g. To make corrections in top-bound manuscripts, first remove the error. Then insert a sheet of paper in the typewriter, advancing the platen until the paper protrudes about 1 inch above the typing scale. Between the paper and the platen at the front of the machine, place the bottom edge of the page to be corrected. Next, reverse the platen until the typewriter grips the sheet. Use the procedure described in Section B–3f to align the work and make the correction.

B

B–4. Cards and Labels

a.   Continuous-feed labels provide the most efficient means for typing labels because they may be easily inserted into the typewriter. When single labels or small cards must be inserted into the machine, however, slippage may occur. To solve this problem, use a pleat sheet to hold the label or card.

Fold a horizontal pleat approximately ¼ inch deep in the middle of a standard sheet of paper. Use the following procedures to make the pleat.

(1)   Fold sheet in half. Crease with ruler.

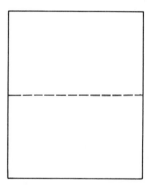

(2)   Lay the sheet flat so that the inside of the fold faces away from you.

(3)   Bring up the bottom edge ¼ inch below the top edge and fold again. Crease with ruler

B

(4)   Arrange sheet in fanfold as illustrated, and <u>crease again with ruler</u> to form a pocket.

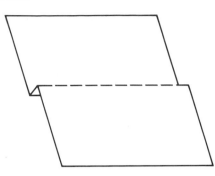

(5)   Tape back side of pocket with transparent tape. Then tape edges of front side so pocket clears platen when inserted in typewriter.

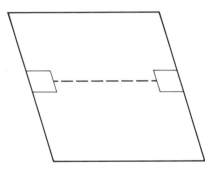

<u>Release the ratchet</u> and roll the sheet into the platen until the fold reaches the edge of the typewriter scale. Insert the label or card into the fold. Then roll back the platen to the desired writing line and secure your ratchet. The pleat will hold the card or label while you type the needed information.

b.   Small cards may be chain fed by feeding the cards from the front of your typewriter. Type the first card in the usual manner. Then roll the card back until just ¼ to ½ inch of the card protrudes above the typewriter scale. Insert the next card at the front of your typewriter by placing the bottom edge of the card between the first card and the platen. Reverse your platen until the card is in position to type. Continue feeding succeeding cards in the same manner. Completed cards will stack neatly on the paper table of your typewriter.

B–5.   Chain Feeding Envelopes

a.   To chain feed envelopes from the front of your typewriter, insert an envelope in the usual manner and type the address. Roll back the envelope until ½ inch of the top edge protrudes above the typewriter scale. Between the first envelope and the platen, insert the bottom edge of the next envelope. Reverse the platen until you reach the appropriate typing line. Type the address and then reverse the platen until ½ inch of the top edge of the envelope protrudes above the typewriter scale. Continue with these insertion and typing procedures until all the envelopes have been addressed. Envelopes will stack neatly on the paper table of your typewriter.

b. For unusually thick envelopes chain feed from the back of the typewriter. Insert an envelope with its flap extended into the typewriter. Roll the platen forward until the top edge of the envelope (the crease between the flap and the envelope) reaches the typewriter scale. With its flap extended, insert another envelope at the back of the typewriter between the first envelope and the platen. Advance the platen to the appropriate writing line on the first envelope and type the address. Again move the platen forward until the bottom edge of the first envelope is released from the typewriter. Then, between the second envelope and the platen, insert into the back of the typewriter another envelope with its flap extended. Advance the platen and type the address on the second envelope. Again, move the platen forward until the bottom edge of the second envelope is released from the typewriter. Insert another envelope with its flap extended into the back of the typewriter between the third envelope and the platen. Continue the above procedure until all envelopes have been addressed.

B–6. Drawing Lines on the Typewriter

a. When possible, use the automatic underscore on the typewriter to draw both horizontal and vertical lines. On typewriters with long carriages, reverse the position of your work and use the automatic underscore key to type vertical lines.

b. To draw horizontal lines with a pen or pencil, insert the writing instrument in the special cut-out on the typewriter scale or in the fork of the ribbon guide. Advance the pen or pencil across the page with the carriage release lever. For stationary-carriage typewriters, advance the machine with the tabulator mechanism, setting tabulator stops at the beginning and end of the horizontal lines. Practice this procedure several times before using it.

c. To draw vertical lines, insert the writing instrument in the special cut-out on the typewriter scale or in the fork of the ribbon guide. Position the carriage where the vertical line is to be drawn and release the ratchet. While holding the pen or pencil firmly, advance the platen to draw the line.

B–7. Blind Carbon Copies

a. To type on carbon copies only, place a piece of paper over the original and over those carbon copies on which you do not wish the typing to appear. Then type the material.

b. When you wish to type on all copies except the original, remove the original from the typewriter. Position the carriage where you wish to begin typing. Then disengage the paper release lever and *carefully* remove the original from the typewriter while firmly positioning the carbon pack. Return the paper release lever to the lock position and begin typing.

Secretarial Procedures

B–8. Follow-Up Files

Ordering priorities and meeting deadlines are the most important tasks of the administrative secretary. Consequently, an appropriate follow-up file should be part of every office operation.

a. The most common follow-up file is one that employs a file-drawer and file-folder system. Number 31 letter-sized folders from 1 to 31. Label additional folders for each month of the year.

follow-up file

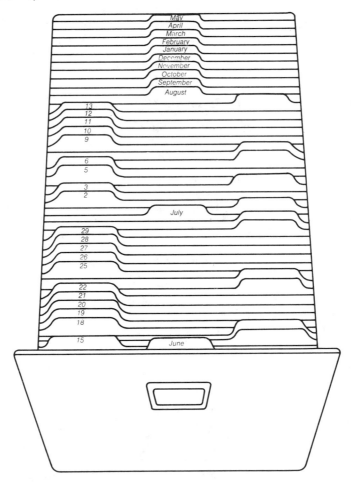

Arrange the folders in your file so that the current month and date appear first. Other folders should be arranged in chronological order with those folders representing nonworking days reversed in the file. Noncurrent month folders are placed in the back of the file until needed. Refer to the illustration of a follow-up file on page 312.

The purpose of a follow-up file is to aid in ordering priorities, meeting deadlines, and serving as a reminder to follow up on previously initiated activities. To use the file effectively, place a reminder notation under the appropriate date for all future activities. The reminder notation may take the form of a note, an *additional* carbon copy of a letter or order, or a photocopy of correspondence received. Use additional copies or make notations on separate sheets of paper for your follow-up file. Documents may be needed intermittently and may not be located easily in the follow-up file. Consequently, place the originating paperwork in its appropriate place in the regular files.

Each day consult the follow-up file to determine what action must be taken on the materials contained in that day's folder. Complete the action or file the material for action at a future date.

b.   A follow-up card system is another method of maintaining a follow-up file. Instead of using folders that contain copies of documents, notations are made on 3- by 5-inch cards to act as reminders of work to be completed by a specific date.

Individual guides are numbered from 1 to 31 and others are labeled with the months of the year. Arranged in a manner identical to the folders in the follow-up file, the card system functions in a similar manner. All items requiring future action are noted on 3- by 5-inch cards and filed under the date on which they are to be completed. A daily consultation of the file enables one to keep up-to-date with the flow of office activities.

B–9.   Filing Procedures

a.   File all correspondence and other office papers in reverse chronological order. Do the same in ordering materials in notebooks or binders. More recent data are likely to be consulted first. Consequently, filing in reverse chronological order saves time by not requiring one to thumb through materials unnecessarily before locating a needed document.

b.   When active folders are removed from the files, use "out folders" instead of "out cards." Label the out folder with the usual information—the date the file was checked out, the name of the file, the name and department of the person checking out the file, and the date the file was returned.

The advantage of an out folder over an out card is that materials received subsequent to the file being checked out may be placed in the out folder until the original file is returned. In this way, important papers will not be lost or destroyed.

B

c. To save filing space, use the back of originating correspondence for typing a carbon to answer routine correspondence. Then only one sheet of paper will be placed in the files.

For two-page letters, use both sides of the carbon copy in making file copies. This procedure also eliminates placing an additional sheet of paper in the files.

d. Use different colored file labels to differentiate filing systems or separate sections of a filing system. The use of colored labels will prevent misfiling and will allow materials to be located more easily.

e. Special containers are available for the filing and storage of records media used with word processing equipment. Magnetic cards, floppy disks, power typing and dictation cassettes, and diskettes may all be filed and later retrieved for use. Various configurations may be used for filing each type of medium. All media may be stored with hard copy in some type of letter- or legal-sized folder or binder. Other storage methods include plastic boxes, vinyl storage cases, revolving storage racks, specially designed storage pockets, etc. Each of these storage methods provides a comprehensive indexing system so that information may be located quickly. There are several different manufacturers of such filing systems. The system selected should be the one that best meets the word processing needs of the specific organization.

B–10. Color Distinctions

a. Use different colored shorthand notebooks for logging different items, taking dictation from different dictators, or for distinguishing among different time periods. Shorthand notebooks may be purchased with green, yellow, blue, pink, violet, or standard white or green-tinted paper.

b. For ease of reference color code sections of duplicated reports by using different colored paper. This technique is especially helpful when many people must make frequent use of different sections of the materials.

c. Color code memos originating from various internal departments within the organization. Such a device distinguishes easily the originating source and enables papers to be located more easily.

d. Differentiate forms similar in size and content by printing the forms on different colored papers. Similarly, in snap-out carbon pack forms, use a different color for each copy to assist in routing the proper form to its appropriate source.

B–11. Time Savers

a. In large, open offices number the desks to simplify the routing of work, the delivery of mail and supplies, the repair of typewriters, and the conducting of general office activities. Persons may be more easily directed to a desk number than to the desk of "Mary Jones" or "Larry Smith."

b. Keep an extra shorthand pad and pen in your employer's office so that you do not have to return to your desk should you be asked to take dictation when in your employer's office for another purpose.

B

c. To seal a group of envelopes rapidly, layer them on your desk with the flaps open and facing you.

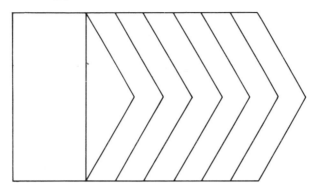

Using a sponge, moisten each flap with your right hand and then press the flap closed with your left hand. Rapidly work through the group of envelopes, moistening them with one hand and sealing and stacking them with the other.

d. To place stamps on a group of envelopes, use stamp strips. Layer the envelopes across your desk so that the position for the stamp is visible.

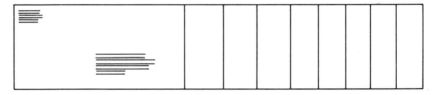

Moisten several stamps with a sponge applicator. Press the first stamp in position with your left hand. With your right hand tear the remaining stamps from the affixed one. Continue this procedure until all the envelopes have been stamped.

e. Eliminate stuffing envelopes by using a postal card instead of a letter where possible. Economize on time, supplies, and postage in this manner.

f. Place alphabetical index labels on your telephone book if it is consulted frequently. Index labels save time in locating names and numbers.

g. When collating large projects, use rubber fingers to assist you in grasping the paper more easily and rapidly.

h. Word processing equipment is ideal for storing information that must be used repetitively—namely, address lists, form letters, paragraphs, etc. This process saves time because once the information is recorded and stored in the memory, it can be accessed and used repeatedly.

Index

A

a
　as an adjective, 8–9
　usage explained, page 124
abbreviations
　in addresses, 5–8
　of business organizations, 5–2b
　of business terms, 5–6, 5–10
　of Canadian provinces, 5–10
　capitalization of, 3–3, 5–9a, b
　comma with, 1–4d
　of dates, 5–3
　diagonal with, 1–64
　exclamation mark and, 5–9d
　of foreign terms, 5–6d
　format for, 5–9
　of general terms, 5–6
　of geographical expressions, 5–8b, c,
　　d, e
　of metric units of measure, 5–5
　of *number,* 4–8b, c, 5–6a
　of organizations, 5–2
　period with, 1–35, 5–9d
　of plurals, 5–7
　question mark and, 5–9d
　of standard units of measure, 5–4
　of states and territories, 5–8c, 5–10
　of telephone numbers, 5–6c
　of time, 5–3
　of titles, 5–1
　underscore with, 1–65
absolute adjectives, 8–10f
academic courses, capitalization of, 3–7a
academic degrees, 5–1c
　capitalization of, 3–7b, c
accede, usage explained, page 124
accept, usage explained, page 124
access, usage explained, page 124
acoustic coupler, defined, page 294
active files, B–9b
ad, usage explained, page 124

adapt, usage explained, page 124
add, usage explained, page 124
addict, usage explained, page 125
addition, usage explained, page 125
address(es)
　abbreviation in, 5–8
　addressee, placement in business letter,
　　10–7
　addressee notations, in addressing
　　envelopes, 10–24
　in automated office terminology, defined,
　　page 294
　buildings in, 9–5
　city names in, 9–7a
　comma in, 1–6
　company names in, 9–4
　courtesy titles in, 9–2
　general format for, 9–1
　for government officials (table), 9–9
　inside, placement in business letter, 10–8
　mailing, in addressing envelopes, 10–23
　numerals in, 4–13
　personal titles in, 9–8
　professional titles in, 9–3, 9–8
　for religious dignitaries (table), 9–10
　return, in addressing envelopes, 10–22
　return, placement in business letter, 10–5
　states in, 9–7b
　street addresses in, 9–6
　units in, 9–5
　word division in, 2–8c
　zip code in, 9–7c
adept, usage explained, page 124
adherence, usage explained, page 125
adherents, usage explained, page 125
adjectives
　absolute, 8–10f
　vs. adverbs, 8–16
　capitalization of, 3–2
　comma with, 1–8
　for comparison, 8–10
　compound, 8–13

compound, hyphenation of, 2–2, 2–4c, d
independent, 8–11
with linking verbs, 8–12
modifying nouns, 8–8
use of articles *a* and *an* as, 8–9
adopt, usage explained, page 124
adverbs
vs. adjectives, 8–16
for comparison, 8–15
double negatives, 8–17
ending in *ly*, 8–14a
function and form of, 8–14
hyphenation of, 2–2e
adverse, usage explained, page 125
advice, usage explained, page 125
advise, usage explained, page 125
affect, usage explained, page 125
ages, format for, 4–12
aid, usage explained, page 125
aide, usage explained, page 125
aisle, usage explained, page 126
allowed, usage explained, page 126
all ready, usage explained, page 126
all right, usage explained, page 126
all together, usage explained, page 126
allude, usage explained, page 126
allusion, usage explained, page 126
all ways, usage explained, page 126
almost, usage explained, page 126
aloud, usage explained, page 126
already, usage explained, page 126
alright, usage explained, page 126
altar, usage explained, page 127
alter, usage explained, page 127
altogether, usage explained, page 126
always, usage explained, page 126
American Standard Code for Information
    Interchange (ASCII), defined, page 294
among, usage explained, page 127
amount, usage explained, page 127
ampersand (&), 1–66
comma with, 1–1d
an
as an adjective, 8–9
usage explained, page 124
and, comma with, 1–7a
and/or, with diagonal, 1–64
anecdote, usage explained, page 127
anniversaries, format for, 4–12
annual, usage explained, page 127
annul, usage explained, page 127
antidote, usage explained, page 127
any one, usage explained, page 127
anyone, usage explained, page 127
any time, usage explained, page 128
anytime, usage explained, page 128
any way, usage explained, page 128

anyway, usage explained, page 128
apartment numbers, 4–13c
apostrophe
additional uses of, 1–56
capital letters and, 1–56b
with contractions, 1–55g, 1–56a
with nouns, 1–55, 8–2f
with possessives, 1–55
with possessive nouns, 8–2f
appositives
comma with, 1–4
pronouns in, 8–3f
titles in, 6–4a
appraise, usage explained, page 128
apprise, usage explained, page 128
Arabic numerals, 4–17
area codes, 4–14
artistic works, titles of, 6–3
as
vs. *like*, 8–22
pronouns after, 8–3e
usage explained, page 128
ascent, usage explained, page 128
assembler language, defined, page 294
assent, usage explained, page 128
assistance, usage explained, page 128
assistants, usage explained, page 128
assure, usage explained, page 128
asterisk, 1–63
dash with, 1–63
with parenthesis, 1–63
asynchronous transmissions, defined,
    page 294
attendance, usage explained, page 128
attendants, usage explained, page 128
automated office, terminology used in,
    pages 294–299
auxiliary storage, defined, page 294
averse, usage explained, page 125
a while, usage explained, page 124
awhile, usage explained, page 124

B

bad, usage explained, page 129
badly, usage explained, page 129
bail, usage explained, page 129
bale, usage explained, page 129
bar charts, 11–9c
bare, usage explained, page 129
base, usage explained, page 129
BASIC, defined, page 294
bass, usage explained, page 129
batch, defined, page 294
bear, usage explained, page 129
beside, usage explained, page 129
besides, usage explained, page 129
between, usage explained, page 127

biannual, usage explained, page 129
bibliography for reports, 11–10
biennial, usage explained, page 129
billed, usage explained, page 129
binary numbering system, defined,
    page 294
bit, defined, page 294
blind carbon copies, B–7
boilerplate, defined, page 295
bolder, usage explained, page 129
book chapters, 6–1b
book titles, 6–1a
    capitalization of, 3–6a
    quotation marks and, 1–49
born, usage explained, page 130
borne, usage explained, page 130
bouillon, usage explained, page 130
boulder, usage explained, page 129
box numbers, 4–13c
brackets, 1–61, 1–62
breach, usage explained, page 130
breech, usage explained, page 130
build, usage explained, page 129
buildings and units, address format for, 9–5
buillion, usage explained, page 130
business letters, *see* letters, business
business organizations
    abbreviations of, 5–2b
    capitalization of, 3–8e
business-reply mail, 12–2b
business terms, abbreviations of, 5–6, 5–10
but, comma with, 1–7a
byte, defined, page 295

C

cablegrams
    charges for, 12–15
    classes of, 12–14
calendar dates, comma with, 1–5a
callous, usage explained, page 130
callus, usage explained, page 130
can, usage explained, page 130
Canadian provinces, abbreviations of, 5–10
canvas, usage explained, page 130
canvass, usage explained, page 130
capacity, metric and standard measures of,
    4–7
capital, usage explained, page 130–131
capitalization
    of abbreviations, 3–3, 5–9a, b
    of academic courses, 3–7a
    of academic degrees, 3–7b, c
    of adjectives, 3–2
    apostrophe and, 1–56b
    of book titles, 3–6a
    of business organizations, 3–8e
    of celestial bodies, 3–12

colon with, 1–28, 3–1d
    of company names, 3–8b
    of complimentary close of business letter,
        3–1c
    of dates and events, 3–10
    of educational institutions, 3–8g
    of ethnic references, 3–11
    of geographical locations, 3–9
    of government organizations, terms, and
        titles, 3–5b, d, 3–8d, f
    of languages, 3–11
    with lettered items, 3–4
    of literary or artistic works, 3–6
    of magazine titles, 3–6a
    of movie titles, 3–6a
    with numerals, 3–4
    of organization names, 3–8
    plural forms and, 8–1j
    of professional titles, 3–5a
    of proper nouns, 3–1b, 3–2, 8–1j
    quotation marks and, 1–53
    quotations with, 3–1a
    of Roman numerals, 4–17
    of salutations, 3–1c
    of titles, 3–5, 6–1a, c, d
capitol/Capitol, usage explained,
    pages 130–131
carat, usage explained, page 131
carbon copies, blind, B–7
carbon copy notations in business letters,
    10–17
cards, typing, B–4
caret, usage explained, page 131
carrot, usage explained, page 131
cathode ray tube (CRT) terminal, defined,
    page 295
celestial bodies, capitalization of, 3–12
censor, usage explained, page 131
censure, usage explained, page 131
census, usage explained, page 131
central processing unit, defined, page 295
cereal, usage explained, page 131
certificate of mailing, 12–10b
certified mail, 12–10a
chain feeding envelopes, B–5
character printer, defined, page 295
choose, usage explained, page 131
chose, usage explained, page 131
cite, usage explained, page 131
city names, address format for, 9–7a
clock time, 4–10
coarse, usage explained, page 132
COBOL, defined, page 295
C.O.D. (collect on delivery) mail, 12–9c
collating, B–11g
collective nouns, verbs and, 8–7j
colleges, capitalization of, 3–8g

collision, usage explained, page 132
collusion, usage explained, page 132
colon
    in business letters, 1–26a, 10–20
    capitalization with, 1–28, 3–1d
    in explanatory sentences, 1–24
    in expressions of time, 1–26b
    with formally enumerated or listed items,
        1–23
    in literary references, 1–26d
    with long quotations, 1–25
    with parentheses, 1–60e
    with parenthetical expressions, 1–2e
    placement of, 1–27
    with question mark, 1–41a
    quotation marks and, 1–54a
    in ratios, 1–26c
    special-purpose uses for, 1–26
color distinctions, B–10
comma
    abbreviations with, 1–4d
    in addresses, 1–6
    with adjectives, 1–8
    with an ampersand, 1–1d
    with *and,* 1–7a
    with appositives, 1–4
    in business letters, 10–20
    with *but,* 1–7a
    with contrasting expressions, 1–12
    with coordinating conjunctions, 1–7
    with dates, 1 5
    with decimal fractions, 1–16c
    with dimensions, 1–16e
    in direct address, 1–3
    with *etc.,* 1–1c
    with exclamation point, 1–46b
    with house number, 1–16c
    with identical verbs, 1–14a
    with independent adjectives, 1–8
    with infinitive phrases, 1–10, 1–11e
    with introductory clauses, 1–8, 1–9
    with introductory phrases, 1–10
    with limiting expressions, 1–12
    with metric measurements, 1–16c
    with nonrestrictive phrases and clauses,
        1–11
    with *nor,* 1–7a
    with numerals, 1–16, 4–3a
    with omitted words, 1–13
    with opposing expressions, 1–12
    with *or,* 1–7a
    with page references, 1–16d
    with parentheses, 1–60e
    in parenthetical expressions, 1–2
    with participial phrases, 1–10, 1–11e
    with prepositional phrases, 1–10, 1–11e
    as punctuation for clarity, 1–14
    with question mark, 1–41a
    with quotation marks, 1–43, 1–54a
    with restrictive phrases and clauses, 1–11
    with Roman numerals, 1–4d
    with series, semicolon and, 1–20
    in series of words or elements, 1–1
    in short quotations, 1–15
    with telephone number, 1–16c
    with time period, 1–16e
    with time zones, 1–5
    in titles, 6–4b
    with transitional expressions, 1–19
    with underscored words, 1–4e
    with volume numbers, 1–16d
    with weight, 1–16e
    with word-numeral combinations, 1–16c
    with years, 1–16e
    with zip code, 1–16c
command, usage explained, page 132
commend, usage explained, page 132
communicating computer or word
        processor, defined, page 295
company names
    in addresses, 9–4
    ampersand in, 1–66
    capitalization of, 3–8b
compass points, capitalization of, 3–9c
complement, usage explained, page 132
complementary, usage explained, page 132
complete thoughts, semicolon with, 1–20
compliment, usage explained, page 132
complimentary, usage explained, page 132
complimentary close for business letters,
        10–13
    address format for, 9–8
    capitalization of, 3–1c
compound adjectives, 8–13
compound nouns
    hyphenation of, 2–1
    plural form of, 8–1i
    possessive form of, 8–2d
compound verbs, hyphenation of, 2–1
confidant, usage explained, page 132
confident, usage explained, page 132
conjunctions
    as vs. *like,* 8–22
    coordinating, *see* coordinating
        conjunctions
    used in pairs, 8–21
conscience, usage explained, page 132
conscious, usage explained, page 132
console, usage explained, page 132
consul, usage explained, page 132
continual, usage explained, page 132
continuous, usage explained, page 132
contractions
    apostrophe with, 1–55g, 1–56a

contractions *(continued)*
  single-word, 5–11a
  verb contractions, 5–11b
contrasting expressions, comma with, 1–12
cooperation, usage explained, page 133
coordinating conjunctions
  comma with, 1–7
  semicolon with, 1–17, 1–18
corespondent, usage explained, page 133
corporation, usage explained, page 133
corps, usage explained, page 133
corpse, usage explained, page 133
corrections, typewritten, B–3
correspondence, usage explained,
    page 133
correspondents, usage explained, page 133
council, usage explained, page 133
counsel, usage explained, page 133
course, usage explained, page 132
courtesy titles, 5–1a
  in addresses, 9–2
credible, usage explained, page 133
creditable, usage explained, page 133
cultural data, capitalization of, 3–11
cursor, defined, page 295

D

daisy wheel, defined, page 295
dash
  with asterisk, 1–63
  format and placement of, 1–32
  to indicate hesitation in verbal reports,
    1–30
  with parenthetical elements, 1–29
  with parenthetical expressions, 1–2d,
    1–29
  question mark and, 1–41a
  before source of quotations, 1–31
  with word division, 2–8f
data base, defined, page 295
dates
  abbreviation of, 5–3
  capitalization of, 3–10
  comma with, 1–5
  numerals with, 4–9
  placement in business letters, 10–6
  word division and, 2–8a
days, format for, 4–11
decent, usage explained, page 133
decimal fractions, comma with, 1–16c
decimals
  numbers containing, 4–5b
  period as, 1–37, 1–39a
declarative sentence, period and, 1–33
dedicated, defined, page 295
default, defined, page 295

defer, usage explained, page 134
deference, usage explained, page 134
delusion, usage explained, page 126
deprecate, usage explained, page 134
depreciate, usage explained, page 134
descent, usage explained, page 133
desert, usage explained, page 134
desks, numbering, B–11a
dessert, usage explained, page 134
device, usage explained, page 134
devise, usage explained, page 134
dew, usage explained, page 134
diagonal, 1–64
differ, usage explained, page 134
difference, usage explained, page 134
dimensions, comma with, 1–16e
direct address, comma in, 1–3
direct question, 1–40
disapprove, usage explained, page 134
disburse, usage explained, page 135
disk, defined, page 295
diskette, defined, page 295
disperse, usage explained, page 135
disprove, usage explained, page 134
dissent, usage explained, page 133
do, usage explained, page 134
documentation, defined, page 296
done, usage explained, page 135
dot matrix, defined, page 296
double negatives, 8–17
doubt, expressions of, question mark with,
    1–42
dual density disk, defined, page 296
dual pitch, defined, page 296
due, usage explained, page 134
dun, usage explained, page 135

E

edict, usage explained, page 125
edition, usage explained, page 125
educational institutions, capitalization of,
    3–8g
effect, usage explained, page 125
electronic mail, defined, page 296
elicit, usage explained, page 135
ellipses, 1–38, 1–52
elude, usage explained, page 126
emigrate, usage explained, page 135
eminent, usage explained, page 135
ensure, usage explained, page 128
enumeration of items
  colon with, 1–23
  letters with, 1–59
  numbers with, 1–59
  semicolon with, 1–21
envelop, usage explained, page 136

envelope, usage explained, page 136
envelopes, addressing
  addressee notation, 10–24
  mailing address, 10–23
  mailing notation, 10–25
  for Optical Character Recognition (OCR),
    10–26
  return address, 10–22
  zip + 4, 10—27
envelopes
  chain feeding and typing, B–5
  folding and inserting correspondence in,
    10–28, 10–29
  sealing, B–11c
  stamping, B–11d
etc., comma with, 1–1c
ethnic references, capitalization of, 3–11
events, capitalization of, 3–10
every day, usage explained, page 136
everyday, usage explained, page 136
every one, usage explained, page 136
everyone, usage explained, page 136
exceed, usage explained, page 124
except, usage explained, page 124
excess, usage explained, page 124
exclamation point, 1–45, 1–46
  abbreviations and, 5–9d
  with comma, 1–46b
  with period, 1–46b
  with question mark, 1–46b
  with quotation marks, 1–46c, 1–54b
execute, defined, page 296
executioner, usage explained, page 136
executor, usage explained, page 136
expand, usage explained, page 136
expansive, usage explained, page 136
expend, usage explained, page 136
expensive, usage explained, page 136
explanations, semicolon with, 1–21
explanatory sentences, colon with, 1–24
explicit, usage explained, page 137
expressions of doubt, question mark with,
  1–42
express-mail service, 12–1
extant, usage explained, page 137
extent, usage explained, page 137

F

facetious, usage explained, page 137
factious, usage explained, page 137
factitious, usage explained, page 137
fair, usage explained, page 137
fare, usage explained, page 137
farther, usage explained, page 137
facsimile, defined, page 296
feat, usage explained, page 137

fete, usage explained, page 137
fewer, usage explained, page 137
fiber optics, defined, page 296
fictitious, usage explained, page 137
field, defined, page 296
file, defined, page 296
files, follow-up, B–8
filing procedures, B–9
finally, usage explained, page 138
finely, usage explained, page 138
first-class mail, 12–2
flagrant, usage explained, page 138
flair, usage explained, page 138
flare, usage explained, page 138
flaunt, usage explained, page 138
flew, usage explained, page 138
flout, usage explained, page 138
flowchart, defined, page 296
flu, usage explained, page 138
flue, usage explained, page 138
follow-up files, B–8
footnote, asterisk and, 1–63
foreign terms, abbreviation of, 5–6d
formal listings, colon with, 1–23
formally, usage explained, page 138
former, usage explained, page 138
formerly, usage explained, page 138
forth, usage explained, page 139
FORTRAN, defined, page 296
fourth, usage explained, page 139
fourth-class mail (parcel post), 12–5
fractions, 4–15
  decimal, comma with, 1–16c
  diagonal with, 1–64
  hyphenation of, 2–4c
fragrant, usage explained, page 138
full-rate telegrams, 12–12a
further, usage explained, page 137

G

general terms, abbreviation of, 5–6
geographical expressions, abbreviation of,
  5–8b, c, d, e
geographical locations
  capitalization of, 3–9
  word division and, 2–8d
gerunds
  possessive form of, 8–2e
  pronouns before, 8–3d
global search, defined, page 296
good, usage explained, page 139
government officials, address forms for
  (table), 9–9
government organizations, capitalization of,
  3–8f
government terms, capitalization of, 3–8d

government titles, capitalization of, 3–5b, d
grate, usage explained, page 139
great, usage explained, page 139
guarantee, usage explained, page 139
guaranty, usage explained, page 139

H

hard copy, defined, page 297
hardware, defined, page 297
he, usage explained, page 139
hear, usage explained, page 139
her, usage explained, page 140
here, usage explained, page 139
herself, usage explained, page 140
hew, usage explained, page 140
him, usage explained, page 139
himself, usage explained, page 139
hoard, usage explained, page 140
holy, usage explained, page 140
horde, usage explained, page 140
hours, format for, 4–10c
house numbers, 4–13a
    comma with, 1–16c
hue, usage explained, page 140
human, usage explained, page 140
humane, usage explained, page 140
hypercritical, usage explained, page 140
hyphenation
    of adverbs, 2–2e
    of compound adjectives, 2–2, 2–4c, d
    of compound nouns and verbs, 2–1
    of fractions, 2–4c
    of nouns, 8–1i
    of numbers, 2–4
    of prefixes, 2–3
    to replace to or through, 2–2e
hypocritical, usage explained, page 140

I

I, usage explained, page 141
ideal, usage explained, page 141
identical verbs, comma with, 1–14a
idle, usage explained, page 141
idol, usage explained, page 141
illicit, usage explained, page 135
illusion, usage explained, page 126
immigrate, usage explained, page 135
imminent, usage explained, page 135
imperative statement, period and, 1–33
implicit, usage explained, page 137
imply, usage explained, page 141
incidence, usage explained, page 141
incidents, usage explained, page 141
incite, usage explained, page 141
indefinite pronouns, verbs and, 8–7e
independent adjectives, 8–11
    comma with, 1–8

independent clauses, semicolon with, 1–17,
    1–18, 1–19
independent phrases, period with, 1–34
indigenous, usage explained, page 141
indigent, usage explained, page 141
indignant, usage explained, page 141
indirect question, 1–33
indirect quotation, quotation marks with, 1–47
infer, usage explained, page 141
infinitive phrases, comma with, 1–10, 1–11e
infinitives, splitting, 8–7i
information processing, defined, page 297
ingenious, usage explained, page 142
ingenuous, usage explained, page 142
initials, period with, 1–35, 1–39a
input, defined, page 297
insight, usage explained, page 141
insure, usage explained, page 128
insured mail, 12–9
interface, defined, page 297
interstate, usage explained, page 142
intrastate, usage explained, page 142
introductory clauses, comma with, 1–8, 1–9
introductory phrases, comma with, 1–10
irregular verbs, 8–5
isle, usage explained, page 126
its, usage explained, page 142
it's, usage explained, page 142

K

karat, usage explained, page 131
keyboarding, defined, page 297

L

labels, typing, B–4
languages, capitalization of, 3–11
laser printer, defined, page 297
later, usage explained, page 142
latter, usage explained, page 138, 142
lay
    usage explained, page 142
    as a verb, 8–6
lean, usage explained, page 142
leased, usage explained, page 143
least, usage explained, page 143
lecture titles, 6–3
    quotation marks with, 1–49
length, metric and standard measures of,
    4–7
less, usage explained, page 137
lessee, usage explained, page 143
lessen, usage explained, page 143
lesser, usage explained, page 143
lesson, usage explained, page 143
lessor, usage explained, page 143
letter placement guide for setting up
        correspondence, B–1a

letter quality printer, defined, page 297
letters, business
addressee, placement of, 10–7
attachment notations, 10–16
attention line, placement of, 10–9
body of letter, placement of, 10–12
carbon copy notations, 10–17
colon in, 1–26a, 10–20
comma in, 10–20
complimentary close, placement of,
10–13
date, placement of, 10–6
enclosures and, 10–16
folding and inserting in envelopes, 10–28,
10–29
full block letter style for, 10–1
inside address, placement of, 10–8
mailing notations, placement of, 10–7
modified block letter style for, 10–2
postscripts for, 10–18
punctuation style for, 10–20, 10–21
reference initials, placement of, 10–15
return address, placement of, 10–5
salutation, placement of, 10–10
second-page headings for, 10–19
signature line, placement of, 10–14
simplified letter style for, 10–4
social business letter style for, 10–3
subject line, placement of, 10–11
of transmittal, with reports, 11–2
levee, usage explained, page 143
levy, usage explained, page 143
liable, usage explained, page 143
libel, usage explained, page 143
lie
usage explained, page 142
as a verb, 8–6
lien, usage explained, page 142
lightening, usage explained,
page 143
lightning, usage explained, page 143
like
vs. *as*, 8–22
usage explained, page 128
limiting expressions, comma with, 1–12
line charts, 11–9d
line printer, defined, page 297
lines, drawing on the typewriter, B–6
linking verbs, adjectives with, 8–12
listings, colon with, 1–23
literary references, colon with, 1–26d
local, usage explained, page 144
locale, usage explained, page 144
long quotations, colon with, 1–25
loop, defined, page 297
loose, usage explained, page 144
lose, usage explained, page 144

M

mag, defined, page 297
magazine articles, 6–1c
magazine titles, 6–1a
capitalization of, 3–6a
underscore with, 1–65
magnate, usage explained,
page 144
magnet, usage explained, page 144
mail
electronic, page 296
express service, 12–1
first-class, 12–2
fourth-class (parcel post), 12–5
insured mail, 12–9
mixed class, 12–6
parcel post, 12–5
proof of mailing and delivery, 12–10
second-class, 12–3
special delivery, 12–7
special handling, 12–8
third-class, 12–4
United Parcel Service, 12–11
mailgrams, 12–12c
manuscripts, *see* reports
manuscript typing guide, B–1b
marital, usage explained, page 144
marshal, usage explained, page 144
martial, usage explained, page 144
mass (weight), metric and standard
measures of, 4–7
may, usage explained, page 130
may be, usage explained, page 144
maybe, usage explained, page 144
me, usage explained, page 141
measures, *see* weights and measures
medal, usage explained, page 144
meddle, usage explained, page 144
medium, defined, page 297
meeting minutes
contents of, 11–12
organization and format of, 11–13
purpose of, 11–12
memorandum (memo)
color coding of, B–10c
preparation of, 10–32
use of, 10–31
memory, defined, page 297
memory, programmable read only (PROM),
defined, page 298
memory, random access (RAM), defined,
page 298
memory, read only (ROM), defined, page
298
menu, defined, page 298
merge, defined, page 298

metric weights and measures, 4–7
    abbreviation of, 5–5
    comma with, 1–16c
miner, usage explained, page 144
minor, usage explained, page 144
minutes, format for, 4–10c
minutes of meeting
    content of, 11–12
    organization and format of, 11–13
    purpose of, 11–12
mode, usage explained, page 144
modem, defined, page 298
money, 4–4
months, format for, 4–11
mood, usage explained, page 144
moral, usage explained, page 145
morale, usage explained, page 145
morning, usage explained, page 145
most, usage explained, page 126
mourning, usage explained, page 145
movie titles, 6–3
    capitalization of, 3–6a
    quotation marks with, 1–49
multiple copies, typing, B–2
myself, usage explained, page 141

N

names
    company, 1–66
    company, in addresses, 9–4
    company, capitalization of, 3–8b
    word division and, 2–8b
naval, usage explained, page 145
navel, usage explained, page 145
negatives, double, 8–17
network, defined, page 298
newspaper column titles, 6–1c
newspaper titles, 6–1a
nonessential expressions, parentheses with,
    1–57
nonrestrictive phrases and clauses, comma
    with, 1–11
nor, comma with, 1–7a
nouns
    adjectives comparing, 8–10a
    adjectives modifying, 8–8
    apostrophe with, 1–55, 8–2f
    capitalization of, 3–1b, 3–2, 8–1j
    collective, verbs and, 8–7j
    compound, hyphenation of, 2–1
    compound, plural form of, 8–1i
    compound, possessive form of, 8–2d
    ending in *ff*, plural form of, 8–1d
    ending in *o*, plural form of, 8–1c
    ending in *s, sh, ch, x,* or *z,* plural form of,
        8–1a
    ending in *y,* plural form of, 8–1b

of foreign origin, plural form of, 8–1f
hyphenated nouns, 8–1i
names and titles, plural form of, 8–1k
numerals, plural form of, 8–1j
plural form of, 8–1
possessive form of, 8–2
number (word) abbreviation of, 4–8b, c,
    5–6a
number
    agreement with verb, 8–7a, g
    usage explained, page 127
numbers
    with decimals, 4–5b
    hyphenation of, 2–4
numerals
    in addresses, 4–13
    apartment numbers, 4–13c
    approximations, 4–1c
    Arabic, 4–17
    area codes, 4–14
    capitalization with, 3–4
    comma with, 1–16, 4–3a
    dates, 4–9
    format for, 4–3
    fractions, 4–15
    general rules for, 4–1
    money and, 4–4
    ordinal, 4–16
    parentheses with, 1–58, 1–59
    percentages, 4–5a
    plural forms of, 8–1j
    related, 4–2
    Roman, 4–17
    round numbers, 4–1d, 4–2b
    with symbols, 4–8c
    telephone numbers, 4–14
    above ten, 4–1a
    with words, 4–8a
    zip codes and, 4–13d, e

O

objective case pronouns, 8–3b
omitted words
    comma with, 1–13
    periods for, 1–38
opposing expressions, comma with, 1–12
Optical Character Recognition (OCR)
    addressing envelopes for, 10–26
    defined, page 298
or
    and/or, diagonal with, 1–64
    comma with, 1–7a
ordinal numbers, 4–16
ordinance, usage explained, page 145
ordnance, usage explained, page 145
organization names
    abbreviations of, 5–2

capitalization of, 3–8
outlines
  period in, 1–36
  Roman numerals in, 4–17a
overdo, usage explained, page 145
overdue, usage explained, page 145
overnight telegrams, 12–12b

P

page references, comma with, 1–16d
pair, usage explained, page 145
pamphlet sections, 6–1b
pamphlet titles, 6–1a
paragraphs, quoted, quotation marks with, 1–51
parcel post, 12–5
pare, usage explained, page 145
parentheses
  asterisk with, 1–63
  colon with, 1–60e
  comma with, 1–60e
  enumerated items and, 1–59
  for letters in enumerated list, 1–59
  nonessential expressions and, 1–57
  numerals with, 1–58, 1–59
  parenthetical expressions with, 1–2d
  period in, 1–39d
  placement of, 1–60
  question mark in, 1–44a
  semicolon with, 1–60e
parenthetical expressions
  colon with, 1–2e
  comma in, 1–2
  dash with, 1–2d, 1–29
  parentheses with, 1–2d
  semicolon with, 1–2e
participial phrases, comma with, 1–10, 1–11e
passed, usage explained, page 145
past, usage explained, page 145
patience, usage explained, page 146
patients, usage explained, page 146
peace, usage explained, page 146
peal, usage explained, page 146
pear, usage explained, page 145
peel, usage explained, page 146
peer, usage explained, page 146
percentages, 4–5a
period
  with abbreviations, 1–35, 5–9d
  as decimal, 1–37, 1–39a
  declarative sentence and, 1–33
  for emphasis, 1–38
  at end of independent phrase, 1–34
  at end of sentence, 1–33
  exclamation point with, 1–46b
  format for, 1–39

indirect question and, 1–33
  with initials, 1–35, 1–39a
  for omission, 1–38
  in outlines, 1–36
  in parentheses, 1–39d
  in quotation marks, 1–39c, 1–54a
  in titles, 6–4b
peripheral, defined, page 298
persecute, usage explained, page 146
personal, usage explained, page 146
personal titles, 5–1c
  in addresses, 9–8
personnel, usage explained, page 146
perspective, usage explained, page 146
piece, usage explained, page 146
pie charts, 11–9b
pier, usage explained, page 146
plaintiff, usage explained, page 147
plaintive, usage explained, page 147
play titles
  capitalization of, 3–6a, 6–3
  quotation marks for, 1–49, 6–3
plurals
  abbreviation of, 5–7
  capitalization of, 8–1j
  of nouns, 8–1
  of numerals, 8–1j
populace, usage explained, page 147
populous, usage explained, page 147
pore, usage explained, page 147
possessives
  apostrophe with, 1–55
  nouns, 8–2
  pronouns, 8–3c
postal money orders, 12–9d
pour, usage explained, page 147
practicable, usage explained, page 147
practical, usage explained, page 147
pray, usage explained, page 147
precede, usage explained, page 147
precedence, usage explained, page 147
precedents, usage explained, page 147
prefixes, hyphenation of, 2–3
prepositional phrases, 8–20
  comma with, 1–10, 1–11e
prepositions
  use of *in, between,* or *among,* 8–18
  used with certain words, 8–19
prey, usage explained, page 147
principal, usage explained, page 148
principle, usage explained, page 148
priority mail, 12–2a
proceed, usage explained, page 147
processing, defined, page 298
professional titles, 5–1b, c
  in addresses, 9–3, 9–8
  capitalization of, 3–5a

program, defined, page 298
programming, defined, page 298
pronouns
  adjectives comparing, 8–10a
  in apposition, 8–3f
  ending in *self* or *selves*, 8–3g
  before a gerund, 8–3d
  indefinite, verbs and, 8–7e
  objective case, 8–3b
  possessive case, 8–3c
  relative, verbs and, 8–7k
  subjective case, 8–3a
  after *than* or *as*, 8–3e
  verbs and, 8–7b, k
proper nouns, capitalization of, 3–1b, 3–2,
  8–1j
propose, usage explained, page 148
prosecute, usage explained, page 146
prospective, usage explained, page 146
protocol, defined, page 299
published works, titles of, 6–1
purpose, usage explained, page 148

Q

question mark
  abbreviations and, 5–9d
  colon with, 1–41a
  comma with, 1–41a
  dash with, 1–41a
  exclamation point with, 1–46b
  with expression of doubt, 1–42
  in parentheses, 1–44a
  placement of, 1–44
  in quotation marks, 1–44a, 1–54b
  with series of questions, 1–43
  statement with questions and, 1–41
  in titles, 6–4c
questions
  direct, 1–40
  indirect, 1–33
quiet, usage explained, page 148
quite, usage explained, page 148
quotation marks
  artistic works and, 6–3
  book titles and, 1–49
  capitalization with, 1–53
  colon with, 1–54a
  comma with, 1–4e, 1–54a
  with direct quotations, 1–47
  with ellipses, 1–52
  exclamation point with, 1–46c, 1–54b
  period in, 1–39c, 1–54a
  placement of, 1–54
  question mark in, 1–44a, 1–54b
  for quotations within quotations, 1–50
  with quoted paragraphs, 1–51
  semicolon with, 1–54a

  short expression and, 1–48
  with slang words, 1–48a
  with technical words, 1–48a
  titles and, 1–49, 6–1b, c, 6–4b
quotations
  capitalization with, 3–1a
  colon with, 1–25
  comma in, 1–15
  dash with, 1–31
  quotation marks with, 1–47

R

raise, usage explained, page 148
ratios, colon in, 1–26c
raze, usage explained, page 148
real, usage explained, page 148
reality, usage explained, page 149
really, usage explained, page 148
realty, usage explained, page 149
receipt, usage explained, page 149
recipe, usage explained, page 149
registered mail, 12–9a
regular verbs, 8–4
related numbers, 4–2
relative pronouns, verbs and, 8–7k
religious dignitaries, forms of address for
  (table), 9–10
reports
  appendix for, 11–11
  bar charts for, 11–9c
  bibliography for, 11–10
  headings for, 11–6
  illustrations for, 11–9
  letter of transmittal with, 11–2
  line charts for, 11–9d
  list of illustrations for, 11–4
  list of tables for, 11–4
  listings for, 11–7
  pie charts for, 11–9b
  sources, methods of citing, 11–8
  table of contents of, 11–3
  tables for, 11–9a
  title page of, 11–1
  typing of, 11–5
reprographics, defined, page 299
residence, usage explained, page 149
residents, usage explained, page 149
respectably, usage explained, page 149
respectfully, usage explained, page 149
respectively, usage explained, page 149
restrictive phrases and clauses, comma
  with, 1–11
rise, usage explained, page 149
Roman numerals, 4–17
  comma with, 1–4d
  in outlines, 4–17a
rote, usage explained, page 149

round numbers, 4–1d, 4–2b
rout, usage explained, page 149
route, usage explained, page 149
rural route numbers, 4–13c

S

salutation
  address format for, 9–8
  capitalization of, 3–1c
  placement in business letter, 10–10
scene, usage explained, page 149
scrolling, defined, page 299
second-class mail, 12–3
secretarial procedures
  color distinctions, B–10
  filing procedures, B–9
  follow-up files, B–8
  time savers, B–11
seen, usage explained, page 149
semicolon
  with enumerations and explanations, 1–21
  with independent clauses, 1–17, 1–18, 1–19
  with parentheses, 1–60e
  with parenthetical expressions, 1–2e
  placement of, 1–22
  with quotation marks, 1–54a
  with series containing commas or complete thoughts, 1–20
senses, usage explained, page 131
serial, usage explained, page 131
set, usage explained, page 150
sew, usage explained, page 150
shall, usage explained, page 150
she, usage explained, page 140
shear, usage explained, page 150
sheer, usage explained, page 150
shone, usage explained, page 150
shorthand notebooks, color distinction for, B–10a
should, usage explained, page 150
shown, usage explained, page 150
sight, usage explained, page 131
single-word contractions, 5–11a
sit, usage explained, page 150
site, usage explained, page 131
slang words, quotation marks with, 1–48a
so, usage explained, page 150
soar, usage explained, page 151
software, defined, page 299
sole, usage explained, page 151
some, usage explained, page 151
some time, usage explained, page 151
sometime, usage explained, page 151
somewhat, usage explained, page 151
song titles, quotation marks with, 1–49
sore, usage explained, page 151

soul, usage explained, page 151
sow, usage explained, page 150
special delivery, 12–7
special handling service, 12–7
splitting infinitives, 8–7i
staid, usage explained, page 151
stamps, time-saving procedure for, B–11d
stand alone system, defined, page 299
standard weights and measures, 4–6
  abbreviation of, 5–4
states
  abbreviation of, 5–8c, 5–10, page 330
  address format for, 9–7b
  post office abbreviation of, 5–8e
  two-letter abbreviation of, 5–10, page 330
stationary, usage explained, page 152
stationery, usage explained, page 152
statue, usage explained, page 152
stature, usage explained, page 152
statute, usage explained, page 152
stayed, usage explained, page 151
street addresses, address format for, 9–6
street names, numerals for, 4–13b
subjective case pronouns, 8–3a
subject-verb agreement, 8–7
subjunctive mood, verbs and, 8–7b
suit, usage explained, page 152
suite, usage explained, page 152
suite numbers, 4–13c
sure, usage explained, page 152
surely, usage explained, page 152
symbols, numerals with, 4–8c

T

tables as illustrations for reports, 11–9a
tabulations, typing, B–1c
tare, usage explained, page 152
tear, usage explained, page 152
technical words, quotation marks with, 1–48a
telegrams
  classes of, 12–12
  sending, 12–13
telephone numbers, 4–14
  comma with, 1–16c
  with extensions, 5–6c
television series, 6–3
terminal, defined, page 299
territories, abbreviation of, 5–10
than
  pronouns after, 8–3e
  usage explained, page 152
that, usage explained, page 152
their, usage explained, page 153
them, usage explained, page 153
then, usage explained, page 152
there, usage explained, page 153

they, usage explained, page 153
they're, usage explained, page 153
third-class mail, 12–4
threw, usage explained, page 153
through, usage explained, page 153
tier, usage explained, page 152
time, expressions of
  abbreviation of, 5–3
  colon in, 1–26b
  comma with, 1–16e
time zones, comma with, 1–5
titles
  abbreviation of, 5–1
  in appositive expressions, 6–4a
  of artistic works, 6–3
  of books, 3–6a, 6–1a
  capitalization of, 3–5, 6–1a, c, d
  comma in, 6–4b
  company names, 9–4
  courtesy, 5–1a, 9–2
  for government officials (table), 9–9
  of lectures, 6–3
  of magazines, 6–1a
  of movies, 6–3
  of newspapers, 6–1a, c
  of pamphlets, 6–1a
  period in, 6–4b
  personal, 5–1c
  of plays, 3–6a, 6–3
  professional, 3–5a, 5–1b, c, 9–3, 9–8
  of published works, 6–1
  punctuation format for, 6–4
  question mark in, 6–4c
  quotation marks in, 1–49, 6–1b, c, 6–4b
  for religious dignitaries (table), 9–10
  of unpublished works, 6–2
to, usage explained, page 153
too, usage explained, page 153
transitional expressions
  comma with, 1–19
  semicolon with, 1–19
turtle graphics, defined, page 299
two, usage explained, page 153
typewritten corrections, B–3
typing practices
  blind carbon copies, B–7
  cards, B–4
  corrections, B–3
  drawing lines, B–6
  envelopes, chain feeding, B–5
  labels, B–4
  multiple copies, B–2
  placement guide, B–1

U

underscore, 1–65
  comma with, 1–4e

United Parcel Service (UPS), 12–11
universities, capitalization of, 3–8g
unpublished works, titles of, 6–2
unrelated numbers, 4–2c
us, usage explained, page 153
user friendly, defined, page 299

V

vain, usage explained, page 154
van, usage explained, page 154
vane, usage explained, page 154
vary, usage explained, page 154
vein, usage explained, page 154
verbs
  adjectives with, 8–12
  collective nouns and, 8–7j
  comma with, 1–14a
  compound, hyphenation of, 2–1
  contractions of, 5–11b
  irregular, 8–5
  pronouns and, 8–7e, k
  regular, 8–4
  subject-verb agreement, 8–7
  subjunctive mood and, 8–7b
  use of *lay* and *lie*, 8–6
very, usage explained, page 154
vice, usage explained, page 154
vise, usage explained, page 154
volume numbers, comma with, 1–16d

W

waiver, usage explained, page 154
waver, usage explained, page 154
we, usage explained, page 153
weather, usage explained, page 154
weeks, format for, 4–11
weights, comma with, 1–16e
weights and measures
  metric, 4–7, 5–5
  standard, 4–6, 5–4
well, usage explained, page 139
whether, usage explained, page 154
which, usage explained, page 152
who, usage explained, page 154
wholly, usage explained, page 140
whom, usage explained, page 154
who's, usage explained, page 155
whose, usage explained, page 155
will, usage explained, page 150
word division
  for addresses, 2–8c
  dash with, 2–8f
  for dates, 2–8a
  for geographical locations, 2–8d
  for names, 2–8b
  for numbered items, 2–8e
  rules for using, 2–5, 2–6, 2–7, 2–8

word-numeral combinations, comma with, 1–16c
word processing, defined, page 299
word processing equipment for storing information, B–11h
words
  numerals with, 4–8a
  omitted, comma with, 1–13
word series, comma with, 1–1
would, usage explained, page 150

Y

years
  comma with, 1–16e
  format for, 4–11

your, usage explained, page 155
you're, usage explained, page 155

Z

zip codes, 4–13d
  address format for, 9–7c
  comma with, 1–16c
  zip + 4, 4–13e, 10–27

Abbreviations of States and Territories

State or Territory	Standard Abbreviation	Two-Letter Abbreviation
Alabama	Ala.	AL
Alaska	Alas.	AK
Arizona	Ariz.	AZ
Arkansas	Ark.	AR
California	Calif.	CA
Canal Zone	C.Z.	CZ
Colorado	Colo.	CO
Connecticut	Conn.	CT
Delaware	Del.	DE
District of Columbia	D.C.	DC
Florida	Fla.	FL
Georgia	Ga.	GA
Guam		GU
Hawaii		HI
Idaho		ID
Illinois	Ill.	IL
Indiana	Ind.	IN
Iowa		IA
Kansas	Kans.	KS
Kentucky	Ky.	KY
Louisiana	La.	LA
Maine		ME
Maryland	Md.	MD
Massachusetts	Mass.	MA
Michigan	Mich.	MI
Minnesota	Minn.	MN
Mississippi	Miss.	MS
Missouri	Mo.	MO
Montana	Mont.	MT
Nebraska	Nebr.	NE
Nevada	Nev.	NV
New Hampshire	N.H.	NH
New Jersey	N.J.	NJ
New Mexico	N. Mex.	NM
New York	N.Y.	NY
North Carolina	N.C.	NC
North Dakota	N. Dak.	ND
Ohio		OH
Oklahoma	Okla.	OK
Oregon	Oreg.	OR
Pennsylvania	Pa., Penna.	PA
Puerto Rico	P.R.	PR
Rhode Island	R.I.	RI
South Carolina	S.C.	SC
South Dakota	S. Dak.	SD
Tennessee	Tenn.	TN
Texas	Tex.	TX
Utah		UT
Vermont	Vt.	VT
Virgin Islands	V.I.	VI
Virginia	Va.	VA
Washington	Wash.	WA
West Virginia	W. Va.	WV
Wisconsin	Wis.	WI
Wyoming	Wyo.	WY